RAJNEETI

ADVANCE PRAISE FOR THE BOOK

'Shri Rajnath Singh is a stalwart of Indian politics who has infused a rare vibrance to its language and idioms. Intensely rooted and deeply connected with people, Shri Singh's story is one of triumph and tribulations; a story of a grass-roots BJP worker who has risen through the ranks due to sheer hard work and commitment. His life journey is a classic case for aspiring and young politicians. I am so happy Gautam Chintamani has tried to capture Rajnath Singhji's extraordinary journey in his book *Rajneeti*, which shall serve as a remarkable reference, and a valued treatise for future generations'—Yogi Adityanath, chief minister of Uttar Pradesh

'When the history of India's national security and the policies and actions taken to strengthen it is written, Prime Minister Modi's leadership and his government's efforts will be regarded as a watershed. In this narrative, the critical role played by Shri Rajnath Singh as home minister will stand out. A policy that is anchored in nationalism, and one that departs from the western liberal construct of liberalism—according to which the state is regarded as the sole violator of human rights—will be hailed as visionary. Under his leadership, regions that were earlier marred by violence and bloodshed are today on the path to attaining peace and prosperity.

'This book is a testament to one of India's finest home ministers. It captures how he has given salience to national interest and dealt a serious blow to those seeking the balkanization of our great nation. I would encourage the younger generation, in particular, to give this account a thorough read. They will find in these pages the journey of an inspiring leader, who has contributed to laying the foundations for a stronger and more robust India'—Hardeep Singh Puri, permanent representative of India to the United Nations, 2009–13; Minister of State (Independent Charge) for Housing & Urban Affairs and Civil Aviation; writer

'Contemporary history tends to be under-documented in India. This book documents the life of an important politician who contributed immeasurably to the the post-1991 growth of the BJP. It weaves together the dynamics of state and national politics through the life story of an important player. A must-read for those who want to understand the BJP'—Swapan Dasgupta, columnist and member of Parliament, Rajya Sabha

RAJNEETI

A Biography of
RAJNATH SINGH

GAUTAM CHINTAMANI

EBURY
PRESS

An imprint of Penguin Random House

EBURY PRESS

USA | Canada | UK | Ireland | Australia
New Zealand | India | South Africa | China | Singapore

Ebury Press is part of the Penguin Random House group of companies
whose addresses can be found at global.penguinrandomhouse.com

Published by Penguin Random House India Pvt. Ltd
4th Floor, Capital Tower 1, MG Road,
Gurugram 122 002, Haryana, India

First published in Ebury Press by Penguin Random House India 2019

ISBN 9780670092369

Typeset in Adobe Caslon Pro by Manipal Digital Systems, Manipal
Printed at Replika Press Pvt. Ltd, India

To
Sir C.Y. Chintamani
(10 April 1880–1 July 1941)

My great-grandfather and the liberal thinker, fearless editor of the Allahabad-based The Leader *from 1909 to 1934, whose uncompromising writing earned him the epithet of the 'Pope of Indian Journalism'*

A man's character is his fate.

—Heraclitus

हतो वा प्राप्स्यसि स्वर्गं जित्वा वा भोक्ष्यसे महीम् च
तस्मादुत्तिष्ठ कौन्तेय युद्धाय कृतनिश्चय: ॥
Bhagavad Gita: Chapter 2, Verse 37

'If you fight, you will either be slain on the battlefield and go to the celestial abodes, or you will gain victory and enjoy the kingdom on earth. Therefore arise with determination, O son of Kunti, and be prepared to fight.'

Contents

Author's Note

As a citizen of the world's largest democracy where, every five years, at times even earlier, each adult gets an opportunity to exercise their franchise, an average Indian cannot remain untouched by politics. Yet there was, till a few years ago, very little interest in who took charge of a particular ministry. But this attitude changed and, as of 2014, people have made political parties answerable in ways like never before.

On 26 May 2014, millions of Indians glued to their television sets and smartphones followed every single moment of the swearing-in ceremony of the Narendra Modi–led National Democratic Alliance (NDA). After Modi became the fifteenth prime minister of India, all eyes turned to the person who was sworn in as the first cabinet minister of the Modi sarkar—Rajnath Singh. As the national president of the Bharatiya Janata Party (BJP), Rajnath Singh had led the party to its biggest electoral victory until then, but more importantly, he delivered on the biggest gamble of his four-decade-long political career when he put his weight behind Narendra Modi as the NDA's prime ministerial candidate in the face of stiff opposition both within and outside the alliance.

There are many leaders in India whose lives would make for a compelling political biography, but few come close to

Rajnath Singh. The manner in which Singh unexpectedly returned as the national president of the BJP in 2013 and, in a matter of months, got like-minded political parties to reaffirm their commitment to the NDA, besides ensuring that the alliance accepted Modi as the prime ministerial candidate and won a massive mandate in the sixteenth Lok Sabha would be more than enough to write about, but Singh's legacy extends way beyond what meets the eye.

My aim in writing *Rajneeti* was to chronicle a life which, unlike many, has traversed the entire spectrum of a political career in India and made thousands of lives better. The title of the book might sound a bit presumptuous, but it was something that Singh himself expressed in the course of one of our conversations that put it all together. For Singh, the word 'rajneeti' means more than mere politicking; it is a word that contains 'neeti' or principle, and he has often questioned why people in public life indulge in 'aneeti' or unprincipled acts. Singh remains one of the few politicians in India who have risen from the ground up and never lost touch with his roots. He has held nearly every single position that is imaginable as a politician in India, including member of the legislative assembly and chief minister of India's biggest state, Uttar Pradesh; the state and national head of the Bharatiya Janata Yuva Morcha (BJYM), the BJP's youth wing; the state and national president of the BJP; a member of both the houses of Parliament—Rajya Sabha and Lok Sabha; Union cabinet minister for surface transport, agriculture and home affairs where he oversaw epoch-making reforms. In spite of the vast experience and achievements that easily outshine some of his much-discussed contemporaries, Singh is rarely spoken about.

This biography of Rajnath Singh is both the story of an exemplary leader as well as an account of a period of India's political history which has seldom been written about. Singh hails from a political thought that for long has been labelled as 'opposition' and, therefore, unjustly undermined on account of not being the so-called popular opinion. As a result, the viewpoint of a considerable section of India's public opinion repeatedly got sidelined. In Rajnath Singh, I found a public figure who remained committed to ideals that did not change with changing sociopolitical winds.

One of Singh's grouse has been that fate rarely gave him enough time to perform a task he had been entrusted with. As the chief minister of Uttar Pradesh, he barely got two years, but even then he heralded policies and schemes that managed the upliftment of the weakest sections of society to a substantial degree. Singh spent only a few months as, first, the minister for surface transport and, later, minister for agriculture in Atal Bihari Vajpayee's government. Within the timeframe he laid the groundwork for the ambitious Golden Quadrilateral project and also constituted the first-ever National Commission on Farmers. As the home minister in the first Narendra Modi government, Singh was part of the ministry that was directly responsible for making Indians feel safe. For the first time in years, under Singh, the Ministry of Home Affairs (MHA) got the upper hand while dealing with internal and external threats. Between 2014 and 2019 there was not a single terror strike on the lines of Mumbai local train blasts, the Varanasi temple bombing, the Mecca Masjid blasts in Hyderabad or the 26/11 Mumbai terror attacks that Indians had come to accept as a way of life. Singh ushered in long-overdue reforms within the paramilitary forces such as the Central Reserve Police Force (CRPF) and modernized it to take on Naxal–Maoist insurgents, militancy in the north-east and Jammu and Kashmir, where the Government of India also successfully and safely conducted local body elections for the first time in over a decade.

One of the tallest political leaders in India today, Rajnath Singh continues to pursue excellence in public office. Even after spending nearly fifty years in public life, Singh takes on every challenge with the same passion that saw him leave the security of a career as a physics lecturer to foray into politics. During the 2019 Lok Sabha elections, Singh was the only senior BJP leader besides Prime Minister Narendra Modi and Amit Shah, the national president, to have over a hundred public engagements and rallies. True to his style, the fight for the Lucknow parliamentary seat was devoid of any personal attacks on his opponents. The thumping victory (he won over 6 lakh votes and defeated his nearest rival, Samajwadi Party's Poonam Sinha, by a margin over 3 lakh votes) reiterated the electorate's faith in him.

With the NDA returning to power with a more significant mandate than in 2014, most political commentators would have expected Singh to continue as the home minister. Hence, many view his appointment as India's defence minister as a demotion of sorts. This couldn't be further from the truth. In the days to come, defence is poised to become the most critical aspect of the Indian government, and there couldn't be anyone better than Rajnath Singh at the helm of affairs.

Defence has always been a tricky ministry where even the best of men and women have fallen short of expectations for reasons that are often beyond their control. For far too long, defence ministers have tried to tread the fine line between managing a political appointment within the Ministry of Defence (MoD) and the needs of the armed forces. It has also been a hotbed of corruption pertaining to defence and arms deals. Singh's first statement as defence minister, that he would leave no stone unturned in lifting the morale of the armed forces, underscored his priority and intention. To my mind, there cannot be a better leader than Rajnath Singh to infuse the armed forces with vigour and drive. His aura as a leader who places the well-being of people before everything else has already inspired everyone within the forces, from the soldier guarding our borders to the men and women who lead them. As defence minister, Rajnath Singh is in charge of the most potent autonomous ministry in India. Every single decision of the MoD, whether in the course of purchasing equipment, or the way our armed forces engage with the enemy, has global ramifications. Today, the defence needs of India go beyond modernization and replenishment of equipment. The need of the hour is for all security agencies to have a synergy to protect 1.3 billion people from threats big or small. Singh's expertise as home minister, where he facilitated great coordination between multiple security agencies including the armed forces in strife-torn areas such as Kashmir, is sure to stand him in good stead as the defence minister.

Prologue

At 11.15 a.m. on 15 February 2019, Rajnath Singh, the minister of home affairs, left for Srinagar to take stock of the situation on the ground. The home secretary, the director general of the Central Reserve Police Force (CRPF), and the additional director of the Intelligence Bureau (IB) and other senior officials accompanied him. Under Singh, the MHA had dealt with terrorist attacks in Jammu and Kashmir, the insurgency in the north-east and Naxal-infested area or the 'Red Corridor' with an iron hand, and the results were more than visible. He was sanguine that the government would give the armed forces a free hand to respond in the manner they deemed fit as they had done on a few occasions in the recent past. But it was the circumstance of his visit that burdened his heart.

Convoys ferrying CRPF personnel were a common sight along the highway that connects Jammu and Srinagar. In the summers, the slew of vehicles would criss-cross the 295-kilometre-long segment of National Highway 44 every alternate day, but snowfall and landslides in the winter months disrupted the pattern and increased the time gap between the convoys. As a result, the number of stranded security forces personnel went up routinely. They would also be shifted between various transit camps like the one in Jammu that could accommodate 1000 personnel at the most. Incessant snowfall in late January 2019 had made it difficult for the convoy to move between Srinagar and Jammu for nearly a fortnight. From 4 February, fresh snowfall had blocked the route and, finally, ten days later, when the road became motorable again, the convoy strength had gone up to more than the usual. The seventy-eight-vehicle convoy carrying 2547 paramilitary personnel left Jammu at 3.30 a.m. on 14 February.

As the convoy hit the halfway mark at Qazigund, some of the vehicles dropped out but the number remained the same as a few 'mobile bunkers' joined the convoy. Post-Qazigund the probability of a terrorist ambush increased drastically and the mobile bunkers were meant to address that contingency. At 2.40 p.m., the convoy left Qazigund and a few minutes after 3 p.m. it crossed Pulwama village. It seemed like a routine exercise for the troops on the move, most of them returning from leave. They found the sights familiar. With the road-opening party sanitizing the Jammu–Srinagar highway for improvised explosive devices (IEDs) and men on guard from any possible lobbing of grenades or firing by terrorists, everything seemed in order. Perhaps this is why a civilian vehicle approaching from the slip road did not seem out of place. Until 2003, the CRPF could stop vehicles entering the convoy path, but being sensitive towards local commuters, non-military vehicles were now allowed to use the highway during convoy movements.

The Maruti Eeco drove along with the convoy for a few metres. As the convoy neared Ladhoo Mode, a point where the curve and the gradient in the mountainous highway compelled vehicles to slow down, the driver moved up to the fifth bus in the convoy. He rammed the car laden with 80 kilograms of high-grade RDX (Research Department Explosive — a type of high explosive) into the convoy and triggered an explosion. The impact was fierce. The forty-five-seater bus was blown to smithereens and two more were damaged. The explosion killed forty jawans in an instant and left five critically injured. The blast radius spread over 200 metres and lay littered with debris mixed with the remains of the slain troopers. Details of the attack emerged as news filtered in. This was the worst terror attack in Jammu and Kashmir in three decades. Initial reports suggested that nearly 300 kg of RDX was used but investigations over the course of the next few days revealed that the fidayeen had used ammonium nitrate and other chemicals along with 80 kilograms of high-grade RDX sourced from Pakistan and smuggled into Kashmir over a period of more than six months in gas cylinders and coal booths.

Minutes after the gruesome attack was carried out, Jaish-e-Mohammed (JeM), a Pakistan-based militant organization, designated a terrorist group by the United Nations, Australia, Canada, India, Russia, the United Arab Emirates, the United Kingdom and the United States, claimed responsibility for the attack. Not long after, a video appeared online, featuring a man identified as Aadil Ahmad Dar, who hailed from Gundibagh in Pulwama district, claiming to have masterminded the heinous attack. In the video testament, Dar, twenty, whose parents believed him to be a C-category militant and hoped that he would someday surrender even if it meant serving jail time, warned that 'more lions will rise across India to wage jihad against you'. The school dropout had joined the JeM's Afzal Guru squad, a homegrown Kashmiri cadre, after the death of Burhan Wani, a commander with the Hizbul Mujahideen, yet another Pakistan-based militant outfit designated a terrorist group by India, the European Union and the United States.

It was a long night for the families of the soldiers who had laid down their lives in the line of duty. It was a long night for millions of Indians who were coming to terms with the new modus operandi of outfits such as Jaish-e-Mohammed: use local radicalized youth to carry out their mission. It was a long night for the armed forces for they knew that come morning it would not be business as usual. It was also a long night for the Government of India.

Under Prime Minister Narendra Modi, India had signalled a change in strategy when it came to addressing threats, both internal and external. Barring a couple of attacks on military establishments, which met a befitting response, or the insurgency strikes, the number and intensity of which were waning, the MHA had managed to get an upper hand in most matters since the Modi government took office on 26 May 2014. Pulwama was an attempt to challenge India by changing the rules of the game.

At 9.15 a.m. on 15 February, as the prime minister chaired a meeting of the Cabinet Committee on Security (CCS), a twelve-member team of the National Investigation Agency (NIA) was dispatched to probe the attack and gather evidence. The CCS meeting would weigh India's options in terms of the response to the attack and was attended by ministers from home, external affairs, defence and finance.

Following the CCS meeting, India withdrew the 'Most Favoured Nation' (MFN) status accorded to Pakistan with immediate effect. The Ministry of External Affairs (MEA) initiated a major diplomatic offensive against Pakistan and briefed representatives of nearly twenty-five countries including the P5 nations—the United States of America, China, Russia, the United Kingdom and France—about the attack and Pakistan's state policy of using terrorism.

When Rajnath Singh reached the regional training centre of CRPF in Srinagar, the remains of the forty slain soldiers were lying in coffins draped with the tricolour. Singh laid wreaths on the coffins of the martyred personnel and paid his tributes to the departed souls. A two-minute silence was observed as a mark of respect for the sacrifice made by the troops.

Singh assured the soldiers that the nation would not let the sacrifice of their brethren go in vain. A few minutes later, in what would perhaps be the only instance in India's history, Rajnath Singh, the home minister, helped carry the coffin of a slain CRPF jawan.

1

The Son of a Farmer

One of Rajnath Singh's earliest childhood memories is his father engrossed in a book on Ayurveda. Ram Badan Singh spent a large part of his day overseeing the farming activities on the tract of land he owned along with some cousins and other relatives. Besides attending to the duties of the land and taking care of his family, Ram Badan barely had any time left but still made it a point to catch up on reading about various natural remedies for ailments in order to help treat people in and around the village.

Rajnath Singh was born on 10 July 1951 into a Rajput family in Bhabhaura village, which at the time was in Uttar Pradesh's Varanasi district and later became Chandauli district. The youngest of the seven children—three sons and four daughters—of Ram Badan Singh and Gujarati Devi, Rajnath would often catch his father listening patiently to people whom he could not recognize and, after a while, scribbling something on a piece of paper that rarely failed to bring a smile to the weary faces. Ram Badan had been a freedom fighter and was a well-known, much-respected figure across the district but chose not to participate in public life post-Independence.

One of Ram Badan's close friends, Pandit Kamlapati Tripathi, had risen to become a stalwart in the state's political arena, but Singh never had any interest in politics. A former journalist, Tripathi had known Ram Badan ever since he became a member of the Uttar Pradesh Legislative Assembly for the first time in 1937 and later a senior Congress leader from Varanasi. By the time Rajnath Singh began to recognize his father's friend, Tripathi was in his third term in the assembly and also the state's information and irrigation minister. Tripathi visited the Singh household once or twice every year without fail and each trip of his would see him urge Ram Badan to play a more active role in public life, but to no avail.

By the time Rajnath Singh turned three, Ram Badan started to home-school his son. Rajnath spent a better part of the day with his father and heard him speak about nearly everything under the sun. Ram Badan taught his son the basics of what books would teach in schools, but at the same time also instilled in the young mind knowledge about the traditions and customs that shaped India. He spoke about the greatness of the nation where common men and women withstood the might of the biggest colonial power in the world. Rajnath displayed a sharp acumen for grasping things and was naturally observant as well as curious about things around him.

Besides learning from his father, a usual day for Rajnath was interspersed with exchanges with his siblings, who also shared with him things they were taught in school, and playing to his heart's content. Rajnath was Gujarati Devi's pet and her fondness for her youngest-born, who always remained 'babua' or the little one for her, grew with each passing day.

Even though babua was given all the freedom a child could hope for, Rajnath and his siblings were far from spoilt. Right from the beginning, Ram Badan and Gujarati Devi had placed a great premium on values. Most of the teachings passed on to their children pivoted around the basic commitment to upholding these moral principles irrespective of the cost.

Later in life, every child of Ram Badan and Gujarati Devi remembered the standard set by their parents, but more than his siblings, Rajnath Singh discovered that the tougher the circumstances, the easier it became for him to function, thanks what his parents had instilled in him.

A few months before Rajnath Singh was born, the country witnessed one of the most significant changes in the way politics was practised. In 1950, Shyama Prasad Mookerji quit the first Central cabinet of independent India following differences with the first prime minister of India, Pandit Jawaharlal Nehru. Mookerji had played a vital role during the struggle for India's freedom and had come to be identified as one of the country's strongest nationalist voices.

Mookerji began his political career in 1929 when he entered the Bengal Legislative Council as an Indian National Congress (INC) candidate, and even though he resigned the next year when the Congress decided to boycott the legislature, Mookerji chose to contest the elections as an independent candidate. Mookerji was appointed the vice chancellor of the University of Calcutta in 1934, which at the age of 33 perhaps made him one of the youngest VCs in the world. He continued on the post till 1938 and it was during his tenure that Bengali was introduced as a medium of regular studies in the University of Calcutta. He won the elections again in 1937 as an independent and served as the finance minister of Bengal Province in 1941–42 under A.K. Fazlul Haq's Progressive Coalition government. Mookerji joined the Hindu Mahasabha in 1939 and was elevated to the post of the organization's working president, a position he held till 1946. He was deeply moved by the Noakhali genocide, a series of organized massacres, rapes, abductions and forced conversions of Hindus to Islam and looting and arson of Hindu properties perpetrated by the Muslim community in the Chittagong division of Bengal (now in Bangladesh).

Mookerji was opposed to any vivisection of India but fate stacked the odds against him in the strangest way. After the Second World War ended, the British prepared ground for an interim national government, but the viceroy of India, Lord Archibald Wavell, did not invite the Hindu Mahasabha to be a part of the Simla Conference where the Congress and the All-India Muslim League agreed on the 'Wavell Plan' for Indian self-government—the self-rule of India that provided separate representation for Muslims and which meant that Hindus or Muslim won't have additional veto power because they were in majority in some regions. But the fall of the Conservative government under Winston Churchill in England led to the new prime minister, Clement Richard Attlee, sending a new high-powered Cabinet Mission to India to decide whether Indians would like to associate with the Commonwealth or prefer to be completely independent and, if so, determine the means for the transfer of power to Indian hands.

By the time the Cabinet Mission landed in April 1946, provincial elections had been held and even though the Congress won 923 seats out of the 1585 (58.23 per cent) and the Muslim League came second with 425 seats (26.81 per cent) the results showed a clear demarcation between the Congress and the Muslim League strongholds.[1] The Muslim League won over 86 per cent of the Muslim votes. Considering that its election manifesto had proclaimed the provincial elections to be a plebiscite for Pakistan and on their claim to represent the whole of Muslim India, the Muslim League saw it as the 'first pitched battle for Pakistan with the enemies of Muslim India'.[2]

The provincial election results bolstered Muhammad Ali Jinnah's demand for a separate state, and while Congress was initially opposed to the idea of a partition of India, its working committee passed a resolution in Poona that it would not coerce any unwilling part to remain in India. Mookerji saw this as a great betrayal and decided to contest the provincial elections. However, a heart attack put paid to his plans and he was unable to galvanize the electorate.

Over the course of seven weeks, Attlee's Cabinet Mission interviewed 742 leaders in 182 sittings, covering every shade of opinion, mainly that of the Congress and the Muslim League, presented by then Congress President Maulana Abul Kalam Azad and Jinnah respectively. By the end it was clear that the Muslim League would have its way and the country would undergo a partition, but Mookerji was not ready to give up easily. He opposed the idea of a united but independent Bengal floated by Netaji Subhas Chandra Bose's brother, Sarat Chandra Bose, in 1947. Recalling the violence of Direct Action Day, 16 August 1946, also known as the Great Calcutta Killings, and the carnage of the Noakhali riots, Mookerji pushed for splitting Bengal in order to safeguard the Hindu population of the state.

According to those close to Mookerji, he was disgusted with the way the Congress had functioned at a crucial juncture in India's history. In the run-up to forming the first-ever cabinet of independent India, Mookerji was certain that Nehru would never consider including the likes of anyone who could question him. He was surprised when both Mahatma Gandhi and Sardar Vallabhbhai Patel insisted that he—along with Sir John Mathai, a noted economist and business magnate, Sir Shanmukham Chetty, a well-known financial expert, and Dr B.R. Ambedkar— be a part of Nehru's cabinet.[3] Once India became a free nation, Mahatma Gandhi also proposed dissolving the Congress to make way for political parties based on distinguishable political and social programme and ideology. Although that did not happen, Gandhi managed to include in the cabinet people from various nationalist forces that also contributed to the freedom struggle.

Mookerji served as the minister for industry and supply under Nehru for two-and-a-half years and it's interesting to see how it was the former and not the latter who perhaps laid the foundation of modern India. Mookerji had been the finance minister of undivided Bengal and possessed a blend of intellectual grasp as well as a realistic comprehension of industrialization in a country that has predominantly been agrarian. Mookerji conceived three of the most successful industrial undertakings of independent India—the Chittaranjan Locomotive Factory, Sindri Fertilizers Corporation and the Hindustan Aircraft Factory—and also planned a steel plant in Bhilai, besides overseeing the country taking its first steps to manufacture newsprint in National Newsprint and Paper Mills, Nepanagar, that finally went into production in 1954. These enterprises provided the blueprint for nearly all future public sector undertakings. It was Mookerji who also initiated the policy of managing state-controlled industries through corporations that were organized on the lines of joint stock companies where the government supplied a major portion of the capital and placed some of its nominees on the board of directors along with private industrialists.

Mookerji was opposed to Nehru's handling of Kashmir and his general demeanour of dealing with Pakistan. During the course of cabinet meetings or debates in Parliament, he routinely took on Nehru, often leading the PM to pull rank on Mookerji to stop his questioning.

The reason Mookerji had agreed to join the cabinet was to ensure some firmness and, more importantly, realism, in dealing with Pakistan. As far as Mookerji was concerned, the first war that the two newly formed nations fought over Kashmir in 1947 had set the tone for Indo-Pak relationship. Pakistan, which was both militarily and economically weaker, had not only committed an act of aggression but had also got away with over 28,000 square miles (72,520 sq km) of Indian territory in the strategic region of Gilgit. Mookerji was supportive of Patel's stand that India take a hard line against Pakistan, but when Nehru's approach of negotiated settlement called the Liaquat–Nehru Pact or the Delhi Pact prevailed, which finally led to an agreement with Pakistan on 8 April 1950, Mookerji resigned from office.

Once Mookerji quit the government, his quest to provide a committed and organized Opposition, both within and outside Parliament, saw him form the Bharatiya Jana Sangh in 1951. The first Parliament of India largely consisted of those who were also a part of the Constituent Assembly and at that time the biggest challenge for them was how to avoid the partition of the country; but once that bridge was crossed, there was nothing truly left to oppose. The Socialist Party of India under Jayaprakash Narayan and Acharya Narendra Deva offered some opposition but their approach to issues was similar to that of the Congress under Nehru. The other form of opposition was offered by the Communist Party of India, but that fell short when it came to appealing to the nation in general. Mookerji found that he had outgrown the Hindu Mahasabha after independence. He was of the opinion that the organization should either cease to participate in politics or open its doors to non-Hindus. As there were no longer separate electorates, Mookerji felt that the Hindu Mahasabha ought to reorient its policies and outlook.[4] Following the assassination of Mahatma Gandhi in January 1948, both the Hindu Mahasabha and the Rashtriya Swayamsevak Sangh (RSS), the other prominent nationalist cultural and social organization, were banned as the government felt they might have been a part of the conspiracy to kill Gandhi. The man who killed Gandhi, Nathuram Godse, at the time of the assassination, was the editor of a pro–Hindu Mahasabha newspaper in Poona. Besides senior leaders of both groups, such as M.S. Golwalkar, the then sarsanghchalak or supreme guide, nearly 20,000 swayamsevaks were arrested for varying lengths of time. But with the government unable to prove any RSS involvement in the killing of Gandhi or a conspiracy to overthrow the government, most of them were released by August 1948.[5] It took a while for the government to lift the ban on the RSS and the interim period saw a long exchange of letters between Golwalkar and Nehru as well as Patel.

The first home minister of India, Patel, was of the opinion that the RSS should let go of its opposition to the Congress, especially its disregard of decency and decorum towards it, and suggested that the RSS cadre carry out 'their patriotic endeavour only by joining the Congress and not by keeping a separate identity or by opposing'.[6] The back and forth exchange between the RSS and the government continued until the former launched a massive satyagraha to urge the latter to lift the ban. The renewed negotiations between the two resulted in the government asking the RSS to revise its Constitution, state its allegiance to the national flag and the Indian Constitution, provide for a democratic system to elect office-bearers and reject violence. The RSS prepared a draft of the revised Constitution under the supervision of Eknath Ranade, a member of the executive committee, aided by P.B. Dani and Balasaheb Deoras, but the government rejected it. Later, a new version was written by Mauli Chandra Sharma, Eknath Ranade and Deendayal Upadhyaya, a young pracharak, who, in time to come, would go on to play a prominent role alongside Mookerji.[7] The Sangh refused to change its stance on fundamental issues, such as participation of pre-adolescents or the selection of the sarsanghchalak. Once the new Constitution was accepted by Sardar Patel, the ban on the RSS was lifted on 11 July 1949.[8]

There had been a fourteen-month period between the time Mookerji quit the Nehru cabinet and his launching of the Bharatiya Jana Sangh. Mookerji was aware of not only the work the RSS had done—he had called it the 'only silver lining in the cloudy sky of India' at a rally in Lahore in 1940—but also the manner in which it remained the only organization that more than demonstrated its determination to exist outside the realm of the Congress and root itself in the age-old culture of the country.[9] Unlike the RSS or the Hindu Mahasabha, Shyama Prasad Mookerji was not tied to a particular dogma or driven by abstract theories. As far as he was concerned, the RSS drew its cadre from the middle and lower classes of Indians, which automatically gave it an extremely wide base, and the restraint its cadre showed in the face of the ban imposed by the government revealed a great sense of discipline. The Sangh had won accolades from the nation for the work it had done in Punjab, Kashmir, the North-West Frontier Province and Sind in 1947 during the Partition and later at the time of the attack on Kashmir by Pakistan. Some factions within the RSS were keen on exploring the possibility of becoming a more politically vocal outfit or at least be a part of a political party that reflected its ideologies.

At the time of the deliberations, a book titled *The Philosophy and Action of the R.S.S. for the Hind Swaraj* written by Anthony Elenjimittam, a Catholic priest from Kerala, who was also an ordained monk of the Dominican Order and completed his theological studies in Rome, pointed out how a common historic Indian culture could be a basis for all citizens of India to unite. Noting how the Hindu Mahasabha has outlived its purpose, and expressing the need for the RSS's participation in politics, Elenjimittam wrote: 'Today the neo-nationalism of the R.S.S., rooted in the neo-Vedantism and strong organizational and disciplinary strength, is the main national force. On this strong nationalism, all citizens of India can unite to fulfill their patriotic mission as common children of Mother India.'[10]

Intriguingly enough, on 7 October 1949, when Nehru was travelling abroad, the Congress Working Committee (CWC) had voted in favour of RSS members joining the party but following a fracas between the supporters of Patel, who supported the move, and Nehru, who opposed it, the order was rescinded. One of Patel's supporters, A.G. Kher, the minister for local self-government in the United Provinces (now Uttar Pradesh), predicted how this action would push the RSS into politics. He argued that swayamsevaks could not participate in active politics unless they joined some political party and this move had compelled the RSS cadre to join opponents of the Congress.[11]

Both Golwalkar and Mookerji had met to discuss the modalities of a partnership, and the reason for a rather long gestation period for them to come to an understanding was perhaps the possibility of a leadership change in the Congress. It was believed that Mookerji, as well as Golwalkar, would have supported the Congress had the party elected Sardar Patel as its leader, but with Patel's death in December 1950, things were not the same. The growing differences between Nehru and Congress president Purushottam Das Tandon, who was not power hungry but was seen as a protégé of Patel, began to impact the relations between the party and the government. Tandon had defeated the Nehru-backed candidate Jivatram Bhagwandas Kripalani to become the party president but things came to a point where Nehru resigned from the Congress Executive and Central Election Committee and all the members followed suit. Following his defeat, Kripalani, who had begun to feel disillusioned with the Congress for abandoning the Gandhian ideal of forming countless village republics post-Independence, left the party and formed the Kisan Mazdoor Praja Party (KMPP). Tandon offered to continue as the president with any new members proposed by the party, but resigned when Nehru refused the compromise solution. In September 1951, the All-India Congress Committee (AICC) elected Nehru president and, consequently, the options for Mookerji drastically reduced.[12]

After much deliberations, Mookerji and the RSS came together to form the Jana Sangh. The understanding between Mookerji and Golwalkar was that the RSS would remain structurally separate from the new party. At the same time, Golwalkar wanted the views of Mookerji's political outfit, especially when it came to nationalism, to be compatible with the Sangh's. The RSS's constitution did not allow it to participate in political activities; however, it 'loaned' a few pracharaks known for their organizational skills to the new outfit. In time, swayamsevaks too joined the political outfit and formed a large part of the grass-roots structure of the Jana Sangh. The first state unit of the Bharatiya Jana Sangh was formally launched on 23 May 1951 in Jullundur (now Jallandhar) where the representatives of Punjab, PEPSU (the Patiala and East Punjab States Union that consisted of eight princely states between 1948 and 1956), Himachal Pradesh and Delhi met.[13] RSS activists took charge of organizing the party in most regions and Mookerji himself worked to garner support in Bengal. Soon there were similar conventions held in Indore, Patna, Jaipur, Nagpur and Lucknow, where Deendayal Upadhyaya was elected the general secretary of Uttar Pradesh Jana Sangh. At the first public meeting of the Jana Sangh in Calcutta in June 1951, a resolution was passed to make Mookerji the first president of the party. Speaking at the event, Mookerji sketched out the Jana Sangh's political stance that would focus on refugee rehabilitation, a harder line towards Pakistan, oppose large-scale government control of the economy and promote a public–private partnership to overcome the country's developmental problems as well as foster regional self-sufficiency. Moreover, unlike the Hindu Mahasabha, the Jana Sangh would be 'open to all citizens of India irrespective of caste, creed or community'.[14] A few months after Rajnath Singh's birth, on 21 October 1951, the Jana Sangh was formally launched in Delhi where its state units met for its first all-India convention.

The Jana Sangh was established on the eve of the first general elections to be held in India. With the help of the RSS workers deputed to the Jana Sangh, the party managed to create a pan-India presence within a few months and was able to connect with the voter. The Jana Sangh fielded candidates in 93 of the 489 parliamentary seats and 717 of the 3383 state assembly constituencies. It won three parliamentary seats and thirty-five assembly seats.[15] Despite the Congress winning nearly 75 per cent of both Parliament and state assembly seats, the Jana Sangh came to be recognized as an all-India party as it had garnered 3 per cent of the vote share. Mookerji was also able to unify the Opposition parties and some independents under the umbrella of a National Democratic Party, which featured thirty-two constituents that saw him as their leader. This was in some way the beginning of the inter-communal, conservative, all-India party he had hoped to found.[16]

By the time the first session of the first elected Parliament of India ended, nearly everyone, including the press, was of the opinion that the mantle of the late Sardar Patel had fallen on Dr Shyama Prasad Mookerji. This was particularly true when it came to the question of total integration of Muslim-majority Kashmir into India. Mookerji travelled to Kashmir in May 1953, by which time the situation in the state had come to a point where Sheikh Abdullah's government had bought into the notion that Kashmir was an independent state that had acceded to India for the limited purpose of defence, foreign affairs and communications. The people of the state had wanted a complete integration with India and a few years later, when the Preamble to the Constitution of Jammu and Kashmir was adopted in November 1956 by the Constituent Assembly of Jammu and Kashmir, a body of representatives elected in 1951, it clearly said it is an integral part of the Union of India 'in pursuance of the accession of this State to India which took place on the twenty-sixth day of October 1947'. Abdullah, however, took refuge in Article 370 of the Indian Constitution that gave the state special status.[17]

In March 1952, Sheikh Abdullah publicly proclaimed that Jammu and Kashmir would become a republic within the Union of India with its own independent constitution, flag, a separate assembly and a president. Mookerji vehemently opposed Abdullah's plans and in June 1952 took Nehru head-on in Parliament, questioning Abdullah's machination and exhorting the prime minister of India to answer whether, after giving up areas that Pakistan had forcibly occupied, India was, in fact, now willing to lose the entire state thanks to what Abdullah had in mind.[18] After meetings with members of the Opposition in Jammu and Kashmir, such as Pandit Prem Nath Dogra of the Praja Parishad, who were in favour of a complete integration with India, Mookerji launched a campaign to make the rest of India aware of what was happening in Kashmir and how the government of the day was letting it slip away with each passing moment. Mookerji's stance was clear and firm and he believed, '*Ek desh mein do Vidhan, do Pradhan aur Do Nishan nahi chalenge*' (A single country cannot have two constitutions, two prime ministers and two national emblems). He travelled to Kashmir on the invitation of the Praja Parishad to get a sense of what was happening on the ground and promised the people he met to fight tooth and nail for them in Delhi.

In July 1952, Sheikh Abdullah and Pandit Nehru signed what came to be known as the Delhi Agreement that allowed the state of Jammu and Kashmir to elect its own head in place of the maharaja, have its own flag, elect its own Sadar-i-Riyasat or the equivalent to the governor of other states, and agreed to the Supreme Court of India having only appellate jurisdiction in the state.[19] The agreement also entailed that the Fundamental Rights enshrined in the Constitution could not be made applicable to the state, particularly to the latter's land reforms programme. The agreement also had the Government of India giving up the residuary powers of legislature over the state and although it insisted on the application of Article 352, empowering the president to proclaim a general emergency in the state, it agreed to the modification in its application to Kashmir by adding the words 'but in regard to internal disturbance at the request or with the concurrence of the Government of the State', at the end of clause 1.[20] If this was not enough, the Constitution Drafting Committee appointed by Abdullah was virtually going to make Jammu and Kashmir an independent state. Mookerji offered his full support to the Praja Parishad in its quest to oppose Abdullah and in December 1952, after he was re-elected president of the Jana Sangh, the party took a decision to aid the Praja Parishad's movement for the integration of Jammu and Kashmir with the rest of India.

Despite his earlier pleas falling on deaf ears, Mookerji began a new dialogue with both Nehru and Abdullah via letters to find a solution. Between January and May 1953, Mookerji had a protracted correspondence with Pandit Jawaharlal Nehru and Sheikh Abdullah. Despite people such as the then vice-president of India Dr S. Radhakrishnan playing intermediaries, all efforts failed.[21] Finally, in May 1953, Mookerji made up his mind to go to Kashmir to protest against the system under which Indian citizens, including the president of India, could not enter without a permit even though it was a part of India.

Mookerji was deemed to have defied the law that made entering the state without the permission of Kashmir's prime minister illegal. He was arrested on the bridge over the Ravi river at 4 p.m. on 11 May 1953. On the day of Mookerji's arrest, the state government had issued an ordinance through the Sadar-i-Riyasat that entering without a state permit was an offence but at the time of his arrest only the Government of India was empowered to issue such an order.[22] Even though Mookerji's then secretary Atal Bihari Vajpayee felt that the Punjab government would arrest Mookerji and prevent him from proceeding further, the deputy commissioner, Gurdaspur, later told Mookerji that the Government of India had allowed him to enter Jammu and Kashmir without a permit.

The news of Mookerji's arrest spread across the country the next day. On 13 May 1953, when one of his fellow parliamentarians, Nirmal Chandra Chatterjee, a Hindu Mahasabha member of the first Lok Sabha and father of future Communist Party of India (Marxist) (CPI [M]) parliamentarian Somnath Chatterjee, questioned Nehru on the basis of the information that he had personally received from the deputy commissioner, Gurdaspur, Nehru denied any knowledge of the arrest.[23] Mookerji was detained in Kashmir which, following the July Agreement, was out of the jurisdiction of Indian courts. On 23 June 1953, he was found dead in his jail cell under circumstances that remain mysterious till date.

Nearly half a century later, Vajpayee accused Nehru of colluding with the Jammu and Kashmir government in Mookerji's death—it was widely believed that there had been a conspiracy to ensure that Mookerji would be allowed to enter Jammu and Kashmir but not be allowed to leave.[24] Mookerji had been denied medical care for the time he was incarcerated, and even Nehru, who visited Kashmir a few days before Mookerji's death, did not call on his one-time cabinet colleague.[25] Mookerji's funeral procession was one of the biggest gatherings ever seen in Calcutta. Soon after, his mother, Jogmaya Devi, wrote to Nehru asking for an investigation. Nehru rejected all demands for an inquiry into Mookerji's death, and while the tragedy led to the abolishment of the permit law, the conundrum that was Jammu and Kashmir would linger.

2

The Student and the Teacher

After home-schooling Rajnath for a few years, Ram Badan Singh enrolled him in a local primary school where the young one topped his class on a regular basis. Much like learning with his father, Rajnath enjoyed studying in the classroom and impressed most of his teachers with his ability to absorb what was being taught faster than his classmates. By his thirteenth birthday, Rajnath got double promotions and raced ahead of his classmates. It was around the same time that one of the local RSS pracharaks, who used to visit the school and other places in the vicinity, noticed Rajnath's fondness for learning and invited him to accompany him to events organized by the sangh. The tehsil pracharak introduced Rajnath to the local shakha, the chief instrument for organizing the community.

The pracharaks formed a communication network outside of the Sangh's constitutional system while serving as a link between the various levels within the RSS and organizing the shakha's core activities aimed at the character-building process of the swayamsevaks. Each shakha would ideally feature fifty to a hundred participants divided into five groups—shishu swayamsevaks aged between six to ten years, bal swayamsevaks aged between ten to fourteen years, taruna vyavasayee between twenty-eight to forty-five years and post forty-five praudh swayamsevaks, who were above twenty-eight and were further divided into groups or a *gata* of twenty participants.[1] Rajnath participated in various games and exercises aimed at fostering bonding at the shakha. He enjoyed participating in kabaddi immensely and went on to become quite proficient in the sport over the years.

Much like what Ram Badan and Gujarati Devi had instilled in their children at home, the mukhya shikshak or the chief instructor of the shakha too spoke about attributes of good character and discussed themes such as fidelity, fortitude, honesty, obedience to superiors, hard work, personal discipline, besides the need for unity in India. The sessions also introduced the participants to heroic tales of India and spoke about heroes such as Shivaji Maharaj, Guru Gobind Singhji, or Maharana Pratap, but it was the special *bauddhik* or intellectual session that Rajnath looked forward to the most.

The bauddhik took place a few times each month with the shakha coming together in the evenings for a lecture delivered by a senior member of the Sangh who specialized in a given subject. The short discourses lasted anywhere between twenty minutes to an hour and covered a vast array of topics ranging from the Sangh's history, the country's spiritual and cultural legacy or current affairs. At times, these bauddhiks also sought the opinion of participants on issues that concerned the society or the nation. Rajnath continued to participate regularly in activities of the shakha. He particularly looked forward to special events including the collective celebrations of festivals and the three-day camps that were conducted throughout the year.

Over time he became intrigued by political leaders across the political spectrum and during his high-school years, whenever possible, Rajnath attended their public rallies. Amongst those who frequented the area, Rajnath rarely missed

an address by the likes of Chaudhary Charan Singh, Atal Bihari
Vajpayee or Kamlapati Tripathi, who invariably called on Ram
Badan Singh after the speech was over. During one such visit,
Rajnath, at that time in the eighth grade, made a dash for his
home to welcome Tripathi along with his father. Later, when
Tripathi was about to leave, Rajnath accompanied his father to
the minister's car parked at a short distance, and as they walked
past the isolated fields, Tripathi asked Ram Badan if he felt safe
out in the hinterland. Before Ram Badan could reply, Tripathi
instructed the collector walking alongside to issue a licence for
a firearm for the family's protection. A smiling Ram Badan
thanked Tripathi for his concern but refused to take a gun and
told him there was no reason to worry.

Rajnath Singh finished his high school from Chakia
Government Inter College (GIC) with flying colours and fell
three marks short of a first division in his intermediate or senior
secondary. He was always fascinated by science and decided to
pursue his bachelor's degree in physics, his favourite subject.
During his undergraduate studies, Rajnath started becoming
aware of the political situation around him. This was an era
when one rarely doubted the newspapers or politicians and
when it came to smaller districts and towns, any news that
trickled down from the cities such as Delhi and Bombay was
considered to be the truth. For youngsters like Rajnath, who
were based in nondescript towns such as Chakia, a subdivisional
headquarters of Varanasi, events such as the Naxalbari uprising
of 1967, which the world considered to be cataclysmic, meant
little more than distant events.

The mid-1960s were a period of great transition in India.
The Jana Sangh had been around for over a decade along with
other Opposition parties such as the Praja Socialist Party (PSP),
which was formed in 1952 to 1972 when the erstwhile Socialist
Party led by Jayaprakash Narayan, Acharya Narendra Deva and

Basawon Singh (Sinha), merged with J.B. Kripalani's Kisan Mazdoor Praja Party; the newly formed Swatantra Party, which was launched in 1959 by the statesman C. Rajagopalachari and parliamentarian Minoo Masani along with others as a reaction to the Nehru-dominated Congress's increasingly socialist outlook; besides the communists as well as a few regional parties like the Dravida Munnetra Kazhagam (DMK) and the Shiromani Akali Dal (SAD). Although the Congress still appeared to be the only one with a pan-India clout, it was fast beginning to lose its hallowed space.[2]

The Jana Sangh had bettered its performance in terms of assembly seats in the second and third Lok Sabha elections held in 1957 and 1962 respectively. It's tally went up from thirty-five in 1951 to fifty-two in 1957 to 119 assembly seats in 1962. It also increased its vote share in the parliamentary seats from 3.06 per cent to 5.93 to 6.44 per cent over the same period.[3] The RSS that had helped Jana Sangh's campaign become effective largely due to its wide base across the country at the time of the first Lok Sabha only helped get more support for the party in the subsequent elections as a series of crises added to a growing anti-Congress sentiment all over the country. The two wars that India fought with China in 1962 and Pakistan in 1965 slowed down development and led to inflation as money had to be diverted to war efforts. There were also widespread agitations in almost all major non-Hindi-speaking states arising from the imposition of Hindi as the national language.

Following its strong stand against China and Pakistan, the RSS had begun to gain both respectability and acceptance. After Nehru invited the Sangh to participate, for the first time, in the 1963 Republic Day parade in New Delhi where almost 2000 swayamsevaks marched in full uniform, the time was ripe for the organization to broaden its base.[4] It was around this period that Balraj Madhok, a pracharak from Kashmir who had not only witnessed Shyama Prasad Mookerji from close quarters and was closely involved with the genesis of the Jana Sangh, but also won the Lok Sabha seat for Delhi in 1961 on a Jana Sangh ticket, suggested that the party unite with the Swatantra Party to form a new outfit. In Madhok's view, the merger could see the emergence of a well-defined ideological alternative to the ruling Congress establishment. However, the then general secretary of the Jana Sangh, Deendayal Upadhyaya, opposed it as he did not want the Jana Sangh to be identified as a completely right-wing party.[5]

In an effort to make the Jana Sangh's ideology clear and why it needed to keep a distinct identity of its own, Upadhyaya came up with the concept of 'integral humanism', a set of principles that stood for a separate political philosophy different from the Western mindset. Upadhyaya believed that the Western political mindset was too occupied with materialism and this came at the cost of the social well-being of an individual. Evoking the philosophy of the 'Advaita Vedanta' or recognition of one's own self in all life, Upadhyaya rejected the intrinsic diversity based on race, colour, caste or religion, and identified all human beings as a part of one organic whole that shared a common political perspective. Upadhyaya's sentiment was adopted by the Jana Sangh as its official statement of fundamental principles. Putting it in a political perspective meant that Hindus, Muslims, Christians and the people of all other faiths and sects were essentially one and that their intrinsic unity should be based on this common consciousness of 'rashtriyata' or nationalism.[6]

In the run-up to the 1967 general elections, which were also the first after the death of Nehru, who passed away in 1964, the Jana Sangh laid down its guidelines in 1965 at its working committee meeting in Vijayawada. It would henceforth question the government on the country's foreign policy, demand the termination of diplomatic relations with China besides pushing for closer ties with other South-East Asian nations to contain China, and also recover areas occupied by both Pakistan and China. The party also decided to push for compulsory military training of all young men and also the development of nuclear weapons.[7]

The impact of the 1967 Lok Sabha elections would be felt for years to come as the electoral system seen so far began to disintegrate. Although the Congress under Indira Gandhi, Nehru's daughter who had succeeded Lal Bahadur Shastri as the third prime minister of India after his death on 24 January 1966, managed to win 54 per cent of the seats, the magnitude of victory was much smaller than earlier, and the party suffered significant losses in seven states. In Madras and Delhi, the Congress lost power to single parties, the Dravida Munnetra Kazhagam (DMK) and Jana Sangh respectively. The Swatantra Party under C. Rajagopalachari won forty-four seats in the Lok Sabha while the Jana Sangh under Balraj Madhok as president experienced its best-ever electoral performance. The elections—the last time India voted to elect the Union as well as the state governments simultaneously—saw the Jana Sangh increase its parliamentary representation from fourteen in 1962 to thirty-five in 1967. It also managed to win 261 assembly seats, which was more than double of what it had won in 1962.[8] The Jana Sangh participated in the formation of many coalition governments in states such as Bihar, which was one of the places where it performed the best, winning twenty-six assembly seats (up from a measly three); Haryana, the new state carved out of Punjab; Madhya Pradesh; Uttar Pradesh and Punjab. Thanks to its impressive performance, the party became a part of many united front governments and formed alliances with the Akalis, the socialists as well as the communists. This was not something that Madhok was too keen on but did not have much say during debates within the party that were led by Atal Bihari Vajpayee, a national-level party secretary.

Upadhyaya had become the party president in late 1967 but the party's experience with alliances was not so satisfactory. Nearly all the states where the party was in partnership saw mid-term elections. Upadhyaya's untimely and unexpected death under mysterious circumstances during a train journey on 11 February 1968—his body was found near Mughal Sarai railway station in Uttar Pradesh clutching a five-rupee note in his hand—saw the elevation of Vajpayee, who was reluctant to change the ground rules for alliances, as the president of the Jana Sangh.

It was after enrolling in the University of Gorakhpur for his master's degree that Rajnath Singh became an active participant in college-level politics. Right from his early days, Rajnath displayed a tendency to take a firm stand when it came to being upright about any issue. Singh became a member of the Akhil Bharatiya Vidyarthi Parishad (ABVP), the Sangh's student association and soon made a name for himself thanks to his impeccable organizational skills and his unwavering dedication to discipline.

The ABVP had come into existence as a result of the ban imposed on the RSS in the aftermath of Gandhi's assassination in 1948. Prior to the independence of India, many swayamsevaks were associated with the activities of the largest association of students in India, the All-India Students' Federation (AISF) but, in 1940, when the outfit split into the pro-communist All-India Students' Federation and the pro-Congress All-India Students' Congress (AISC), the majority opted to join the latter. At the time the RSS was banned in 1948–49, the swayamsevaks found themselves shunned from most organizations and ended up forming sports, devotional and student associations to sustain their ideology. This period also saw some RSS members such as Balraj Madhok organizing students groups on their own, but by July 1948 some student organizers, who were all RSS members, met in Delhi to make an official body that would link such groups that were scattered across India.[9]

The ABVP was different from most other student organizations of the period in its overall commitment to academics. It was not focused on students' trade unionism alone but also invited teachers to join, and made it a point to offer a kind of surrogate family environment to students who hailed from lower-middle-class backgrounds. Up until the 1960s it tried to avoid getting embroiled in student protests or campus politics by choosing to concentrate on providing students with a wide range of extra-curricular activities and counselling, which were not so common in the period. It organized study circles presided by a faculty member, and while it espoused the Sangh's cause and ideology, it also gave an opportunity to widen the RSS's base with students who were not swayamsevaks.

The reasons for its origins notwithstanding, the ABVP was seen as a force to counter the spread of communism on college campuses in India. The ABVP's foray into mainstream campus politics increased over the years as it continued to promote activities on nationalism and national integration, social and gender justice and promote youth leadership as well as help spread the Sangh's ideas.[10] In urban areas, the ABVP had bureaus that introduced foreign students to Indian culture and also offered a chance to young boys and girls from smaller towns to spend time with older members in cities and, as a result, experience diversity.

At the time of its inception, almost half of the ABVP's cadre was drawn from RSS members but the number had steadily declined by the time Rajnath Singh joined. His years in the RSS laid the foundation of his mobilizing skills while his willingness to support or stick up for what was right made him an inspiration for several people. Singh slowly evolved into a strong leader when it came to students' well-being, and although he was assertive, he was not aggressive or combative, which enamoured him to even professors and other staff.

One such instance that highlighted Singh's leadership abilities and in which he won the faith of both his fellow students as well as the university administration—unlike anyone else in the recent past—came when he championed the agitation against the quality of the food served in the hostel. It was during the third semester examination when students in the university hostel got fed up with the quality of food served, and campaigned against the administration a day before an examination. The then vice chancellor, P.T. Chandi, a retired Indian Administrative Services (IAS) officer, was aware of Singh and even liked him enough to indulge in conversation on occasions. It took a whole day of non-stop agitation from the students for the administration to give in and call them for talks. By the time the matter was resolved, it was late evening and Chandi was convinced that the moment they agreed to the demands, the students would ask for the next day's examination paper to be postponed. Most of the students were even convinced that they might be able to swing an extra day to prepare, but they did not know that their own leader would put his foot down.

Chandi called Rajnath for a chat and smilingly told him to come out with the 'new' demand, but much to his surprise, Singh told him there was no question of rescheduling the exam. The more Chandi tried to reason with the young man, the more Singh convinced him that not only he but all the students would appear as per the schedule and assured him that he would get everyone on board. As Singh took leave of the vice chancellor, Chandi said that he might not get the first division or an A grade, and Singh smilingly added that with his blessing he just might. Singh managed to score over sixty per cent and maintained his first-division streak.

Although Ram Badan Singh had never entertained the idea of politics, calls to run for public office continued to knock on the family's door. Village folk beseeched his son and Rajnath's eldest brother, Suryanath, to become the pramukh or president of the Panchayat Samiti (Block) but he refused as, like his father, he too found politics tedious. It was after Ram Badan's death in 1969 that Rajnath Singh became the first member of the family to hold a political post when he was made the organizational secretary of ABVP's Gorakhpur division. The time when Singh was involved with the ABVP was one of its most dynamic phases and by the time Singh left the ABVP in 1971, the organization had nearly 100,000 members and had begun taking up issues that impacted the lower middle class such as government inertia and corruption.[11]

Upon completing his master's, Singh began to teach physics at the K.B. Postgraduate College in Mirzapur. The city got its name from the East India Company and owed much of its modern-day creation to the British, but for centuries it was also known to be the place where the holy River Ganga met the Vindhya Range and was home to the Vindhyavasini Devi temple. In addition to being the city where he got his first job, Mirzapur also became home to Singh in more ways than one. He married Savitri Singh on 5 June 1971, and as the young couple started their life in Mirzapur, the country too was witnessing a metamorphosis.

In March 1971, Indira Gandhi returned with a thumping majority in the fifth Lok Sabha elections in which her party, the Indian National Congress (Requisitionists), which was created after a split in the Congress, won 352 of the 518 parliamentary seats. In 1969, the Congress president S. Nijalingappa had expelled Indira Gandhi from the party for fostering a personality cult, and the sitting prime minister of India walked away with 446 of the 705 party members.[12] While the 'Old Congress' retained the party symbol, a pair of bullocks carrying a yoke, Indira Gandhi's faction used a new symbol—a cow with a suckling calf. The Jana Sangh was part of the Opposition that came together in a pre-poll alliance called the Samyukta Socialist Party along with the Indian National Congress (Organization), the Praja Socialist Party (PSP) and the Swatantra Party to take on Indira Gandhi. However, for the first time since it was created, the Jana Sangh did not improve upon its previous performance.

During the time he taught at the K.B. Postgraduate College, Rajnath Singh became the RSS karyavah or general secretary of Mirzapur in 1972. The RSS once again came into focus when fissures within the Jana Sangh came out in the open after the debacle of the 1971 Lok Sabha elections and the 1972 assembly elections where the latter lost more ground. The Jana Sangh cadre was critical of the leadership, which came as a shock to observers, for the Jana Sangh was seen as a party that took into account the views and opinion of the cadre more than any other political party. Vajpayee took responsibility for the poor show and while the leadership blamed the Congress for walking away with the credit of the victory over Pakistan in the 1971 war, the general perception amongst the cadre was that the party had begun to appear as a party of the rich.[13]

Although the 1971 elections had come as a relief to Indira Gandhi, the RSS, for what it was worth, could play a great role in unifying the Opposition. Since the early 1970s, the ABVP became a major force on campuses where student politics was practised and came to be seen as a significant part of the collective Opposition that ultimately became too big a force for Prime Minister Indira Gandhi to ignore. By the mid-1970s, the ABVP became ensconced in mainstream politics of the period where its involvement in student agitations in Bihar and Gujarat transformed into massive campaigns against the governments of the states. The ABVP had participated in campus protests to curb the influence of radical revolutionary communists and to draw the governments' attention to the demands of the students. In Gujarat, the ABVP participated in the Nav Nirman movement that led to the resignation of the incumbent chief minister, Chimanbhai Patel, and imposition of President's Rule, while in Bihar, the students' protest got support from Jayaprakash Narayan, referred to as 'JP', who converted the agitation into a mass movement seeking a 'total revolution' that would non-violently transform Indian society.[14] The ABVP also won the Delhi University elections in 1974 when Arun Jaitley, a future member of the Jana Sangh, became the president of the students union and represented its liberal and sophisticated face.[15]

It was in the middle of such strong winds of change that Rajnath Singh stepped into national politics. Singh became the secretary of the Bharatiya Jana Sangh's Mirzapur unit in 1974 by when the party had not only initiated a more activist approach by participating in demonstrations against price rise, but had also become very intricately involved with JP's movement. The party shifted gears internally as well. The former speaker in the Delhi Metropolitan Council, Lal Krishna Advani, replaced Vajpayee as the president. As he enjoyed the full support of the party, as well as the RSS leadership, he did not flinch from taking some harsh decisions. One such move involved the expulsion of Balraj Madhok from the party for a period of three years for indiscipline.[16]

Madhok had opposed the manner in which the Jana Sangh had become left-leaning in its policies. After he was thrown out, he wrote to the cadre sharing his anguish that while he did not oppose the RSS he was against its dominating influence in the party. It was Madhok who had ushered Advani into the Jana Sangh by introducing him to Upadhyaya to help him translate press statements, resolutions and other party material into English.[17]

The path ahead for the Jana Sangh became clear after the 25–26 November 1974 meeting between the Jana Sangh top brass with their counterparts from other Opposition parties. JP called for this meeting after his meeting with Indira Gandhi on 1 November 1974 to end the deadlock between the two that had hit a wall.[18] Besides Jana Sangh, the conference included leaders such as Charan Singh, who headed the Bharatiya Lok Dal (BLD) that was a fusion of seven parties opposed to Indira Gandhi, namely, the Swatantra Party, the Utkal Congress, the Socialist Party and Charan Singh's own party, the Bharatiya Kranti Dal, as well as the Akali Dal and the Congress (Organization). They concluded that a people's charter of demands would be submitted to the prime minister and discussed issues that could be projected based on what people thought on the ground to give more teeth to the movement.

In early 1975, only a few months after he had joined the Jana Sangh, Rajnath Singh was promoted to district president, Mirzapur, and became the coordinator for the JP movement in Uttar Pradesh's largest district. Singh's reputation as a steadfast organizer whose skill set would serve best at the grass-roots resulted in the mass movement covering great ground in a relatively short period of time. The district consisted of four tehsils or administrative divisions—Mirzapur (Sadar), Lalganj, Marihan and Chunar—that were further divided into twelve blocks. As JP's call for reform spread from states such as Bihar and Gujarat to the entire country, it was party personnel like Singh who ensured news of every single development reached the last person.

By the time the Opposition parties met again in February 1975, it was more than apparent that only a mass movement could prevent the complete collapse of democracy.[19] On 6 March 1975, an estimated crowd of 300,000 gathered at the Boat Club lawns, adjacent to Parliament in New Delhi to hear JP's speech. Even as the seventy-two-year-old JP was greeted with shouts of 'Lok Nayak zindabad', he called for a total revolution, which, he underlined, was the only way to put an end to the Indira Gandhi-led Congress's authoritarianism.[20] The rally consolidated the Opposition parties and some within the Congress such as Chandra Shekhar, a future prime minister, tried to broker peace, but an aggressive group within the Congress (R), led by Sanjay Gandhi, Indira's younger son, was not in favour.[21]

As rallies and demonstrations became a common sight, Indira Gandhi also became the first Indian prime minister to be cross-examined in a high court case of election fraud filed by Raj Narain, who had lost the 1971 parliamentary election to her. Narain's counsel, Shanti Bhushan, questioned her for allegedly misusing state machinery for election purposes and, in June 1975, Justice Jagmohanlal Sinha of the Allahabad High Court found the prime minister guilty.[22] Declaring her election victory null and void, the verdict unseated Indira Gandhi in the Lok Sabha besides banning her from contesting any elections for the next six years. Gandhi challenged the Allahabad High Court verdict in the Supreme Court, but on 24 June 1975, Justice V. R. Krishna Iyer upheld the high court judgment, ordering all privileges she received in the capacity of a member of Parliament to be stopped and debarring her from voting, but allowing her to carry on as prime minister till her appeal was resolved.[23]

A day after the Supreme Court judgment, on 25 June 1975, at a rally in Delhi, JP called for daily anti-government protests till Indira Gandhi continued to be in office. He even asked the police and the army to defy 'illegal' orders from a government that had lost all its moral authority.[24] It was certain that a great change in the history of independent India was around the corner. For an entire generation that had only heard stories from their parents about the struggle for freedom and liberty from the British, this was nothing less than the moment of reckoning. For Rajnath Singh, the events of 25 June 1975 and what followed became an instrinsic part of his life thereafter, and came at a great personal cost.

3

The Emergency and Its Aftermath

History books define the Emergency imposed by Indira Gandhi between 25 June 1975 and 21 March 1977 as a period when, under Article 352 of the Constitution of India, the president of India, Fakhruddin Ali Ahmed, effectively bestowed upon Gandhi the power to rule by decree. The dramatic turn in the history of independent India saw a suspension of nearly all civil liberties, fundamental rights and legal recourse available to the average Indian for a period of twenty-one months.

The judgment of the Allahabad High Court that declared Indira Gandhi's election null and void and banned her from contesting any elections for a period of six years was stayed for a period of twenty days during which the Congress party was to appoint a successor to the prime minister. Later, when the Supreme Court quashed Indira Gandhi's appeal for a complete and absolute stay, granting her a conditional stay, which in effect would have allowed her to not only continue as prime minister but also as an MP, the cries for her resignation grew louder. At the public rally held in the shadow of these developments, on 6 March 1975 at Boat Club in New Delhi where hundreds of thousands came to hear the veteran leader, JP called for a civil disobedience movement in order to put pressure on Indira Gandhi to quit.

The Allahabad High Court judgment indicting Indira Gandhi had been based on comparatively less serious charges such as the building of a dais by the state police, the height of the dais and the use of electricity; the more damning charges like bribing voters and election malpractices were dropped. This dilution had led the press to call the judgment akin to firing the prime minister for a traffic ticket.[1] Twenty-eight years after Nehru's famous 'tryst with destiny' speech, where at the stroke of the midnight hour India awoke to a new dawn, the night of 25 June 1975 saw his daughter Indira bring the world's largest democracy to a grinding halt.

In a midnight swoop, the government, now armed with absolute power, jailed nearly the entire Opposition including Jayaprakash Narayan, Atal Bihari Vajpayee, L.K. Advani, Morarji Desai, Ashok Mehta, Chandra Shekhar, Charan Singh, Madhu Dandavate, Ramakrishna Hegde, Biju Patnaik, Nanaji Deshmukh and Sikander Bakht, among others. It banned the RSS and went on to censor the press to such an extent that a few days into the Emergency, the Bombay edition of the *Times of India* carried an anonymous obituary that read: 'O'cracy D.E.M., beloved husband of T. Ruth, loving father of L.I. Bertie, brother of Faith, Hope and Justicia expired on 26th June 1975.'[2]

In 1971, the Parliament had passed the controversial Maintenance of Internal Security Act (MISA) that gave the administration and law enforcement agencies powers to detain individuals indefinitely, search and seize property without warrants, and wiretap to quell civil and political disorder in India besides countering foreign-inspired sabotage, terrorism, subterfuge and threats to national security. The MISA was amended many times during the course of the Emergency and it got more teeth thanks to Article 352 under which the courts could not inquire into the validity of the grounds upon which Emergency was called. Indira Gandhi also introduced a twenty-point programme that used the Emergency's 'discipline of the graveyard' to raise agricultural and industrial production, improve public services and fight poverty and illiteracy.[3] The powers that were given to the Central government virtually had no limits and the government did not shy away from practices such as amending laws in order to safeguard itself.

On 10 August 1975, Indira Gandhi put into effect the thirty-ninth amendment of the Constitution of India that placed the election of the president, the vice-president, the prime minister and the Speaker of the Lok Sabha beyond the scrutiny of the courts. Sanjay Gandhi practically shared authority with his mother, the prime minister, and ran a parallel government that openly indulged in excesses such as forced mass sterilization where, in just 1976, nearly 6.1 million men were sterilized.[4]

A few weeks into the Emergency there were widespread arrests across the country. With nearly the entire top brass of the Opposition incarcerated, the secretaries and the cadre followed a wait-and-watch approach but despite being cautious it was impossible to not oppose the tyranny of the government. There were programmes such as cleanliness camps that became the point of contact for those opposed to the government. Additionally, the production and distribution of underground literature such as *Lok Sangharsh*, in English and Hindi, and another local bulletin, *Jana Vani*, started in mid-July 1975 in Delhi, put out information about the government's autocratic functioning in the adjoining states.

The day of 12 July 1975 started like any other day for Rajnath Singh and after his morning exercise and bath, as he was about to step out, he was arrested by the Mirzapur police under MISA. By the time of his arrest, Singh had become known as a formidable force who had galvanized the JP movement programmes, and the authorities were instructed to not take him lightly. No one arrested under MISA was allowed any access to people outside, and Singh being one of the prominent detainees in the area, all contact was ruled out.

After he had spent a few days in Mirzapur jail, Singh was transferred to the Naini Central Jail near Allahabad. Hearing about the transfer, Savitri and Gujarati Devi decided to meet Singh at Mirzapur railway station where the train carrying him was scheduled to make a brief stop. Savitri had not seen her husband since the day he was arrested, but it had been a few months since Gujarati Devi had seen her son. On the day Singh was being ferried by train, both reached the station hours before the train was due. Every moment that passed filled them with anxiety. No one knew how long he would be under detention and the news of thousands more being hauled up across the country added to their fears.

The train arrived slightly later than it was due and soon the platform was full of police personnel. In a matter of seconds, Gujarati Devi and Savitri were separated from the train by a sea of humanity dressed in khaki. Handcuffed and held by policemen at the elbows, Singh emerged from the train hoping to meet his wife and mother. He spotted them at some distance but the sheer number of policemen between him and his family made it impossible for him to meet them. At twenty-four, Singh, who had been a physics lecturer at a local college a few years ago, was just a young man taking his first steps in politics but the security personnel treated him like a hardened criminal. Some of the people whom Singh had worked with during the JP movement had also made it to the railway station and they began sloganeering. It was impossible for Singh to hear his mother or Savitri in the middle of all the cacophony and sloganeering, asking him to carry on with his struggle. As the policemen whisked Singh away, he finally heard Gujarati Devi. Even in the face of uncertainty about what lay ahead for her son, the only thing Gujarati Devi told him was not to bow down. '*Babua, maafi maange ki naheen! Chahe umar bhar kaal-kothri mein kyon na katt jaye . . . kabhi sar mat jhukana.*' (Never beg for forgiveness, my son, even if you have to spend your entire life within the confines of a prison . . . never bow down). Hearing his mother urging him to never give in filled Singh with pride as he fought back the tears that had welled up. Many policemen too were moved by Gujarati's comment. That was the last time Singh ever saw his mother.

By August 1975, nearly 50,000 people had been arrested under MISA. In the wake of the government suspending all the rights offered under Article 19 of the Constitution of India that included the freedom of speech and expression, the right to assemble peaceably and without arms, the freedom to move freely throughout the territory of India, it was anybody's guess how long the imprisonment would last. Like Rajnath Singh, many Jana Sangh members were arrested and transferred to various jails. Advani was picked up in Bangalore and spent the next year and a half between the central jails at Rohtak and Bangalore; Vajpayee too spent some time in the Bangalore jail after which he was put under house arrest. Besides senior leaders such as Bhairon Singh Shekhawat and Vijaya Raje Scindia, several future leaders of the party—including Venkaiah Naidu, Pramod Mahajan, Ravi Shankar Prasad, Mukhtar Abbas Naqvi, Gopinath Munde, Shushil Modi and Arun Jaitley—were imprisoned for varying periods. Some other leaders such as Subramanian Swamy managed to not only evade arrest but also escaped to the United States from where he built public opinion abasing the Emergency. Swamy, in fact, escaped the police during a visit to Ahmedabad railway station, disguised as a Sikh, where he was received by a then twenty-five-year-old pracharak called Narendra Modi, who was also disguised as a Sikh. Later, Swamy used the same disguise to enter Parliament and mark his presence as a member in the middle of heavy security.

During the first few weeks in Naini Central Jail, Rajnath Singh was put in solitary confinement. Despite the bleak scenario and the uncertainty, Singh never lost faith. This enforced isolation gave him the time to reflect on the ideals and the principles instilled in him by his father and the values for which his mother was willing to let go of the chance to see her youngest son ever again.

A while later, when the solitary confinement ended, Singh saw some of his friends move applications for release on parole but he refused to do so. For Rajnath Singh, the time in jail made him reassess the ideals for which he was willing to put his life on the line. There were times when he caught himself thinking about how things had come to such a pass in the political history of the country. Irrespective of the differences in ideology or political affiliation, most politicians and people in public life, he believed, had one goal: serve the people and the country. Despite the cynicism about politicians that was beginning to set in among the public, the idea of making India a strong nation, one that would attract the envy of the world, was perhaps still the singular thought amongst people operating in the political sphere. In this context, the total disregard for propriety and decorum, and the high-handedness that the government displayed towards those in the Opposition and anyone who questioned it, in the process pushing the country into an era of darkness where basic civil liberties were snatched away, did not make much sense for young people such as Singh. For them, politics, at least up until the Emergency was declared, was about a debate between two or more theories and ultimately it was the voter who decided on which set of ideas suited them.

In the days leading to the Emergency, stories about Indira Gandhi using state machinery for her own benefit had become common knowledge. Even then reports about how a certain percentage of chemicalized ballot papers were pre-stamped in her favour—where stamps put by the voters in polling booths would disappear and the invisible stamp on the cow-and-calf symbol would become visible after some days—were ignored by leading Opposition members.[5] Some unnamed government officials sent anonymous letters to people such as Atal Bihari Vajpayee, S. Nijalingappa, Charan Singh and Nayantara Sahgal—Indira Gandhi's cousin and acclaimed author, who had been asked by JP to write a paper on the situation in Bihar and reported extensively for JP's newspaper *Everyman's Weekly*—appraising them of the degree of election malpractice that Indira Gandhi was said to have indulged in. The 1971 Lok Sabha elections and the state assembly elections later also witnessed a change in the process of counting, whereby ballots in each box, rather than being counted separately at the end of polling, were mixed with ballots in boxes from several polling stations. This resulted in a lapse of time, sometimes days, before counting could begin. Despite the enormous implications it possibly had, the change was not put to the Parliament for any debate and, in fact, was introduced after the session was dissolved. The Opposition maintained that such deviations would lead to massive misconduct and when the results were declared, the scale of Mrs Gandhi's victory had surprised even her own party men.

The Emergency was a tool to elicit a political price from those who challenged Indira Gandhi, but, for many, it extracted much more. Gujarati Devi had kept abreast of the unfolding situation and counted the days to her son's return. She often asked the same question every time she met any of her nephews: '*Babua kabhin aayen?*' (When will my lad return?) One of Rajnath Singh's cousins told Gujarati Devi that MISA would be retracted in a year's time and so, if everything went off well, Singh would probably be released on 25 June 1976. Through the course of the first year of the Emergency, scores of mothers like Gujarati Devi kept track of the days and waited with bated breath for someone to repeal the law or the government to release those detained under it.

A year later, on the said date, 25 June 1976, Gujarati Devi asked the same nephew about Singh's release, and unable to give her any good news, he told her that the government had extended MISA and no one had any idea how long it would take. It could well be another year. Gujarati Devi was unable to take it any more and suffered a stroke. She was rushed to the hospital and the doctors concurred she had had a brain haemorrhage. Her condition worsened over the next few days and, preparing for the worst, the doctor asked Savitri to inform her husband.

Upon hearing the news, Singh refused to move an application for a furlough to visit his mother in the hospital, preferring to absorb the blow silently. Every morning at sunrise, he hoped against hope that any news about his mother would be delayed by yet another day. The jail and the treatment meted out to him had not succeeded in breaking his spirit. The jail authorities were following orders from a dispensation powerful enough to brush away basic rights of one of the world's most populous countries by a mere stroke of the pen. They had dented the self-esteem of many of the inmates and ensured that the person eventually walking out was not the same as the one who had gone in.

Singh remained determined to not letting anything undermine him mentally and more so when the news about his mother's condition became public knowledge. He reminded himself of what his mother would have expected from him and carried on. It was in jail that Singh got to learn about his mother's passing away and performed all the post-death rites including shaving his head within the confines of Naini Central

Jail. To this day, Singh finds it difficult to stop tears welling up in his eyes every time he remembers his mother.

The news of Gujarati Devi's death spread across the district and, a few days later, when Madhav Prasad Tripathi, a Jana Sangh leader who had come to be a mentor of sorts to Rajnath, met Uttar Pradesh chief minister Narayan Datt Tiwari, he chastised the government for being so hard-hearted and told him about what had transpired. Madho babu, as Tripathi was fondly known, was assured by Tiwari that Singh would be back home for a few days to take care of the formalities. Singh was granted a fifteen-day furlough by the government, but the fortnight seemed too long for him to spend at home. He could not sit idly lest the pain and the anguish start to gnaw at him and weaken his spirit. Even during the parole, Singh began to organize cleanliness campaigns in the neighbourhood as a means of opposing the Emergency. He was happy to be home with Savitri but knew that this was not the kind of freedom he had wanted. A day before the parole ended, Singh returned to Naini Central Jail and remained there till the Emergency was finally lifted on 21 March 1977. Towards the final months, when many of the detainees were given the option of shifting to house arrest, he refused to leave Naini jail for any other confinement.

On 18 January 1977, Indira Gandhi called for fresh Lok Sabha elections that would be held in the month of March and although she also ordered the release of those her government had detained, the Emergency officially ended on 21 March 1977.[6] The Opposition soon galvanized people and left no stone unturned to make it amply clear that this was their last chance to pick between democracy and dictatorship. After his release, Singh found great support within his community that was aware of the hardships he had undergone during the Emergency. An entire generation of India's political class that had been put through the strongest of fires was about to graduate and Singh was amongst them.

Unlike the decision to not give tickets to some rising stars such as the ABVP students as the Jana Sangh felt they had been overly politicized during the Emergency, which could lead them to look at things in a different light, there was no predicament when it came to Singh. He became an automatic choice for the Lok Sabha ticket from Mirzapur. The principal Opposition parties— the Jana Sangh, the Bharatiya Lok Dal, the Socialist Party and the Congress (organization)—had come together as the Janata alliance to fight the elections against Indira Gandhi. Singh began campaigning in full swing for the elections that were to be held between 16 and 19 March 1977. But before voting day, an internal understanding between the Jana Sangh and the Lok Dal relegated him to the sidelines.

Uttar Pradesh had traditionally been a state where political battles decided the political future of the Indian Parliament and an eleventh-hour seat-sharing arrangement between the parties that constituted the Janata alliance saw the Jana Sangh giving up Mirzapur in favour of Faqir Ali Ansari. As a result, the Jana Sangh could not pitch its candidate and the Lok Dal decided to field a locally recognized carpet manufacturer as the contender from Mirzapur.

The news of the change sent shockwaves across the city. Not just the Jana Sangh party workers but also the RSS and ABVP cadre offered their support to Singh. Much like the earlier elections, the RSS cadre was bound to play a significant role in mobilizing the electorate in favour of the Janata alliance as it had done for the Jana Sangh in the past. The word on the ground suggested that the joint cadre was willing to go against the executive if Rajnath Singh was not picked and some had even begun suggesting that he should fight the elections as an independent.

Singh made his way to the district collector's office to withdraw his candidature, accompanied by a swarm of supporters.

The sight was perhaps too intimidating for Ansari, the Lok Dal candidate, a soft-spoken Muslim gentleman who was known to Singh as well. As he entered the office, Singh offered him his best wishes. The district collector informed Singh that the time to withdraw candidature was over and his name would remain on the ballot paper. As Singh pondered over how to avoid a situation that would be detrimental for both the Jana Sangh and the Janata alliance, the clamour urging him to fight as an independent candidate grew louder amongst the cadre. Singh took a moment to think and decided to stand by the party. He told everyone that if the party was right in thinking of him as worthy enough to contest, how could it be wrong if it changed its mind due to some unavoidable circumstance? In a practical display of walking the talk, doing the right thing irrespective of the situation, which was also fast becoming a much-talked-about trait of Rajnath Singh, he offered all his support to the Janata alliance candidate. As he stepped out of the DC's office, Singh addressed the crowd, underlining that it was his bad luck that the rules did not permit his name to be struck off the ballot paper. He told everyone present that if he got even one vote it would be tantamount to dishonouring his name. When the votes were cast and the ballots counted, Rajnath Singh did not get a single vote. To this date, he considers it to be a victory unlike any other in his entire life.

A few months before the 1977 elections, senior Congress member Jagjivan Ram, who was Indira Gandhi's defence minister, quit the party and formed the Congress for Democracy (CFD) along with Hemvati Nandan Bahuguna and Nandini Satpathy that joined the Janata alliance. A major advocate for Dalit rights, Jagjivan Ram's defection swung the Dalit vote away from Indira Gandhi. With Charan Singh influencing the rural vote and a swing in the Muslim vote due to some of the actions during the Emergency that specifically targeted the community, such as bulldozing of slums near Jama Masjid in Delhi and the forced sterilization drive that by design targeted the population of the poor at large, especially Muslims and in Muslim-majority areas, it was no wonder that the Congress lost heavily.[7]

The Janata alliance won 271 seats and along with allies such as the Shiromani Akali Dal, the DMK and CFD, garnered an absolute majority of 345 seats. Morarji Desai became the first non-Congress prime minister of India in March 1977 and his cabinet included two deputy prime ministers, Charan Singh and Jagjivan Ram, who also held on to home and defence portfolios respectively. The cabinet also included the two senior Jana Sangh leaders, Atal Bihari Vajpayee (minister of external affairs) and Lal Krishna Advani (minister of information and broadcasting) besides Brij Lal Varma, a mild-mannered district lawyer from Raipur, who was initially given the industry ministry but later swapped portfolios with George Fernandes to handle the Telecommunications portfolio.

Both Indira Gandhi and Sanjay Gandhi lost their seats and, for the first time since Independence, the Congress did not win a single seat in Uttar Pradesh. In one of its first moves, the Janata government amended the Constitution of India to its pre-1976 status. The forty-fourth amendment put in place a provision that Article 19, which provides freedom of speech, and Article 21 that provides right to life and right to personal liberty, could not be suspended or amended even during an Emergency.[8]

A lot had changed for Rajnath Singh by the time the Uttar Pradesh state assembly elections were due in June 1977. Word about Singh and his 'sacrifice' had reached the Lok Dal leader Chaudhary Charan Singh, who had come to regret his decision of snatching the Lok Sabha ticket from the young man. Charan Singh's party decided to not field any candidate against Singh in the assembly elections, and, as expected, Singh won handsomely. Singh dedicated his maiden speech in the Uttar Pradesh Legislative Assembly to the memory of his mother and spoke about the trials of the small-scale industries of his constituency. Singh's oratory skills impressed the house and also caught the attention of many senior members, including Narayan Dutt Tiwari, who, while walking past the treasury benches, congratulated him and told him to feel free to approach him should he ever feel the need.

There was a lot of hope from the Janata government as well as the state governments that replaced the Congress party. The scars of Emergency would take a while to heal, but for the common citizen, the act of putting new custodians of democracy in power was reason enough to expect an unbridled overhaul of the system in the shortest time possible. However, that was not to be. The alliance had come together with the common cause of throwing Indira Gandhi out of power and once that objective was achieved, it displayed a lack of direction. By August 1977, Jagjivan Ram had publicly admitted the party was working more as a conglomeration of various ideological groups rather than as a unified political party.[9] Desai faced initial teething troubles but the writing was becoming clearer with each passing day. The decision to appoint Desai as the leader and, therefore, the prime minister had been taken by JP and J.B. Kripalani, another senior functionary of the movement. Charan Singh, for one, did not take too kindly to the decision. Despite some impressive work in its first few months, the cracks within the Janata government became more and more apparent with each passing day, the tussle between Charan Singh and Desai highlighting just one aspect of what was going wrong with the alliance.

Immediately after Emergency, the RSS witnessed a surge in its membership as the number of shakhas went up from 8500 in 1975 to 11,000 in 1977 and to 13,000 a year later in 1978.[10] RSS affiliates, such as the Bharatiya Mazdoor Sangh (BMS) and the

ABVP, also saw a spurt in membership. This led to a sense of unease among other constituents of the Janata alliance which probably feared that the Sangh could help further strengthen the Jana Sangh, which, already, was the single largest element in the group. The top brass of the Janata Party suggested a merger between the RSS and any one of the Janata Party's affiliates. This, however, was not acceptable to the RSS that continued to reject any direct role in politics. Once the merger was ruled out, Jana Sangh leaders were asked to cut their ties with the RSS on the pretext that such dual membership was not permitted under the interim constitution of the Janata alliance. The demand arose on the grounds that the Janata Party did not permit members belonging to another 'political party, communal or other, which has a separate membership, constitution and programme', to which Vajpayee and others pointed out that the RSS was not a political party.[11]

In early 1979, as the issue reached a fever pitch, Vajpayee warned that the Jana Sangh could pull out of the government. Despite being the single and largest party in the alliance and having the organizational spread of the RSS that played a decisive role in the elections, the Jana Sangh never negotiated for a proportionate share in the government.

The government began to appear increasingly unstable as the relationship between Desai and Charan Singh worsened, with the latter openly advocating the former's ouster. Things had come to such a pass that both Charan Singh and Desai, who at the time were in their late seventies and early eighties, had started to talk about each other's death to resolve the leadership issue.[12]

Charan Singh's ambition also fuelled the return of Indira Gandhi, who fought and won a by-election in Chikmagalur in Karnataka and returned to the Lok Sabha. When Singh withdrew his support to the government, Desai was forced to resign as prime minister on 19 July 1979. The Jana Sangh had tried to get Jagjivan Ram to replace Desai, which would have silenced the critics who were hinting that the RSS was controlling the government or the party, but that did not work out. Charan Singh managed to succeed as the prime minister and, close on the heels of his elevation, the party's constitution was unanimously amended by adding a provision specifying that 'no member of any organization having faith in a theocratic state can be a member of the party'.[13]

Although the Janata Party and its president Chandra Shekhar feared that following the split of the party, the Jana Sangh would capture the party thanks to its mass base and a large army of dedicated workers, the reality was different.[14] The Janata Party needed all the votes it could keep and, in July 1979, Chandra Shekhar met Balasaheb Deoras, the then sarsangchalak to ask the RSS to bar swayamsevaks and pracharaks who held office to not participate in the activities of the RSS. There were positive indications from Deoras that such an arrangement could be worked out but the central assembly of the RSS did not meet till March 1980 to consider it. Within three weeks of being in office, Charan Singh resigned after most of the partners abandoned the alliance; he even tried to woo Indira Gandhi's Congress that by now was called Congress (Indira). With no other political party left in the position of establishing a majority, President Neelam Sanjiva Reddy called for fresh elections in January 1980.

The in-fighting between leaders of the Janata Party and the political instability in the country worked in favour of Indira Gandhi's Congress (I). She apologized for the Emergency and came back to power, reminding the voters to elect a stable government. The 1980 elections also saw a near-eclipse of the Jana Sangh in the Lok Sabha where its tally came down to sixteen seats.[15] In April 1980, the Janata Party adopted a resolution prohibiting members of RSS from continuing in the Janata Party. On 6 April 1980, Rajnath Singh along with scores of Jana Sangh members from across India travelled to New Delhi to witness the end of an era and the beginning of a new one. The Jana Sangh decided to part ways with the Janata Party and it was on the same day that the Bharatiya Janata Party (BJP) emerged from the remains of the Jana Sangh.

4

Sun-ward Climb

Indira Gandhi's announcement to hold the state assembly elections in May 1980 hastened the process of the Bharatiya Jana Sangh's transformation into the Bharatiya Janata Party (BJP). Both the Janata Party and the Rashtriya Swayamsevak Sangh could not arrive at any consensus and even mediations by senior figures such as Morarji Desai did not seem to help. The Jana Sangh felt that the RSS should decide on the matter of dual membership while the Janata Dal believed it was up to them to decide their own membership requirements. The Jana Sangh had called for a national convention a day after the Janata Party was scheduled to have its national executive meeting where they were to vote on the dual-membership issue. The Janata Party voted against dual membership, and the 17–14 vote put paid to all hopes of the Jana Sangh and the Janata Party continuing as partners.[1]

At the Kotla grounds in Delhi, over 3000 delegates of the Jana Sangh, along with a few who had left the Janata Party, formed the BJP. The emergence of the BJP was clearly a result of the confusion within the Janata Party that refused to get its act together. The newly formed party, which aimed to be the real representative of both Jayaprakash Narayan and Deendayal Upadhyaya, did not intend to be a rejigged Jana Sangh. In

fact, Atal Bihari Vajpayee, who became the first president of
the BJP, made it amply clear that the party aspired to a much
broader following. The party might not have had a traditional
organization as yet, but it had its erstwhile Jana Sangh cadre and
many aspirants amongst the RSS. Vajpayee also picked many
non–Jana Sangh individuals for his working committee and one
of the secretaries, Sikander Bakht, was a Muslim. The party
was clear that it wanted to include members of the RSS even
though publicly many pracharaks expressed a disenchantment
with politics after the Janata experience. In fact, many of them
such as Nanaji Deshmukh even questioned the legitimacy of
politics as a vocation.[2]

The BJP, however, resolved the issue of dual membership
by including in its basic statement that 'members of all those
social or cultural organizations which are working for the social
or cultural uplift of the masses and are not engaged in any
political activity are welcome to join the BJP'. The BJP adopted
the 'lotus' as its new symbol in place of the lamp of the Jana
Sangh. Its flag also featured both saffron and green instead of
the solid saffron that adorned the Jana Sangh flag. In its bid
to be different from its past, while not abandoning it, the new
party tried to combine the RSS cadres' organization skills and
JP's idealism. This could also explain why it appeared to adopt
the Gandhian brand of socialism rather than continuing with
Deendayal Upadhyaya's path of integral humanism.

Beginning in April 1980, the BJP moved cadres to set up
units across the country and, by December 1980, when the
party's first plenary was held in Bombay, it had managed to
enrol nearly 25,00,000 members. The assembly elections held
in nine states in May 1980 gave the new party hardly any time to
prepare for the polls. The results revealed a general acceptance
of the BJP amongst the voter but, more importantly, it showed
that the party had managed to retain its 'Jana Sangh' base,

especially in Rajasthan where it picked up thirty-two seats. The party's maiden plenary held between 28 and 30 December 1980 was attended by over 55,000 workers from across the country and was addressed by Muhammedali Currim Chagla, a veteran ex-Congressman who had opposed the Emergency. Chagla not only felt that the Congress had become a party of 'hypocrites, opportunists and sycophants' but also argued that the BJP has 'completely established its credentials as the alternative that can replace' the Congress government.[3]

The ideological change that BJP had now decided to implement became a bone of contention during the plenary. There was some criticism of the Gandhian socialism approach by Vijaya Raje Scindia, a vice-president of the party, whose apprehension was that it hardly differentiated the BJP from Indira Gandhi's Congress.

Despite the initial argument within the executive, the party continued to perform well on the ground. Its members Rajendra Agnihotri and L. Bachani won the 1981 by-elections in Jhansi, Uttar Pradesh and Naroda, Gujarat, respectively, and in 1982, the BJP managed to emerge as the single largest party in Himachal Pradesh. Within three years of its formation, there was also a sense emerging both within the party and power circles that the BJP could, in fact, become a national-level alternative to the Congress. There was also the question of alliances at the national level and there were two divergent camps within the leadership on how to approach this. The Emergency had firmly put the spotlight on the Jana Sangh, which L.K. Advani once described as suffering from 'political untouchability'. However, the party's primary face, namely Vajpayee, was far from being a political pariah. As far as Indira Gandhi and the Congress were concerned, there was no doubt that the Congress projected itself as the one party for all, but the electorate had constantly witnessed instances where the party routinely failed to live up to its secular tag.

In 1981, after hundreds of low-caste Hindus converted to Islam in Meenakshipuram, a village in the Tirunelveli district of Tamil Nadu, amidst media reports of the conversion taking place using foreign funding, Indira Gandhi considered introducing anti-conversion legislation. Later in 1983, the government's decision to hold elections in Assam despite stiff local opposition largely due to the appeasement of nearly four million immigrants from Bangladesh, whom Indira Gandhi also gave the right to vote, led to one of the worst massacres in human history, the Nellie massacre.

The All Assam Students Union (AASU) that had constituted the All Assam Gana Sangram Parishad (AAGSP) along with representatives of various local organizations and political parties and went on to form the Asom Gana Parishad (AGP), called to defer the elections until the names of the 'foreign nationals' or migrants who had relocated in the early part of the twentieth century as well as the ones who had illegally moved from Bangladesh, were deleted from the electoral rolls. The locals often complained that the Congress government did not take effective measures, and instead protected Muslims in order to gain power in the state and used them as 'vote banks'.[4] On 18 February 1983, when the state was under President's Rule, an attack by the locals against the migrant population left over two thousand people across fourteen villages—Alisingha, Khulapathar, Basundhari, Bugduba Beel, Bugduba Habi, Borjola, Butuni, Dongabori, Indurmari, Mati Parbat, Muladhari, Mati Parbat No. 8, Silbheta, Borburi and Nellie—of Nagaon district dead. The Nellie incident has been compared by many to the 'Great Calcutta Killings'.

Indira Gandhi's most famous political misadventure in terms of vote-bank politics saw the Congress party nurture Jarnail Singh Bhindranwale, a leader of the Sikh educational organization Damdami Taksal, as a 'Sant' to challenge the Akali government in Punjab. According to many sources, it was Sanjay Gandhi who along with Kamal Nath—in an effort to replicate Punjab chief

minister Pratap Singh Kairon's tactics of fighting the Akalis—
selected Bhindranwale in 1977 and assisted him financially,
besides giving him political clout to establish himself as a power
centre.[5] Bhindranwale's radical plans to secede from India had the
backing of Pakistan's Inter-Services Intelligence (ISI) that also
supplied his group with arms and ammunition.[6]

By July 1982 he had taken up residence inside Sri Harmandir
Sahib (the Golden Temple), the most important pilgrimage
site of the Sikhs. It was from there that he led the terrorist
campaign in Punjab. Later, after repeated negotiations between
the Government of India and Bhindranwale failed, Indira
Gandhi ordered a military operation called Operation Blue
Star in June 1984 to remove Bhindranwale from the complex.
It witnessed the use of tanks and heavy artillery to attack the
militants who responded with anti-tank and machine-gun fires
from the heavily fortified Akal Takht, one of the five seats of
power of the Sikhs, located inside the Golden Temple complex.

The events of June 1984 led to the assassination of Indira
Gandhi on 31 October 1984 by two of her Sikh bodyguards.
Although it might not have been known to many in the party,
according to a close aide of Vajpayee, Indira Gandhi had spoken
to the president of the BJP before putting Operation Blue Star
into play.[7] On a secure telephone line, Vajpayee, who was in
Bangalore at the time undergoing naturopathy treatment, was
told by the prime minister that she was planning to order the
army into the Golden Temple. Vajpayee warned her against
such action and told her there could be other ways of flushing
out terrorists, but to no avail.

What followed Indira Gandhi's assassination was a state-
aided pogrom against Sikhs in Delhi in which thousands of
Sikh men, women and children were mercilessly butchered on
the streets of Delhi, with the authorities turning a blind eye.[8]
Indira Gandhi's son, Rajiv Gandhi, was anointed the president
of the party and also made the prime minister of India. He

justified the massacre of a community with his 'When a big tree falls, the earth shakes' statement.[9] For decades there was not a single conviction even though subsequent governments formed many commissions to investigate the cold-blooded killings.

A few electoral setbacks around 1983, primarily in Delhi and Jammu where the BJP had enjoyed a traditional base, might have compelled Vajpayee to think of alliances in a new light. In Jammu, Indira Gandhi's criticism of the independent-line tactic employed by Dr Farooq Abdullah, the son of Sheikh Abdullah and the new leader of the NC, saw the Congress shift gears in the state. The younger Abdullah's ploy was too reminiscent of his father, who had died in 1982. Farooq Abdullah's independent line became a cause of bigger worry for Indira Gandhi when the former began to make his presence felt on the national political scene by sharing the stage with major Opposition leaders such as the Telugu Desam Party's N.T. Rama Rao and Akali Dal's Prakash Singh Badal. Mrs Gandhi did not take too kindly to Abdullah's pro-regional autonomy sentiments and began appeasing the 'Hindu' vote in the state.[10] She was particularly accommodative of the Vishwa Hindu Parishad's (VHP) *Ekaimata Yagna* or Rite for the Union of Souls where ninety-two caravans conducted yagna across temple towns in India.[11] The intensive campaign saw her indulge in fear-mongering, which according to analysts, intensified the Hindu–Muslim polarization in the state of Jammu and Kashmir.[12] The NC won forty-four of the seventy-one seats in the state and although the Congress could only manage one seat in the Kashmir Valley, it nonetheless shifted the BJP's vote in Jammu where it walked off with twenty-three of thirty-two seats.[13] However, the real shocker came in Delhi where the BJP won only nineteen of fifty-six metropolitan council seats and thirty-seven out of 100 corporation seats.[14]

The press was rife with rumours of the RSS cadres' somewhat 'neutral' position that led to such a result. It was inferred that the cadre in Delhi that largely consisted of Punjabi Hindus was supportive of Indira Gandhi's tough stand towards the growing demand for an autonomous Punjab and, as a result, the BJP suffered due to a disaffected RSS being on the sidelines.[15] In a somewhat surprising turn of events, the BJP managed to pick up unexpected votes amongst Muslim voters. The Muslin community voted against the Congress and not a single candidate of the Congress returned from areas with a high proportion of Muslims such as Ballimaran, Farash Khana, Bara Hindu Rao and Matia Mahal from where the BJP's Begum Khurshida Kidwai won hands down.[16] Vajpayee asked the party to bring together 'nationalist democratic forces' and, as a result, Advani met leaders of thirteen other Opposition parties, including the communists, at a conclave called by the chief minister of Andhra Pradesh, N.T. Rama Rao. There were many such meetings and even though the BJP and Charan Singh's Lok Dal formed a National Democratic Alliance (NDA), the latter went ahead and merged with some other Opposition parties without even bothering to inform the former.[17]

But the biggest electoral shock the BJP faced was in the 1984 Lok Sabha elections. Held in the aftermath of Indira Gandhi's death, the Congress swept the polls, winning 404 of the 514 seats on which the elections were held as the voting in Punjab and Assam was delayed. Once again there was widespread speculation that the RSS cadre had backed the Congress party because of its hard stance against secessionist ideology both in Punjab and Kashmir. Contrary to the impression of some people that the RSS did not oppose the 1984 genocide in Delhi, writers such as Khushwant Singh acknowledged that some leaders of the Sangh Parivar and the RSS, including Vajpayee, went out of their way to help the Sikhs.

In the year where Indian politics was undergoing tumultuous change, and the BJP commenced its second attempt to start afresh in four years, Rajnath Singh was appointed the state secretary of the party's Uttar Pradesh unit. If between its inception and 1984, the BJP's aim was to project itself as a national alternative to Indira Gandhi's Congress, post-1984, it became a question of political survival. The state assembly elections held a few weeks later, in early 1985, came as a breather for the BJP where it managed to improve its tally in UP (sixteen seats, up from eleven in 1980), Rajasthan and Madhya Pradesh, but it was still a far cry from posing a real challenge. The manner in which it was reduced to two seats in Parliament called for a reinvigoration of the party at the grass-roots level, and states such as Uttar Pradesh were bound to play a significant role.

Most Central governments in India tend to micromanage politics in the state of Uttar Pradesh, which is not surprising given that every sixth legislator in the Lok Sabha is elected from the state. Before the spilt in the Congress in 1969, the Centre's intervention in UP politics was limited but the realization that the state's fortunes had a direct influence on the national governments changed the terms of engagement. Indira Gandhi's efforts to centralize power by controlling the distribution of tickets to contest elections for state legislative assemblies transformed the organization structure of the party in the state. The steady decline of the independent state politicians within the Congress in Uttar Pradesh began in the 1970s where committees and party offices were filled by appointment rather than election.[18] As a result of this, factionalism no longer decided the outcome of the state party's leadership.[19]

The Congress won a whopping 309 seats out 425 in the 1980 assembly elections and, beginning with the appointment of Vishwanath Pratap Singh as the chief minister, the state saw an intervention of the Congress high command irrespective of who the party president was or where political decisions were made outside of the dynamics of the state. Singh was nothing less than a rising star in the Congress and the erstwhile raja of Manda commanded great loyalty amongst the Thakur community. Yet, within two years, he was replaced by Sripat Mishra, a former Speaker of the UP Legislative Assembly, who barely had a following of any significance when compared with V.P. Singh but met Indira Gandhi's criteria. On the face of it, Mishra's elevation was a result of V.P. Singh's inability to carry the 'Brahmin'-dominated bureaucracy but more than curbing the imagined dissidence or the Thakur lobby, which was highlighted by most political commentators, there was little doubt that Mishra being 'nobody' would not be a threat to Mrs Gandhi.[20]

Such factionalism might have existed within the echelons of Indian politics, but earlier in Uttar Pradesh, it at least attempted to work around divisive caste and religious groups within the state and give them a fighting chance to compete for the top post. But this changed as the decade progressed.[21] Between 1982 and 1987, three chief ministers of the state were selected the same way as Mishra—N.D. Tiwari (1984), Vir Bahadur Singh (1985) and Tiwari again (1988)—and their appointments seemed to represent the Brahmins and Thakurs caste and religious lobbies.[22]

Within a few months into his appointment as the party's state secretary, Rajnath Singh could see how UP was slowly becoming the hotbed of political upheavals, some of which were bound to have a long-term impact on the nation's politics.

In April 1985, the Supreme Court of India upheld the decision of the Madhya Pradesh High Court directing alimony to be paid to a sixty-two-year-old woman, Shah Bano Begum, who had filed a criminal suit against Mohammad Ahmed Khan, her husband, who had divorced her. Shah Bano had married Khan in 1932. Bano had five children with Khan and had been living in the same house with Khan when he married and brought home his second wife. When Khan asked her to move out and refused to pay maintenance, she filed a lawsuit, claiming maintenance for herself and her five children under Section 123 of the Code of Criminal Procedure, 1973, which was applicable to all Indians. Khan, who was a lawyer, contested the claim on the grounds that the Muslim Personal Law in India required the husband to only provide maintenance for the duration of the *iddat*, the ninety-day period after the divorce. Khan lost the case in Madhya Pradesh High Court and appealed against it in the Supreme Court. The case was heard by a five-judge bench comprising the then Chief Justice of India, Y.V. Chandrachud and Justices Ranganath Misra, D.A. Desai, O. Chinnappa Reddy and E. S. Venkataramiah. On 23 April 1985, the Supreme Court, in a unanimous decision, dismissed the appeal and confirmed the judgment of the Madhya Pradesh High Court.

In a blatant display of vote-bank appeasement, Rajiv Gandhi passed The Muslim Women (Protection of Rights on Divorce) Act, 1986, that not only nullified the Supreme Court's judgment in the Shah Bano case but also adhered to the tenets of the Muslim Personal Law by allowing maintenance to a divorced woman only during the period of iddat according to the provisions of Islamic law. Even in the wake of much opposition, including from one of Rajiv Gandhi's colleagues Arif Mohammad Khan, a minister in his cabinet, who resigned from both the post and the party in protest, the government's huge majority in Parliament allowed it to violate the sanctity of the country's highest court.

A few months later, in February 1986, in a desperate bid to balance his action of giving in to Muslim zealots, Rajiv Gandhi ordered the locks on the Babri Masjid to be opened and allowed religious rites to be performed at the Ram Mandir site in Ayodhya. The action saw a revival of the movement for the temple at Ramjanmabhoomi, the birthplace of Lord Ram in Ayodhya, where Mughal Emperor Babur's general Mir Baqi built the Babri Masjid in 1528. The Ayodhya dispute—which included aspects pertaining to access to a site traditionally regarded among Hindus to be the birthplace of the Hindu deity Ram and whether a previous Hindu temple was demolished or modified to create the mosque—had been on the socio-political back burner since Independence. The issue had nearly run out of steam in mainstream circles, and very few people in India probably had any idea about its contentious history, but Rajiv Gandhi's decision revived it. Though it was again a blatant act of appeasement aimed at the majority community this time so as to offset the earlier act in the Shah Bano case, Rajiv's decision sent out a message that on the face of it he favoured the Hindu claim.

A few months before the opening of the locks of the Babri Masjid, the BJP, in March 1985, set up a twelve-member working group to probe the ills that were plaguing the party. Vajpayee asked the group consisting of Krishanlal Sharma, Bhairon Singh Shekhawat, Shanta Kumar, Sunder Lal Patwa, Makrand Desai, Pramod Mahajan, Vijay Kumar Malhotra, K. Jana Krishnamurthi, Murli Manohar Joshi, Suraj Bhan, Arif Beg and Mridula Sinha to present a report on what could help the party in the days ahead. The committee asked over fifty questions pertaining to past performance, ideology, the organization, discipline, finances, the relationship between the legislative and organizational wings and election strategy, besides a few more areas via a questionnaire that was circulated among thousands of cadre.

What followed was a shift in the party's perspective when, at the July 1985 Bhopal national executive, the BJP reverted to Upadhyaya's integral humanism as its core philosophy. Another aspect that emerged from the working group's report was the emphasis on the ideology of any political party which, to the cadres' mind, distinguished it from the rest. When it came to

ideology, the BJP was different from the rest thanks to the
adoption of certain policies such as advocating the repeal of
Article 370 of the Indian Constitution that gave special status to
the state of Jammu and Kashmir and backing of India's nuclear
capability. In 1986, when Advani became the party's national
president, the BJP made building a Ram temple on the site of
the mosque an election issue. In his inaugural presidential speech
in May 1986, Advani chided Rajiv Gandhi's legislation forcing
the courts to apply traditional Islamic law instead of common
civil code in alimony cases involving Muslim women and also
called for a uniform civil code.

At the time he was appointed the party's state secretary,
Rajnath Singh was also given the position of the Uttar Pradesh
state president of the Bharatiya Janata Yuva Morcha (BJYM),
the BJP's youth wing. Assigning dual responsibilities was not
uncommon in the BJP, but what made Singh's appointment
intriguing was the state in which he operated—Uttar Pradesh.
While the Ram Janmabhoomi movement was steadily gaining
momentum at the grass roots, the Congress was losing political
ground equally steadily. Astute observer that he was, Rajnath
Singh realized that this was the foundation on which the next
general election would be based.

Uttar Pradesh was fast becoming synonymous with Singh's
name as he was with the state and he was soon given charge of
organizing rallies and drives to connect with the electorate. As
the state president, Singh became the point of contact for the
BJYM's national president Pramod Mahajan, who had begun
to make a name for himself as one of the emerging faces that
would lead the party in the foreseeable future. The BJYM had a
near-similar organizational structure to the BJP, and its national
president was also a part of the BJP's national executive. Rajnath
Singh enjoyed a great working relationship with Mahajan and,
thanks to the organizational structure being similar that of the

parent party, got to learn and grow exponentially along with the BJYM. As Singh had been closely involved with the RSS and the ABVP, he was more than familiar with the arrangement in terms of organization, and as senior leaders within the party made it a point to make the youth wing participate in the decision-making process, Singh's generation also played its role in shaping the party's political destiny.

At the BJP's national executive held in Agra in 1988, the party announced Rajnath Singh as BJYM's new national president after Pramod Mahajan. Singh had attended the plenary following the national executive in Agra and witnessed first-hand how the city showered flowers on Atal Bihari Vajpayee as the senior leader made his way to the convention.[23] Following the three-day convention, a BJP wave swept the city and it initiated the process of the party's emergence as a major political force across the municipal corporation, legislative assembly and the Lok Sabha from Agra. Singh had been earmarked to succeed Mahajan both by the senior leadership and Mahajan himself, who had asked him to also assume charge as BJYM's general secretary in order to get him to Delhi. With an alliance between the BJP and the Shiv Sena on the horizon, which was largely facilitated by Mahajan's efforts, the only person Mahajan felt confident of easing into the space that he would leave was Singh.[24]

At the time, Singh was not too keen to leave Uttar Pradesh and politely refused Mahajan's offer. At party meetings, Singh was routinely asked by other party members, including Kushabhau Thakre and Madhav Bhandari, to shift to Delhi or convey Mahajan's reluctance to appoint anyone else in his place. Mahajan refused to appoint any other general secretary. Singh eventually relented. When Singh returned home to Mirzapur after the Agra convention, he read in the newspapers about his sudden elevation as the national president of the BJYM. It was on the same day that Singh was also nominated to the Uttar

Pradesh Vidhan Parishad, the Legislative Council or the Upper House of the state legislative.

At thirty-seven, Rajnath Singh found himself at the helm of affairs of one of the fastest-growing youth wings of a political party in the world. A tectonic shift in the way politics operated was under way and it would be the youth wing at the forefront that drove this change, with Singh having a vital part in the shaping of the BJP's transition. In the mid-1980s, the BJYM played a big role in bringing to the fore issues affecting the youth and making them aware of national issues in states such as Uttar Pradesh.

During this time, Singh wrote a book on one of the issues that plagued the youth the most anywhere in the country: unemployment. In a detailed treatise titled, *Unemployment: Its Reasons and Remedies*, Singh articulated the major reasons for unemployment amongst the youth in Uttar Pradesh and, based on his interaction with the young across districts and constituencies, offered remedies that would cut the Gordian knot strangling the potential of the country.

The country had been independent for four decades but instead of transforming into a superpower that everyone dreamt of, India was experiencing a growing sense of disenchantment with the promises that the political dispensation had made. Barring a brief period of three years where the Janata Party government was at the Centre, the Congress had been in power for the entire period and the lack of direction, as well as confusion in terms of policy, had become too conspicuous to ignore. Many Indians and, particularly, the young started questioning the policies of the first prime minister of India and the so-called 'Nehruvian' dream as well as the actions of his grandson and the then prime minister of India, Rajiv Gandhi.

Things got tough for Rajiv Gandhi when, on 16 April 1987, Radio Sweden broke the story of the reputed Swedish artillery manufacturer Bofors paying kickbacks to politicians, members of the Congress party and bureaucrats to secure a Rs 1,500-crore contract. The deal was to supply 410 155-mm calibre Howitzer guns for the Indian Army but most Indian newspapers were not even aware, and the course of history might not have changed as much had the story not been picked up by Chitra Subramaniam, a journalist from *The Hindu*, who happened to be in Sweden at the time. On 20 April 1987, Rajiv Gandhi told the Lok Sabha that no kickbacks were paid and no middlemen were involved. As the Bofors mystery unravelled and it became clear that the Swedish manufacturer had reportedly paid Rs 64 crore (US $8.9 million) as kickbacks to top Indian politicians and key defence officials, it triggered Gandhi's downward spiral.[25]

The euphoria of Rajiv Gandhi's initial years in office was giving way to despair and disappointment and talks about Gandhi lacking 'moral authority' became common in the national press.[26] Amongst many of his actions, the two that stuck out included the blatant rigging of the state assembly elections in Jammu and Kashmir in 1987 and sending the Indian Peacekeeping Force (IPKF), a military contingent of the Indian military, into Sri Lanka to end the Sri Lankan civil war between militant Tamil nationalists such as the Liberation Tigers of Tamil Eelam (LTTE) and the Sri Lankan military.

In Kashmir, elections were said to be rigged to the extent where, in some constituencies, many dejected contestants who left the counting centres convinced of their defeat, were summoned back to be declared the winner by presiding officers.[27] The elections were triggered to prevent the Central government from losing control of the state's politics and, years later, Farooq Abdullah, the president of the Jammu and Kashmir National Conference that won the elections, told a journalist, 'I am not saying the elections weren't rigged, but I didn't rig them.'[28]

In 1989, Rajiv Gandhi's government became the first in the world to ban Salman Rushdie's controversial novel *The Satanic Verses* a full two weeks before Muslims in Britain even petitioned their government. Based on a plea by Syed Shahabuddin, a former diplomat and Janata Party politician, the ban was believed to be a part of a package of concessions by the Rajiv Gandhi government to calm him down in exchange for an annulment of a Muslim 'march to Ayodhya' in 1988, the same day on which the Vishwa Hindu Parishad was to hold a rally.[29] The banning of *The Satanic Verses* in India 'without even reading it' resonated across the world from South Africa to Indonesia and created such a climate of opinion that Ayatollah Khomeini felt emboldened to issue a global fatwa against Rushdie on 14 February 1989.[30]

Right from the moment Advani became the BJP president he was extremely vocal about the threat that such tactics on Gandhi's part posed to India. As the Lok Sabha elections approached, the writing on the wall was clear for the Congress and, in the face of impending defeat, Gandhi once again played the appeasement card to try and secure some lost ground. In November 1989, Rajiv Gandhi allowed the *shilanyas* ceremony, in which the first stone of the planned Ram temple was put in place and, with it, essentially attempted to assuage the anger that the 'Hindi belt', particularly Uttar Pradesh and Bihar, had towards the Congress. The Intelligence Bureau is said to have provided Congress with a detailed report about the tenor of the voter in the region and, as a result, Gandhi even kick-started his election campaign from Faizabad, the Lok Sabha constituency in which Ayodhya is situated, on 4 November 1989.[31]

Walter K. Andersen and Shridhar D. Damle's *The RSS: A View to the Inside*, mentions a former Nagpur-based Congress leader Banwarilal Purohit as saying that he was approached by Rajiv Gandhi to ask whether the RSS would support the Congress in the 1989 general elections in exchange for it facilitating the construction of a Ram Mandir at Ayodhya. According to Purohit, the then RSS chief, Balasaheb Deoras, agreed to consider the deal if the construction were to take place. Many years later, Purohit went public and suggested that the purported deal fell through in the wake of the shilanyas or foundation-stone laying at Ram Janmabhoomi when the Congress, facing a Muslim backlash, pulled back from the second part (permitting construction to start) of the reported bargain.[32]

The electorate, however, saw through the pathetic ploy and with the Bofors scandal gaining steam, the Congress lost over 200 seats from its tally in 1984 and emerged with 197 seats in the elections for the ninth Lok Sabha held between 22 and 26 November 1989. Gandhi's erstwhile finance and defence minister, V.P. Singh, whom he had sacked after the Bofors controversy, became the prime minister by uniting nearly the entire Opposition, including the Telugu Desam Party, Dravida Munnetra Kazhagam and Asom Gana Parishad to form the National Front. Along with the Janata Dal's 143 seats, he got additional outside support from the Bharatiya Janata Party that had won eighty-five seats and the Communist Party of India (Marxist), which had thirty-three. After quitting the Congress, V.P. Singh, along with Arun Nehru and Arif Mohammad Khan, formed the Jan Morcha party and later merged it with the Janata Party, the Lok Dal and the Congress (S) to form the Janata Dal.

Enough drama ensued before V.P. Singh became the prime minister. Singh had proposed Devi Lal be made the prime minister but the Jat leader from Haryana opted to be the 'elder uncle' to the government and, in turn, suggested Singh's name. This came as a surprise to Chandra Shekhar, who was Singh's rival for the top spot and felt he had been betrayed, for both had agreed on Lal being their unanimous choice. Chandra Shekhar continued to support Singh but his refusal to serve in the cabinet made it clear that he would not forget anything in a hurry.[33]

In an attempt to move forward on the social justice front, the National Front government implemented the recommendations of the Mandal Commission that suggested a fixed quota of all jobs in the public sector be reserved for members of the historically disadvantaged so-called 'Other Backward Classes'. The Commission had submitted its report in 1980 but, for nearly a decade, it had been kept aside. V.P. Singh decided to implement it in what political commentators believed was unplanned haste. Singh was aware that the highly controversial issue could blow up in his face but rumours of an internal power struggle within the National Front made him take the plunge. The Congress vehemently opposed V.P. Singh's decision and the BJP, despite supporting the government, was informed just a few hours before the implementation of the recommendations.

The decision saw protests across north India where many students, following the actions of Rajiv Goswami, a student of the Deshbandhu College, Delhi, immolated themselves in protest against the government's action.[34] V.P. Singh's affirmative action saw nearly 200 students setting themselves ablaze, out of which sixty-two succumbed to their burns.[35] The BJP was internally divided on what course of action to take. Some of the members wanted to pull the plug on the V.P. Singh government, but a few also dug their heels in stating that opposing affirmative action did not make sense.

While the decision to withdraw support was deferred, the political discourse did not remain static. The increase in BJP's seats from two in 1984 to eighty-five in 1989 showed that the party had recovered well. It had also gone into the elections without any pre-poll alliance and, therefore, the performance was solely to the credit of the party and its cadre. The results of the Lok Sabha elections were seen as an affirmation of its policies and ideology that also included its plea for the Ram temple.

While the National Front government was reeling under the severe reaction from the implementation of the Mandal Commission report, Advani decided to undertake a 'Rath Yatra' or a march from the ancient temple of Somnath in Gujarat to Ayodhya, the birthplace of Lord Ram, to take the cause of the Ram temple to the people. In a Toyota van that was made to look like a rath or chariot, Advani started from Somnath on 25 September 1990 with the intention of covering 10,000 kilometres till Ayodhya, where the government would be urged to allow the construction of the temple. The VHP had called kar sevaks or volunteers from across the country to reach Ayodhya on 30 October 1990 to begin work on the construction of the Ram temple. Covering nearly 300 kilometres and addressing up to six public rallies every day, Advani traversed across several cities, towns and villages in Gujarat, Maharashtra, Andhra Pradesh, Madhya Pradesh, Rajasthan, Haryana and Bihar. The level of popular mobilization in each state was much beyond what the press had anticipated and the yatra received great media coverage.

Advani made a long halt in Delhi as well where rumours of V.P. Singh attempting a preventive detainment or even arresting Advani began to do the rounds. A week before he was due to arrive in Ayodhya, Advani was arrested on 23 November 1990 at the Bihar–Uttar Pradesh border in Samastipur by Bihar chief minister Lalu Prasad Yadav.[36]

Even after Advani's arrest, the kar sevaks continued to move towards Ayodhya and the then chief minister of Uttar Pradesh, Mulayam Singh Yadav, ordered the arrest of all activists bound for Ayodhya. Depending on different reports, nearly 150,000 kar sevaks were jailed but some, again depending on various accounts, ranging from 40,000 to 70,000, managed to reach the site. In the face of a threat to the Babri Masjid, the police responded by using tear gas to expel the crowd and, later, opened fire on the order of Mulayam Singh Yadav. The incident led to the death of twenty volunteers.[37]

The arrest of Lal Krishna Advani led to the BJP withdrawing its support to the V.P. Singh government. Like V.P. Singh's stint as the prime minister, Rajnath Singh's stint as the national president of BJYM also ended in 1990. Much like his party that was about to make history by forming its first independent government in Uttar Pradesh, Singh too, unknown to him at the point, stood on the precipice of a great change, where he would forever etch his name in the history books.

5

Standing, Falling, Standing Again

By the time the BJP formed its first government in 1991 in Uttar Pradesh without aligning with any other party, the state had witnessed political upheavals on many fronts. The previous decade had seen seven chief ministers from various parties, the emergence of new fronts and the near-eclipse of the Congress in the state that had the largest representation of MPs in Parliament.

The build-up to the change in the political landscape of the state had been in the making for some time. The advent of both the Bharatiya Jana Sangh and Janata Dal in newer avatars have been largely credited for the change. The revival of the Ram Janmabhoomi movement at Ayodhya in 1986 (initiated by the then Congress chief minister Vir Bahadur Singh and later the Congress government at the Centre in 1989),[1] too, has been seen as event that shifted gears. The then prime minister V.P. Singh's Mandal campaign also claimed responsibility for the transforming politics in Uttar Pradesh, the seeds, however, were sown much before.

The mid-1980s were also a period of change in the fortunes of the BJP, both within the state as well as the country. From only two seats in all of India in the 1984 general elections and sixteen in the 1985 UP state assembly elections, it went on to win eighty-five seats in the 1989 general elections and fifty-seven in the assembly elections held in the same year. By 1989, the Congress president's constant interference in the state's functioning had corroded the party's potency and it suffered a historic defeat under N.D. Tiwari. Thirty years later, the party is yet to recover from that rout.

The drubbing the Congress suffered both at the Centre and the State saw a Janata Dal coalition led by V.P. Singh form the government in Delhi and call the shots in Lucknow. There were two chief ministerial contenders for the state—Ajit Singh and Mulayam Singh Yadav—and mirroring the situation at the Centre where the BJP supported the Janata Dal from outside, the latter became the Janata Dal's chief minister. A few months later, when the BJP withdrew support owing to the arrest of party stalwart L.K. Advani in October 1990 when his rath yatra reached Samastipur, Bihar, Mulayam Singh Yadav carried on being the CM. Only this time with the outside support of the Congress, which had also put its weight behind Chandra Shekhar's faction of the breakaway Janata Dal at the Centre. After the Congress withdrew its support in just seven months, Chandra Shekhar resigned as the prime minister of India on 6 March 1991, and the nation went to polls again.

Despite no party getting a clear majority, there was a clear swing towards the Congress, which emerged as the single largest party. However, when it came to Uttar Pradesh, the Congress managed only forty-six seats while, for the first time, BJP not only fought the polls without an alliance with anyone but also emerged victorious with a resounding majority. The party won 221 seats out of 419 and formed its first-ever government in the state.[2]

During the campaign, the BJP had put forth a handful of issues that it would address and while it supported reservation for backward castes in accordance with the Mandal Commission report, it nonetheless believed in economic condition and not caste as the criteria.[3] The BJP had projected Kalyan Singh, a popular leader who hailed from the OBC Lodh community, as its chief ministerial candidate. Buoyed by the renewal of the Ram Mandir movement, the state cadre worked aggressively to connect with the voter under Kalyan Singh.

The messy situation left behind by Mulayam Singh Yadav's regime, one that was marked by turbulence and a stalled administration, might have helped the Kalyan Singh-led government come to power, but in just a few days after assuming office, Singh made it more than evident that he meant business. Kalyan Singh established himself as a tough and able administrator with a no-nonsense approach in hardly any time and this became his signature. There were instances when he jailed criminals, including MLAs, and also fired a minister from his own cabinet for violating his orders.[4] He went on to be known for not only the hard stance he personally took, but also of some of the members in his ministry, and the one who stood out was Rajnath Singh.

Singh was given charge of education of a state, which according to experts, had been deeply affected by political considerations and where the education system had become too politicized.[5] Uttar Pradesh was one of the few states in India that still had a Legislative Council—the upper chamber of the state legislature, a body in which teachers had guaranteed representation. Teachers had traditionally been held in great regard in Indian society and, perhaps, that could be the reason why they were also given a special legal status by the Constitution of India which provided for representation to teachers and members who are elected by teachers in the Upper House of the state legislature.[6] UP's council of ministers since 1952 had always had a representation of teachers, barring once when, in 1967, Chandra Bhanu Gupta as chief minister formed his thirteen-member cabinet that lasted for fifteen days.[7]

The significance of education in the politics of Uttar Pradesh can be gauged from the fact that many chief ministers have been former teachers, beginning with Sampurnanand, Sucheta Kripalani, Tribhuvan Narayan Singh, Mulayam Singh Yadav and Kalyan Singh. Rajnath Singh too had joined a long list of education ministers in the state who had been teachers in the past, for instance, Acharya Jugul Kishore, Kalicharan and Swaroop Kumari Bakshi. During Rajnath Singh's stint as education minister, teachers wielded considerable influence both within and outside the state legislature. There were other problems plaguing the education system that needed immediate attention.

Even after four decades of freedom from the British and despite an increase in the number of institutions, the education system in India had little to show in terms of achievements as well as what was being taught in schools. The Kalyan Singh government gave more powers to management committees of private-aided schools, initiated self-financing courses and allowed self-financing schools besides transferring the power of pay disbursement to private management.

In addition to wide-ranging alterations in lessons taught at the secondary-school level, including the introduction of Vedic mathematics and the addition of a chapter detailing the contributions of Keshavrao Hedgewar, the founder of the RSS, the teaching community took exception to many of Rajnath Singh's reforms.[8] The introduction of Vedic maths raised many an eyebrow despite the fact that the world over, mathematicians found it helpful for children at pre-primary and primary levels to calculate complex numbers in a shorter time frame and sculpt young minds.[9] Questions were also raised about teaching children about the RSS even though historically the RSS had not only been a part of mainstream nation-building activities but had also been invited to participate in the Republic Day parade in 1963 by then prime minister, Pandit Jawaharlal Nehru.[10]

At the same time, the teachers under the Madhyamik Shikshak Sangh (MSS), the strongest teachers union in Uttar Pradesh, were up in arms too. The education minister's 'anti-teacher' measures did not go down well and they announced a call for a boycott of examinations.[11] Things came under control only after assurances from the state government that there was no move to change legislation regarding the transfer of secondary teachers from one district to another or empowering the authorities to prolong indefinitely the suspension of any teacher.

If the field of education had become a springboard for successful politicians and a fecund garden for political activism, it had also spawned an industry with cheating in examinations as its mainstay. In 1992, Rajnath Singh presented the historic anti-cheating law that declared cheating in examinations a cognizable offence. The Anti-Copying Act, 1992, promised changes aimed at clearing the system like never before, whereby students caught cheating could be jailed. This was accompanied by the simultaneous deployment of police in all examination centres across the state and its effect was more than palpable. The percentage of students clearing the UP board high school exam came down from 57 in 1991 to under 15 in 1992.

Singh was told in no uncertain terms that his action would have far-reaching implications, or, in other words, his political future was at stake. Even at the time of framing and, later, tabling the Act, there were well-wishers who sprung to advise the first-time minister. Some of them went to the extent of hinting that the CM could probably try to fire from his shoulder and the credit, if it worked, would be Kalyan Singh's while all the brickbats, the more likely outcome, would come his way. But Rajnath Singh had no doubt about the measure. As a teacher, he had often found students not being inspired enough to do the right thing and the only way to bring about a change in the manner the young approached not just studies, but life, in general, would only be possible if they assumed greater responsibility, and what better place to start but one's own self.

There were far greater things happening around the Kalyan Singh government for anyone to focus on the transformation inside the state's education system. Close on the heels of his swearing-in ceremony, the chief minister had undertaken a trip to Ayodhya along with his entire cabinet and some senior member of the BJP where it was said they took a vow to construct the temple. Amongst the slogans echoing across Uttar Pradesh during the run-up to the 1991 assembly poll, the one most prominent after '*Ab ki baar, bhajapa ki sarkar*' (This time it will be the BJP government) was '*Ram lalla, hum aaenge, mandir waheen banaaenge*' (We will come and build the temple there).[12]

As a result, the more ensconced Kalyan Singh's government became, the more pressure it faced to fulfil its promise to build a Ram temple at the site where the Babri Masjid stood. There were demands from outfits such as the Bajrang Dal and the VHP to do away with the barricades around the disputed shrine. The party had repeatedly raised and prioritized the Ramjanmabhoomi issue during its election campaign and the CM himself reiterated there was no question of pressuring him as he himself was committed to building the temple.[13]

In October 1991, Singh's government acquired 2.77 acres of land around the disputed structure at Ayodhya to begin the construction of a Ram temple and the passage of time saw the CM push for the agenda. The acquisition was challenged in the Allahabad High Court which issued an order prohibiting the government from building a permanent structure on that piece of land. There were talks about VHP setting a deadline of sorts for the party to deliver on its promise, but efforts to remove the hurdles in the way before talking about construction continued. Several leaders were said to have asked the Centre to approach the courts to expedite its judgment on the 2.77-acre plot so that the VHP could perform kar seva and build a temple.[14]

Even in the midst of all the turbulence, Kalyan Singh, in an interview given in May 1992, reiterated BJP's stance of exploring either a negotiated settlement and, if that failed, the enactment of a law to remove the legal hurdles to the construction of a temple.[15] Dissent was brewing in the party as well, and with rumours of state BJP chief Kalraj Mishra replacing Kalyan Singh gaining momentum, hardliners were certain that it was a matter of time before Singh was shown the door. As the CM, Singh was also negotiating with the Centre where Prime Minister P.V. Narasimha Rao was possibly as anxious for a solution.[16] In July 1992, Singh in his capacity of the chief minister of the state, submitted an affidavit[17] to the Supreme Court to maintain the status quo on the land around the disputed site, but later in the same month a platform was constructed near the mosque, which Singh said was a space to perform bhajans but was interpreted as a kind of foundation of a Ram temple.[18]

Following the demolition of the Babri Masjid on 6 December 1992, Kalyan Singh took moral responsibility and resigned from the post of chief minister. The next day the Central government dismissed the Uttar Pradesh government under Article 356 of the Constitution of India. Narasimha Rao also dismissed the BJP governments in Madhya Pradesh, Himachal Pradesh and Rajasthan citing 'common thread' as a theory. The counsel appearing for the Centre argued that states ruled by the same political party had felt the same seismic vibration of unconstitutional action by the state government in Uttar Pradesh during the demolition of the mosque.[19]

At the time it was dismissed, the Kalyan Singh government was in the process of putting into place a new approach to uplift one of India's most backward states. Despite being the one state to give India nearly all its prime ministers up until 1991, Uttar Pradesh never really benefited from the symbolic status this gave the state. The Kalyan Singh government was the first ever government in the state of Uttar Pradesh that was directly opposed to the Centre since Independence, and had managed to focus on implementing socio-economic policies to lift the state from the doldrums.

Despite the charge of failing to perform its duty at the time it was sacked in 1992, the state BJP machinery managed to connect well with the electorate in the run-up to the assembly polls in 1993 after almost a year of President's Rule. As the party went to the people with their agenda, it focused more on national issues including threats from both internal as well as external forces, social justice, price rise and not as much on religion. Special attention was given to issues like international Islamic terror in the aftermath of the 1993 Bombay serial blasts orchestrated by the fugitive underworld don Dawood Ibrahim with the help of Pakistan, the role of Pakistan in promoting terrorism especially in Kashmir, bringing to the fore the issue of ethnic cleansing of Kashmiri Pandits and the illegal immigration of Bangladeshi nationals, besides highlighting the widespread corruption of the Congress government at the Centre.

It was not like that the BJP abandoned the Ram Mandir movement, which continued to remain an emotional issue irrespective of whether the party was in power or not. The Rao government had proposed two bills aiming to ban religion from public life. There was little doubt that the Constitution (Eightieth Amendment) Bill and the Representation of People (Amendment) Bill were aimed to deny political space to the BJP, which had come to be seen as the only national party that could challenge the Congress. As the UP assembly elections approached, the party leadership, including Atal Bihari Vajpayee, L.K. Advani and Murali Manohar Joshi, besides Kalyan Singh, met people across constituencies both in the state and the country to garner public opinion against the separation of religion from politics.

Advani planned a four-pronged yatra, the Janadesh Yatra, which commenced from four corners of India and traversed fourteen states and two Union territories seeking the people's mandate against the two bills. On 11 September 1993, Advani started from Mysore, Bhairon Singh Shekhawat from Jammu, Murali Manohar Joshi from Porbandar and Kalyan Singh from Calcutta. They congregated in Bhopal a fortnight later, on 25 September.[20] The massive outreach attempt was a runaway success. If the response seemed to suggest the electorate sharing the same sentiment as the party, it also became a barometer to gauge the party's acceptability amongst the electorate.

The preparation for the assembly polls also saw the emergence of Rajnath Singh as one of the future leaders of the party in the state. Some factions within the party, as well as sympathetic organizations such as the RSS, started talking about nurturing the next generation of leadership. Rajnath Singh was amongst the more popular names in the state machinery and there was hardly anyone or any group that had not come in contact with him. Singh's reassured demeanour and the manner in which he always found common ground across various camps and groups both within the party as well as across party lines made him a well-rounded and acceptable option to fill the leadership vacuum. One could say Singh being a Thakur also had some part to play in his name popping up as a potential leader besides the old horse Ram Prakash Gupta, who had been a deputy chief minister in the Charan Singh-led Samyukta Vidhayak Dal government that in 1967 became the first non-Congress government in the state.

If the grapevine were to be believed, the move to push for Rajnath was also meant to keep Kalyan Singh's rising popularity in check. During the Janadesh Yatra, Kalyan Singh had attracted large crowds in Calcutta and the fact that he was chosen to participate along with Advani, Joshi and Shekhawat also suggested his stock was on the rise.

A look at the manner in which the BJP distributed tickets for the 1993 elections where less than a hundred candidates belonged to lower castes could be interpreted as a ploy to undermine Kalyan Singh's soaring popularity. But when viewed from a different prism the same could be interpreted in another way. There might have been a play in place to shift Kalyan Singh to the Centre as one of the faces for the next Lok Sabha elections and, if that be the case, it made sense to invest in someone younger like Rajnath Singh. Irrespective of all these the elections promised many surprises and threw up realities that only a few months ago no one would have believed were even possible.

The 1993 Uttar Pradesh assembly election saw 9726 contestants vie for 422 constituencies with an average of twenty-three individuals fighting for a single seat, which remains an unbroken record of the highest number of candidates per seat in any election in the history of India. The epoch-making election from nearly every single perspective saw seventy-seven aspirants for a single seat, Agra Cantonment. A staggering 8652 candidates or nearly 89 per cent lost their deposits.[21]

The BJP emerged as the single largest party with 177 seats, accounting for approximately 33.4 per cent of the vote share but it still could not manage to form the government. A coalition between Kanshi Ram's Bahujan Samaj Party (BSP) and Mulayam Singh Yadav's new party, the Samajwadi Party (SP) that he formed in April 1992 after breaking away from the Janata Dal, joined hands to form the government. The BSP had won sixty-seven seats and the SP had emerged victorious in 109 but it was the outside support of the Congress, which had twenty-eight seats, that helped the coalition sail through. This was also an election that witnessed a revival of vote-bank politics with Kanshi Ram openly admitting that the sole purpose of joining hands with Mulayam Singh was to be 'able to form the government'.[22] The delicate alliance continued with constant hiccups in some form or the other with support and vote groups of each party becoming more assertive and often antagonistic towards each other.

Apart from the setback of not being able to garner a majority despite being the single largest party, the elections also saw Rajnath Singh pay a price for pushing education reforms especially the Anti-Copying Act. He lost the Mohana seat to SP's Rajendra Yadav by a small margin of 7968 votes. Located about 25 kilometres from the state capital, Lucknow, Mohana is one of the towns that flourished under both the Mughals and the British thanks to its people who were counted amongst the most literate in Uttar Pradesh. The town was also known for its hakims or traditional physicians practising the Unani system of medicine based on the teachings of the Greek physicians Hippocrates and Galen and, in fact, was referred to as Mohan Khitta-e Unan or 'Mohan—a part of Greece'. A student-dominated area, Mohana would always be a tall order and, especially for Rajnath Singh, the man who practically changed the way many of them operated. The former teacher ended up paying a heavy price for his conviction.

Within months it became evident that the relationship between the two partners who had formed the government was steadily deteriorating and every new dawn brought forth either Mulayam Singh or Kanshi Ram holding each other to ransom. However, even the infighting between the SP and the BSP did not yield any benefit for the BJP, which lost many by-elections where it was the front runner. In the short period that the alliance lasted, Mulayam Singh reversed some of the major decisions of the Kalyan Singh government. Besides the administrative changes, the SP–BSP government undid some of Rajnath Singh's decisions to win over the student community. Mulayam Singh restored the changes in the syllabus initiated by Rajnath Singh, added some new chapters and announced reservation for weaker sections of society in admissions to government schools and colleges from the ninth grade onwards. Above all, he struck down the Anti-Copying Act calling it 'draconian'.[23]

Once the BSP withdrew its support to the SP in June 1995, the BJP decided to extend its backing to Mayawati, who became the state's first Dalit chief minister, thus giving a voice to nearly 21 per cent of the state's population. The rivalry reached a flashpoint when some SP cadre allegedly attempted to assault Mayawati at a guest house in Lucknow after she withdrew support to Mulayam Singh.[24] There were reports of a BJP MLA, Brahm Dutt Dwivedi, stepping in to save Mayawati. The government lasted for four months till October 1995 when the BJP withdrew support.

Through the course of first the SP–BSP and later the BSP–BJP alliances, Rajnath Singh was far removed from all the proceedings. He was elected as a Rajya Sabha MP in April 1994 and featured on a number of committees in the Upper House of Parliament. An important link between the Parliament, the executive and the general public of the country, parliamentary committees often play a significant role in the parliamentary system. The reason such committees assume greater responsibility than what is generally believed is their ability and power to assist the legislature in discharging its duties and also regulating its functions. The sheer volume of work makes it near impossible for each and every matter before

Parliament to be either examined in detail or even considered on the floor, but the presence of parliamentary committees can ensure expertise on any matter referred to it without expending too much time of the House. Constituted by members from across party lines, parliamentary committees have the luxury of systematically debating matters in a businesslike, calmer atmosphere. Parliamentary committees also provide a moral compass for the executive and it became more important in an era of alliances marked by politics of appeasement.

During his first term, Rajnath Singh was involved in committees on industry, agriculture, business and also human resource development. During that period, Singh worked closely with fellow parliamentarians from not only different parties but also different governments. It gave him a great insight into influencing policy without direct control, offering advice to ensure a sense of continuity of the overarching goals for the benefit of the common citizen and, most importantly, preventing any misuse of power at the hands of the executive.

Rajnath Singh's initial years in the Rajya Sabha were a period of great transition for him personally, his party and also his country. A noticeable change was the replacement of party president Advani as the projected candidate for prime ministership during the eleventh general election by Vajpayee after the former opted out once he was charge-sheeted in the hawala case.[25] In 1996, BJP's campaign pivoted on five major aims: *Shuchita* (cleanliness in public life), *Suraksha* (national security), Swadeshi (economic nationalism), *Samrasta* (social equality) and the all-encompassing *Sanskritik Rashtravad* (cultural nationalism). The party manifesto also stated the BJP's resolve to the creation of a Uniform Civil Code, its focus on encouraging the establishment of small-scale industries besides reducing the role of the public sector in all industries except in sensitive areas like defence, the abrogation of Article 370, prevention of illegal infiltration of Bangladeshi migrants in India, and making forceful religious conversions by promising socio-economic privileges a punishable offence. The BJP had also proposed the creation of a National Human Rights Commission in place of the Minorities Commission, which was met with much criticism. It assured the continuation of reservation for OBCs and also extend an additional 10 per cent reservation for economically weaker sections of society.[26]

The party created a Minorities Cell under Arif Muhammad Beg to connect with the Muslim electorate. The cell communicated BJP's idea of how to offer *taaleem* (education), *tanzeem* (organization) and *tijarat* (employment) if it came to power.[27] Unlike Advani, who ended every speech with an exhortation to the people to raise the chorus of 'Jai Shri Ram', the party's mascot Vajpayee never made the Ayodhya temple the most prominent item on the agenda. Vajpayee spoke about corruption in the previous government, criminalization of politics, inflation and neglect of the poor, which seemed to strike a chord with the people.[28]

While the stint in the Rajya Sabha broadened Rajnath Singh's horizon, providing him an opportunity to witness the difference between the politics of consensus and politics of consent, the party also was in the process of redefining the spectrum. In March 1994, at the party's national executive meeting, Advani as party president had said, Hindutva was not just a slogan for the BJP but it was the most distinctive feature of its identity and approach, and its manifesto defined Hindutva in terms of 'cultural nationalism'.[29] However, there was little doubt in the mind of Vajpayee that for BJP to become a force to reckon with in elections it must catch enough votes and go beyond Hindutva.

The results of the eleventh Lok Sabha elections that were held in April–May 1996 were hardly surprising. The election delivered an unclear mandate and resulted in a hung Parliament with the BJP getting 161 seats and the Congress managing to win 140, which till then was its worst performance. Invited by President Shankar Dayal Sharma to form the government as it was the single largest party, Vajpayee was given two weeks to prove his majority on the floor of the house. On 27 May, it became clear that Vajpayee had the support of only 200 members of the 545. He decided to resign instead of facing the vote of confidence. But before he exited, Vajpayee delivered one of the greatest speeches ever heard in the Indian Parliament.

It was the first time a vote of confidence was being telecast live on television and the kind of viewership that tuned in was usually reserved for a cricket match. In his hour-long address, Vajpayee touched upon many facets of democracy and the faith reposed by people in elections but, more importantly, for the first time he put on record the open disdain that politically opposed parties had for the BJP. Those watching Vajpayee speak included Rajnath Singh, who was also BJP's chief whip in the Upper House. In the course of the impassioned speech, Vajpayee filled his party men with immense pride as he made it amply clear how neither he nor the party would do anything immoral to attain power. He mentioned how those on the other side of the House simply brushed off the BJP's support base as 'cow belt' and questioned the Opposition to point out which part of India they singled out as the cow belt when the BJP got votes in states such as Karnataka and West Bengal. He highlighted how everyone from a single-member political party to one who had lesser seats than the BJP were collaborating to keep the BJP at bay and while they had all the right to do so, Vajpayee felt the BJP was being held in the dock without any real reason. Towards the end, as he told the Speaker he was going to give his resignation to the president, Vajpayee expressed doubts about the strange assemblage in the name of the government which would replace the BJP but wished

them luck and assured how his party would work as an able
Opposition in the days to come.

Once Vajpayee resigned, the Congress as the second largest
party refused to form the government but chose to support a
Janata Dal-led coalition that unexpectedly led to then chief
minister of Karnataka H.D. Deve Gowda emerge as the
prime ministerial candidate. The United Front coalition had
the Congress, the Janata Dal, the Communist Party of India
(Marxist) and the Communist Party of India (CPI), Samajwadi
Party, the Dravida Munnetra Kazhagam, Telugu Desam Party,
the Asom Gana Parishad and the breakaway Congress factions
such as the All India Indira Congress (Tiwari), which featured
dissident INC leaders N.D. Tiwari, Arjun Singh, Natwar Singh
and R. Kumaramangalam, and the Tamil Maanila Congress led
by G.K. Moopanar on the same side of the fence.

Pramod Mahajan, by then one of BJP's young leaders,
best summarized this strange phase in India's parliamentary
democracy in a conversation he had had with a member of the
National People's Congress (NPC), the national legislature of
the People's Republic of China during his visit as a part of a
parliamentary delegation. When asked about the functioning
of democracy in India, Mahajan smiled and told his Chinese
counterpart that he would simply introduce a few of the Indian
delegates present, which would provide the answer. Mahajan
introduced himself and said he belonged to the largest party and
he was in the Opposition. The already confused NPC member
was further flummoxed when Mahajan pointed to a Congress
MP and said he belonged to the second largest party and was
outside the government but supporting it. Then he pointed to
another MP and said he was from the third largest party, which
was outside the coalition in power but inside the government.
Mahajan finally introduced an MP who was the single member
of his party and said he *is* the government.

Gowda came to head the alliance in June 1996 once V.P. Singh and Jyoti Basu, the long-standing CPI(M) chief minister of West Bengal, passed on the offer to lead. Basu called the CPI (M)'s refusal to let him be the PM a 'historic blunder'.[30] There were rumours of Chandrababu Naidu too refusing the top job. The manner in which most coalition players sought influence without responsibility soon proved to be too big a burden for Gowda. Trouble between the Congress and Gowda led him to resign and I.K. Gujral took over the mantle in April 1997. Unlike Gowda, Gujral had a great working relationship with Congress but his own party, Janata Dal, had issues with him.

The Central Bureau of Investigation (CBI) sought permission from Gujral to prosecute Lalu Prasad Yadav in the fodder scam and when Gujral asked him to step down he revolted and quit the alliance to form the Rashtriya Janata Dal (RJD) on 3 July 1997. Lalu Yadav took seventeen of the forty-five Janata Dal MPs but the government survived as it continued to enjoy the support of the newly formed RJD from outside.

The saga of the United Front government came to an end in November 1997 when the Congress withdrew support in the wake of the Jain Commission, investigating the conspiracy behind the Rajiv Gandhi assassination, reportedly indicting the DMK for tacitly supporting the Tamil militants in the death of the former prime minister.[31] Congress president Sitaram Kesari demanded the immediate sacking of DMK ministers from the United Front government but Gujral refused and once the Congress pulled the rug from under him he submitted his resignation to President K.R. Narayanan. While Gujral was asked to continue for an interim period till an alternative arrangement was made, the Congress offered to form its own government, but nearly every political party in India refused to support either a Congress- or a BJP-led coalition, triggering another round of polls.

Political uncertainty notwithstanding, both tenures of Gowda and Gujral were marked by the smooth functioning of the committees that helped the Parliament operate better than what could have been assumed keeping the greater picture in mind. During the entire period of the United Front at the Centre, Rajnath Singh worked with people who were not just rivals but politically opposed to him to the extent of going to any length to keep the BJP away from power. Singh had never let rivalry come in the way of finding common ground and the two years in Rajya Sabha gave him ample occasions to put this philosophy of his to practice.

If the lack of a clear mandate made things go awry at the Centre, a similar result emerged from the 1996 Uttar Pradesh assembly elections. For the assembly election in UP, the party raised issues which were removed from what many had come to expect from the BJP. It offered to provide free education for women up to the university level and advocated many schemes in rural areas while projecting Kalyan Singh as the *rakshak* (protector) against the *bhakshak* (oppressor).[32]

The BJP emerged as the single largest party in the state with 174 seats, the SP won 110 seats and the BSP sixty-seven, but the absence of a clear majority meant that President's Rule imposed on 18 October 1995 would continue. Mulayam Singh Yadav refused to support the BSP and there was no question of the Samajwadi Party abiding by a BJP-led government. The stalemate continued; so did President's Rule.

A region-wise assessment of the seats won by the BJP in the general elections revealed it had performed well in the Muslim-dominated areas of eastern UP such as Faizabad, Varanasi and Gorakhpur and had managed to replace both the Congress and the BSP in central UP, but in the assembly election, the party secured lesser seats than it did in the 1993 election.[33]

At the beginning of 1997, Rajnath Singh was sent to Uttar Pradesh to head the party in the state and lead it out of the morass. This was the highest position ever given to Singh within the party and, in March 1997, he managed to pave the path for a BSP–BJP coalition.

The BJP was not unaware of the risks involved with any engagement with the BSP. Besides other factors influencing the decision to go ahead with the coalition, the Dalit vote too could have been at play. The manner in which the party fell short of numbers in the Lok Sabha elections did raise the question of attracting voters, who might have been channelized to vote against the BJP. It is worth pondering that had the state alliance between the two parties not fallen apart in 1995, the BSP might have supported the BJP in the 1996 Lok Sabha elections. Both parties came to a tacit understanding of having a CM for six months by rotation, beginning with Mayawati and followed by Kalyan Singh.

On 21 March 1997, Mayawati became the CM of Uttar Pradesh but even though she relinquished the office to the BJP at the end of her six months, she withdrew support in less than a month, citing fears of Kalyan Singh revoking orders issued by her in the interest of Dalits.

Under a drive launched on the ground of undoing past injustice, Mayawati had allowed Gram Sabha land on lease to thousands of Dalits, unsettling Punjabi settlers who had come in the early 1950s in response to the invitations from the UP government to develop the Terai region. A 14-kilometre wide and 175-kilometre long strip of land called Udham Singh Nagar became the nerve centre of protests and in the time to come it would go on to become a major issue between the Punjab government and the Centre once the decision to transfer the district in the new proposed state of Uttaranchal (later renamed Uttarakhand) came close to fruition.

Mayawati's move had evoked opposition from Hindu traders, Muslim businessmen, Bengali farmers and agricultural labourers of the area, but as long as she was in power she refused to relent even when the then Punjab chief minister Parkash Singh Badal sent a two-member ministerial team to request her to reconsider her stand.[34] Was it this action, carving new districts, or the reinstatement of over 100 previously suspended bureaucrats that Mayawati felt would be reversed by Kalyan Singh?

Survival in Indian politics is often defined by two distinctive features: one, keeping one's flock intact, and two, make the most of the opportunity when the opponents' pack begins to wander. Not willing to let it all slip away, Kalyan Singh responded by making a move that dented both the BSP and the Congress. Rajnath Singh kept his own party intact while Kalyan Singh—who had already been in touch with Naresh Agarwal, a former Congress member who had left the grand old party to join N.D. Tiwari's All India Indira Congress (Tiwari) and formed the splinter group called Akhil Bharatiya Loktantrik Congress with Jagdambika Pal, Bachcha Pathak, Rajeev Shukla and Shyam Sunder Sharma—garnered support from twenty-one non-BJP MLAs. In a matter of days, Kalyan Singh also got the support of twenty-six MLAs from the BSP after a faction split it to form a new party, the Janatantrik Bahujan Samaj Party (JBSP).[35]

With help from Rajnath Singh's leadership, the BJP managed a semblance of stability, at least for the time being, allowing the Kalyan Singh government to work without worrying about appeasing a coalition. But the troubles were far from over thanks to the new members pushing their luck. Kalyan Singh shed the conciliatory approach and got tough by sacking three ministers from the JBSP on charges of corruption, which sent a signal to others such as Naresh Agarwal, who seemed to be nurturing ambitions of their own.[36] Kalyan Singh's emboldened attitude and his zeal to push certain OBC policies[37] and reforms to make UP corruption-free led to an increased power struggle within the state unit, which Rajnath Singh tried to keep in check but certain things were simply out of his control.

Things came to a pass in a dramatic fashion when the UP governor Romesh Bhandari dismissed the Kalyan Singh government on 21 February 1998 and swore in Jagdambika Pal of the Loktrantik Congress as the new chief minister. Naresh Agarwal decided to withdraw his support to Kalyan Singh and shifted to Pal but the development saw Atal Bihari Vajpayee oppose the governor's action and go on a fast unto death. The Allahabad High Court stayed the order and reinstated Kalyan Singh's government. As a result, Pal's three-day tenure became the shortest chief ministerial stint of Uttar Pradesh. Many from the Loktrantik Congress opposed their party leadership's actions and stood by Kalyan Singh and once Singh proved his majority on the floor of the House, Agarwal too returned.[38]

As things inched back to normalcy after the high drama, Kalyan Singh appeared to be all set to finally manage to complete a full term but the cracks within the party were visible. During the 1998 general elections, the BJP won a total of sixty seats where it got fifty-eight seats along with two allies, Maneka Gandhi from Pilibhit, who fought as an independent, and Hari Kewal Prasad, who was the Samata Party candidate from Salempur, out of the eighty-five seats. The inner tussle in the state resulted in the tally coming down a year later, when the second Atal Bihari Vajpayee government fell and the country went to elections again in 1999.

The BJP's tally of twenty-nine out of eighty-five seats in 1999's Lok Sabha elections was its worst performance[39] in the state during the last three elections and it was time to change things. Kalyan Singh's ouster was a foregone conclusion following the poll debacle as was perhaps Rajnath Singh's, till then being considered one of the top contenders for the CM's post. An unexpected name emerged at the meeting in Delhi that was attended, among others, by the BJP president Kushabhau Thakre along with Vajpayee, who was also the prime minister of India, and Advani. Rumours were afloat that the senior leadership felt that choosing one of the favourites of any 'group', including Rajnath Singh could cause more harm considering the scuffle within the state unit amongst the Thakur, Brahmin and other factions. Veteran leader Ram Prakash Gupta was named the new chief minister of the state.[40]

Kalyan Singh did not take too kindly to the development and publicly expressed his displeasure that led to a party disciplinary committee recommending his immediate expulsion. The ousted CM questioned the party's policies and its leadership, besides suggesting that a campaign for his removal had been under way for the past ten months. The party rejected all his claims and expelled him for a period of six years for anti-party activities.[41]

Unlike Kalyan Singh, Rajnath Singh did not show his disappointment, if he felt any, and as the state BJP president extended all support to the newly elected chief minister. Singh had always placed the organization before individuals and saw no reason to not do so now, even if it came at the cost of his own promotion. As the younger one in the relationship, Rajnath Singh was more aware of the nuances of contemporary politics. Unlike in the 1960s, when Gupta was at the forefront, politics no longer operated solely on the basis of caste and pressure groups. Even as he helped the seventy-six-year old CM navigate the choppy waters of UP's state politics, Delhi beckoned Rajnath Singh again.

6

On the Road

Atal Bihari Vajpayee was sworn in as the prime minister of India for the second time in as many years in May 1998. The BJP won the highest number of seats in the general elections and formed the National Democratic Alliance (NDA) with a number of political parties, including some that did not necessarily espouse BJP's ideology. If there was a leader who could naturally lead the thirteen parties in the absence of a formal understanding of any governing structure or executive board, it was Vajpayee.

In his second term as PM, Vajpayee got down to business as soon as the NDA took oath and, on 11 May 1998, India conducted five underground nuclear tests at Pokhran in the Thar Desert in Rajasthan, following which Vajpayee convened a press conference to declare India a full-fledged nuclear state. Vajpayee's decision to go ahead with the tests came in the wake of the groundwork done by P.V. Narasimha Rao, who was all set to conduct them in 1995 when American spy satellites picked up signs of preparations. Under pressure from the then US president, Bill Clinton, Rao halted the programme but informed Vajpayee that everything was in place for him to undertake the tests. Two weeks after India conducted Pokhran-II, Pakistan too conducted its own nuclear tests and the US imposed sanctions against both the countries. The tests boosted the country's confidence in Vajpayee and the NDA as well as the BJP. The US lifted the sanctions after six months, enhancing the government's image further.

There were regular bumps that Vajpayee had to endure due to coalition compulsions but not only did he seem to be able to negotiate them well enough but also drove agendas as if his was a government with absolute majority. Vajpayee pushed for an all-out diplomatic relationship with Pakistan wherein, beginning in late 1998, he opened a communication channel with Prime Minister Nawaz Sharif and, in February 1999, initiated a new peace process between the countries with the historic Delhi–Lahore bus service Sada-e-Sarhad or the Call of the Frontier. Vajpayee invited eminent Indians from all walks of life who shared a connection with Pakistan either due to their personal history, such as Kuldip Nayar and film icon Dev Anand, or were popular across the border like legendary cricketer Kapil Dev, screenwriter and lyricist Javed Akhtar, Mallika Sarabhai, and actor Shatrughan Sinha, who also happened to be the rakhi brother of the daughter of the former military dictator of Pakistan, General Zia-ul-Haq, to seek permanent peace between the neighbours.[1] The Lahore Declaration signed by Sharif and Vajpayee promised a better tomorrow between two nuclear powers in South Asia, but it was not to be.

Vajpayee and the NDA were also battling constant pressure from one of the coalition partners, the All India Anna Dravida Munnetra Kazhagam (AIADMK). The AIADMK leader J. Jayalalithaa kept making demands, be it pushing for cabinet berths for her party members or tightening the noose on the DMK government in Tamil Nadu that was pursuing as many as eight cases of corruption against her, including one involving the purchase of TV sets during her chief ministership for which she had been incarcerated for a month in December

1996.[2] Throughout the NDA tenure there was communication between Delhi and Chennai at times via letters and at other times with a little help from emissaries. For a while it seemed like the ship would stop rocking after the BJP leadership impressed upon Jayalalithaa how a vulnerable Centre might not be able to sack the M. Karunanidhi-led DMK government. But external players such as the then Janata Party president Dr Subramanian Swamy urged her to withdraw support to the Vajpayee government for its continued failure to take action against DMK leader Karunanidhi and his government, which, he alleged, had a nexus with the Pakistani intelligence outfit, Inter-Services Intelligence.[3] In the end, Vajpayee's government could not last beyond thirteen months and Jayalalithaa withdrew support in May 1999. Vajpayee lost the ensuing vote of confidence in the Parliament by a single vote and became the caretaker PM till the elections that were to take place in October. Between losing his government and facing the nation for the third time in three years, Vajpayee and India were tested by a surprise war.

Within two months of the resumption of the Delhi–Lahore bus service, militants and non-uniformed soldiers of the Pakistan army's Northern Light Infantry (NLI) regiment infiltrated into hilltops and unmanned border posts on the Indian side of the Line of Control (LOC), the de facto border between India and Pakistan. The Indian Army launched Operation Vijay on 26 May 1999 and fought thousands of militants and soldiers under heavy artillery shelling in extremely cold and treacherous high-altitude terrain. The three-month-long Kargil war saw over 500 Indian soldiers lay down their lives as the Indian Army pushed back the enemy by eliminating over 4000 Pakistani troops and officials.[4] Vajpayee even reportedly sent a 'secret letter' to President Clinton making it clear that India would get the Pakistani infiltrators 'one way or the other'; in other words he was not opposed to crossing the Line of Control or even using nuclear weapons.[5]

Sharif was not notified by the then Pakistan army chief, General Pervez Musharraf, and with Pakistan suffering heavy losses and both the United States as well as China refusing to restrain India, the Pakistani prime minister ordered the infiltrators to withdraw.[6] The militants refused to budge and were eliminated by the Indian Army but the NLI soldiers, identified from the official documents found on them besides the Pakistan Army's customary weapons, opted to return to their base, abandoning the war.

The thirteenth Lok Sabha elections were held between 5 September 1999 and 3 October 1999 and made history as it was the first time a pre-poll alliance managed to attain a majority. The last two elections had not given a clear mandate to anyone. However, close on the heels of winning the Kargil war, the people of India chose Atal Bihari Vajpayee to run the country with the BJP-led NDA winning 303 seats, thus ensuring a stable government for the next five years.

Vajpayee took oath as prime minister for the third time on 13 October 1999 and began his third term that was filled with visionary ideas, which, if executed as planned, could usher in a golden period for India. Vajpayee emphasized that the government changed its attitude when conducting business in the sectors in which it had a presence and some of the changes initiated by the NDA government laid the foundation of transforming India. Vajpayee made a great push for privatization of central public sector enterprises (CPSE) through a major disinvestment drive of public sector undertakings, which had initially been started by P.V. Narasimha Rao through minority stake sales. The NDA set up a dedicated Department of Disinvestment in December 1999.

One of Vajpayee's dream projects was to usher in India's next-generation infrastructure ahead of its time in the form of a visionary road structure connecting north–south and east–west of the country through a network of highways. Named the Golden Quadrilateral, the network would join the country's major industrial, agricultural and cultural centres by forming a quadrilateral connecting the four major metro cities of India— New Delhi in the north, Calcutta in the east, Mumbai in the west and Chennai in the south. The ambitious project was launched within the first month of Vajpayee's third-term and he turned to Rajnath Singh for its execution.

Despite a large network of highways that were maintained by the National Highway Authority of India (NHAI), the term 'Indian roads' had come to define not just the condition of most roads in the country but also, in a way, a state of mind. In addition to the 'emotional' integration of a country as wide and diverse such as India, tools for the 'physical' connection of Indians needed to be worked upon and this dual purpose made the project important in more ways than one. Rajnath Singh joined the Atal Bihari Vajpayee government as minister for surface transport on 22 November 1999 and undertook the implementation of the largest highway project in India. At 5846 kilometres (3633 miles), the Golden Quadrilateral was a part of the National Highways Development Project (NHDP) and entailed construction of new highways and extension of the existing ones to four- and six-lane express highways that would be built at a cost of 600 billion INR ($8.3 billion).

Although the project's foundation stone was laid by Vajpayee in January 1999, a major portion of the work consisted of planning and getting things in order before work could commence full-steam in 2001. Between the end of 1999 and through a better part of 2000, Singh's ministry did the legwork for the four sections of the project which included the mammoth task of overcoming land acquisition constraints and dividing the work into sections for awarding individual construction contracts.

As someone who hailed from a small village in Uttar Pradesh, Singh was aware of the role roads played in the lives of farmers and their families, with direct and fast access from the hinterland to markets in towns and cities impacting their fortunes. Roads could spell the difference between prosperity and the lack of it. The significance of the project can be gauged from the fact that in the first five decades of Indian independence (1947–1997) only 556 km of National Highways were four-laned. These 556 km accounted for only 20 per cent of the highways but carried 40 per cent of the national traffic.[7] Rajnath Singh's ministry was setting in place the mechanism to convert over 24,000 km of roads into four lanes before the end of Vajpayee's term.[8]

Under Vajpayee's leadership, the BJP-led NDA was undoing decades of lethargy and aimlessness that had seeped into not just governmental policies but also the bureaucracy. Nearly every minister was in for some shock in the way the bureaucracy went about its daily business. There were instances when Rajnath Sigh also found himself ranged against the NHAI, but he was a fast learner who understood that there was a lot to do and hardly any time to waste. Another minister, Ram Naik, the minister of petroleum and natural gas, surprised most of his staff through his tenure simply by reaching his office before everyone else. The cabinet was a mix of experienced and young minds, people who were open to thinking out of the box and pushing the envelope to ensure that the India growth story did not lose momentum.

Most ministries in the Vajpayee government adopted a lateral structure arrangement that helped overcome the barriers in a traditional centralized organization and also fostered teamwork and quick decision making. An example of this was the execution the Pradhan Mantri Gram Sadak Yojana (PMGSY), which endeavoured to connect villages across India with all-weather roads. The programme was launched in 2000 to provide roads to all villages with a population of 1000 and above within three years and, subsequently, villages with a population of 500 people by 2007. The project was under the authority of the Ministry of Rural Development but blended seamlessly with the mission of the Ministry of Surface Transport. Villages in hill states, tribal areas and deserts that had a population of 500 people or more were also included in the first phase and it's perhaps this initiative that saw the 'tyranny of distance'—a reason given to not include places outside of road connectivity while talking about the idea of India—being addressed for the first time. The roads built under PMGSY played a major role in changing the lifestyle of many places in the north-eastern states of India.[9]

Rajnath Singh's work as the surface transport minister was not limited to building roads. More than building roads, the Golden Quadrilateral project generated employment opportunities for both skilled and unskilled labour across India, boosted the rural economy by enhancing its reach and potential, jump-started many industries including cement, steel, automobile and tourism, with the annual average consumption of cement and steel going up from 2.5 to 4 million tonnes and 0.25 to 0.3 million tonnes respectively between 2001 and 2004.[10]

In a short span of time, Singh oversaw a great many other changes in India's road transport sector. The ministry worked with a number of NGOs to spread awareness about road safety and managed to bring down the number of accidents per 1000 vehicles from ten in a day in 1997 to seven in a day by 2002 despite an increase in the number of vehicles on road. During the same period, over 35,000 drivers of heavy motor vehicles in the unorganized sector were also provided refresher training that helped in increasing road safety standards.

One of Singh's big achievements included the measures he took to tighten emission norms and safety standards of motor vehicles. At a time when the Indian economy was breaking free of shackles, Singh's decision to change the name of the emission standard EURO II to Bharat Stage II (BS II), which was followed by BS III and BS IV, instilled a sense of pride in the burgeoning Indian motor industry. The ministry mandated wearing of seat belts in motor vehicles fitted with seat belts and amended the Solatium Scheme, 1989, by waiving the requirement for filing claims within a period of six months to facilitate victims of road accidents or their heirs in obtaining compensation.

In August 2000, Singh also oversaw the amendment of the Motor Vehicles Act, 1988, that legislated use of environment-friendly fuels like compressed natural gas (CNG), liquefied petroleum gas (LPG), solar power electric batteries, etc., as automotive fuel and also notified norms such as testing, type approval and safety-related aspects for vehicles operating on CNG and LPG. His ministry also increased efforts to phase out lead in just six years while most developed countries took a decade to achieve the same.[11]

Later, in the same month, August 2000, Singh reminded the NHAI to not only award all civil works contracts for the Golden Quadrilateral project by the June 2001 deadline so that work commenced as per schedule but also called for a stringent adherence to the time frame of forty days in awarding the bid and check cost escalations. Singh's urgency had to do with the NHAI raising Rs 13,800 crore by issuing highway development bonds, of which Rs 500 crore had to be in place by September 2000.[12] The work on the Golden Quadrilateral was to commence in 2001 and had a December 2003 deadline, which Singh wanted to meet.

Anyone vaguely familiar with how public infrastructure projects worked in India might have had serious doubts about the timelines but Singh felt confident because a review had revealed how, out of the total length of nearly 6000 kilometres, 588 km was already four-laned by June 2000 and an additional 686 km was under implementation.[13] In order to streamline the entire exercise, Singh's ministry had to avoid delays in land acquisition and, for this, it was important that the NHAI kept the 'pre-qualification exercise' for the contractors intact. There was a lot at stake. Although much of the project in terms of success or failure would be visible to the eye, a large part of what the country could achieve from the realization of the Golden Quadrilateral project was indirect, in a manner of speaking. A World Bank study suggested the completion of the Golden Quadrilateral would result in an annual saving of Rs 8000 crores (1999 prices) on account of fuel savings, reduced wear and tear of vehicles and faster transportation.[14]

The extent of Rajnath Singh's seriousness about the timely execution of the project was evident from the manner in which he took on the very tools he was working with. He openly opposed NHAI chairman Deepak Dasgupta awarding a certain contract to a private party. There were murmurs of some high-ranking and experienced senior party members advising Singh to avoid being so vocal, but Singh's zero tolerance of anything that could even remotely suggest impropriety saw him dig his heels in. Ultimately, Singh's opinion was upheld by the law ministry and the NHAI had to call for fresh bids.[15]

The new chief minister of Uttar Pradesh, Ram Prakash Gupta, had spent as much time at the helm of affairs as Singh had been in Delhi. If things were testing Rajnath Singh in ways he had not imagined, the situation in Lucknow was not getting any easier for the veteran Gupta as well. Those who had an ear to the ground could sense the party staring at imminent defeat in the next assembly elections scheduled in early 2002.

Once Singh had shifted to Delhi, another senior state functionary Kalraj Mishra had been named the Uttar Pradesh BJP president but there were times when Singh caught himself thinking about UP. He could not emotionally distance himself from the state. The BJP's internal assessment had come to conclude a shift amongst the upper-caste voter towards Mulayam Singh Yadav and there was a general consensus to get someone charismatic to become the party's chief ministerial candidate. Singh abhorred the idea of being referred to as the 'Thakur' face of the party in the state and always maintained that if caste were the criteria, the electorate would have blindly selected leaders who played that card.

Rajnath Singh seemed more capable than Ram Prakash Gupta of handling difficult situations, which included instances such as coalition partners like the Loktantrik Congress opting to go solo in state municipal elections. Singh had come close to being the chief minister on many occasions in the past and did not want to think about it again. But destiny had already made its plans. In a strange twist of fate, the same people who had shot him down a year ago, such as senior party leadership including Vajpayee and Advani, and Kalraj Mishra, who till a year ago was a fellow contender, selected him to go to Lucknow as the chief minister of Uttar Pradesh and turn the party's fortunes around.

Although Singh left Vajpayee's cabinet before he could truly shine, he had nonetheless managed to do significant spadework and set the standard for the ministry that would go on to become one of the biggest legacies of Atal Bihari Vajpayee's prime ministership. He was aware of the great responsibility that awaited him and what could be more for a man who had taken his first steps in public life in Uttar Pradesh to return as the chief minister of the state. Being in Lucknow would put Rajnath Singh through his biggest test; it would see him push himself to the end of the line and beyond to revive the party.

7

The Chief Ministerial Years

With a little over a year to go for the 2002 UP Legislative Assembly elections, the BJP made Rajnath Singh the chief minister of UP. The development might have seemed sudden given how any decision to change a sitting CM always appears to be made to avert a crisis. However, unlike Ram Prakash Gupta, who had essentially been made the CM in order to contain the infighting within the various factions of the party, Singh's assignment was to portray a better image to the people than what it had in the state.

Gupta had been given the job to please all; and in order to placate most factions within the BJP, he had a ninety-six-member-strong cabinet. He had been out of active politics for nearly fifteen years before he was made the CM and, aware of his limitations, he turned to an army of officers on special duty (OSD) and other staff members. As a result, there were times when Gupta's ability to govern or even lead the party was questioned. His lack of political sensitivity and acumen only made it worse, as he tripped from one crisis to another. In one widely reported matter, Gupta apparently sent a confidential letter with comments 'for immediate action' to the very same officer against whom the party vice-president had complained of bribing certain politicians of the Samajwadi Party and the Bahujan Samaj Party for plum postings.[1]

There were other things that Gupta did which only pushed the administration to a state of flux. In just four months since he took over, the CM was instrumental in nearly 350 transfers because he could not afford to offend anyone. He allowed many MLAs and ministers personal security guards and even lifted the ban on overseas trips by members of his cabinet.[2] Things began to worry the leadership when Gupta's inability to wield a strong hand resulted in some of the party members openly announcing their support to the ousted Kalyan Singh. Moreover, Gupta was not keen on fighting elections and appeared rootless, which did not inspire any confidence in the cadre and boded ill for the BJP.

Before the state elections, the party's own organizational elections were to be held in February 2000 and Gupta was given the task of shortlisting the candidates.[3] In some ways, Gupta was perhaps more than aware of his limitations and rarely reacted to criticism. His mission was to curb the hidden conflict within the party, which he had somewhat managed and, once that was done, it was a matter of time before the axe fell.

Gupta might not have been shunted out in such a hurry had it not been for the mismanagement of the Regulation of Public Religious Buildings and Places Bill, 2000, which aimed to regulate, if not ban, construction of places of worship or the conversion of old buildings into religious places. The Bill applied to all religions, and the provisions clearly stated that no building which was not already used as a public religious place before the Bill came into effect, could be used as one without the prior permission of the district authorities. It gave enough teeth to the bureaucracy to disallow any construction if it felt it was not in the interest of public order and gave it the power to demolish any unauthorized structures.

Since the late 1990s, Islamic fundamentalists along the India–Nepal border had been active and there was enough evidence pointing at Pakistan's Services Intelligence (ISI) trying to recruit agents among frustrated, unemployed youth from across the states of UP, Bihar and Assam. Following a few statements from ministers in the state government, including the state parliamentary affairs ministers, Hukum Singh, who categorically stated that the government was targeting masjids and madrasas in border districts to curb the ISI menace, the Bill came to be perceived as anti-minority.[4]

Despite the fact that the demography of the border districts had altered in the past few years and there was an influx of foreign funds to promote religious activities, mostly setting up religious schools and building new mosques, the Bill was opposed tooth and nail by all quarters. In the Centre, Congress president Sonia Gandhi wrote to President K.R. Narayanan that the Bill in its present form was 'totally unacceptable' and urged him to return it and also add provisions that would reinforce the confidence of secular citizens.[5] Intriguingly enough, there was similar legislation in two Congress-ruled states, Madhya Pradesh and Rajasthan, since 1984 and 1954 respectively, with the latter amending it in 1988. While the Congress president informed Narayanan that she had asked the CMs of both the states to consider amendments, if necessary, to safeguard the minorities, she reiterated that the UP Bill threatened the rights of minority educational institutions, which were protected under the Constitution.[6] Several Muslim leaders felt that the proposed law harmed the Muslim community in particular, and Christians, Buddhists and Sikhs in general as it gave unlimited discretion to the district magistrate, the highest bureaucratic authority at the district level.[7]

Around the time the Bill was presented to the president there was ample substantiation of ISI's activities in cities such as Azamgarh, Jaunpur, Maunath Bhanjan, Ghazipur, Deoria and Siddharthnagar where a spurt in madrasa buildings made the danger clear and present. Intelligence Bureau reports from the region pointed towards the money to these madrasas filtering through hawala channels operated by ISI and Dawood Ibrahim, the underworld don said to be based in Karachi who was the mastermind behind the 1993 Bombay blasts.[8]

The statewide agitation against the Bill gained momentum when the protests spread to the national capital where thousands of Muslims from neighbouring states such as Haryana, Punjab and Bihar congregated at New Delhi's Jama Masjid where the Shahi Imam, Syed Abdullah Bukhari, appealed to the president to not give his assent to the legislation aimed at 'destroying the secular fabric of the country'.[9]

The president rejected the Bill and the misadventure only brought immense criticism to the BJP government. The execution might have been questionable but the Bill in itself was a much-needed tool to address a new kind of threat to India where the fine line between forces external and internal was getting blurred with each passing day. In just eight years from the time President Narayanan rejected the Regulation of Public Religious Buildings and Places Bill, some of the towns which had popped up on the ISI's radar would go on to become hubs of international terror. The town of Sarai Mir in Azamgarh district figured prominently in ISI's roster and intelligence officers would often find spotters hanging around looking for young men willing to be recruited. Funds came in as remittances from the Gulf, where a huge bunch of people from this area flocked to in the 1970s in search of work.

By 2008, nearly forty-four out of fifty-four terror strikes in India could be directly linked to Azamgarh and neighbouring areas such as Sarai Mir, from where Abu Salem, the former driver of Dawood Ibrahim, who rose in ranks after he strategized hiring unemployed Muslim youth from this area to execute shootouts in Mumbai, hails.[10] In the mid-noughties, Azamgarh had become the location preferred by Abdul Subhan Qureshi or Tauqeer, one of the most wanted terrorists in India and often called 'India's Bin Laden', to set up base for the terrorist group he founded, Indian Mujahideen. Tauqueer was apprehended by the Delhi Police in 2018 and revealed that he used to visit the border areas of UP via Nepal and distributed funds to local entities.[11] The Bill could have enabled the state government to heighten the vigilance against ISI-related acts. It could have induced the elders within the community to become a part of the effort to stop the youth from being misled. By 2017 it was more or less clear that madrasas did, in fact, play a key role in radicalizing Azamgarh's Muslims.[12]

Although it took the BJP's central leadership a few months to clear the decks, the writing on the wall was clear for Ram Prakash Gupta. The CM had nearly accepted his destiny and, as a result, kept away from pressing matters of governance, which began to have serious ramifications on the party's image in the state. There were times when Gupta ignored state duties and simply awaited orders from Delhi. The internal assessment of the party had made it clear that the lack of decisive leadership was hurting its prospects and a possible rout was imminent. This pushed the state BJP president Kalraj Mishra, Prime Minister Atal Bihari Vajpayee and L.K. Advani to finally bite the bullet and replace Gupta with Rajnath Singh.

In the period between Singh being sent to Lucknow and Gupta moving out of 5 Kalidas Marg, the official residence of the CM, the latter became momentarily inaccessible to the central leadership. Was Gupta miffed with the way things had turned out? Although he unofficially told reporters that he had no objection to the high command's decision to replace him with a better leader, he apparently refused to entertain calls from the party headquarters. The central leadership did not want to take any chances with the transition and the BJP president Bangaru Laxman dispatched a party general secretary to control the situation in Lucknow. The person entrusted with the responsibility of ensuring that the state's legislature party meeting went off without any major trouble and that the path paved for Rajnath Singh as smoothly as possible was none other than Narendra Modi.[13]

There was little doubt in the minds of everyone concerned that Singh was made the CM with the sole intention of preventing a possible rout in the 2002 assembly elections and he got down to business immediately. He took a series of policy and administrative steps to galvanize the government and the party. Taking inspiration from Deendayal Upadhyaya's Integral Humanism that was also deeply inspired by Gandhian principles of *Sarvodaya* (progress of all), *Swadeshi* (Indianization), and *Gram Swaraj* (village self-rule), Singh announced a number of reliefs and benefits for almost all sections of society in UP. With the idea of transcending the trappings of caste and religion and economic strata, Singh's measures were aimed to ensure that no one was left behind and there was something for everyone.

For the farmers, he started organizing Kisan Panchayats, made it a state policy to purchase as much paddy and wheat that came to the purchase centre, ensured timely payment to sugar cane farmers that also included raising the price by Rs 5 per quintal, offered seeds to potato farmers at a lower price and introduced subsidies, besides ensuring uninterrupted power supply for irrigation. He attacked poverty alleviation by implementing rural development programmes like Jawahar Gram Samridhi Yojana aimed at generating employment opportunities for men and women and other employment assurance schemes, in addition to making the rural drinking water supply programme more robust.

Singh was aware of the charges of corruption levelled against government officials irrespective of who was in power and decided to push for full computerization at the tehsil and the district levels to provide transparency in the functioning of the bureaucracy. He also tried to promote the state's food- and agricultural-related industries by proposing five special agro-industrial parks at Haridwar, Hapur, Lucknow, Allahabad and Varanasi. He offered much-needed relief to the state's industrial units with a green channel facility by doing away with trade tax outposts on the borders and also gave tax concessions on many products.

Singh also made a pitch to revive sick units including turpentine and resin at Bareilly and made efforts to reinvigorate sugar mills and cement factories across Uttar Pradesh. He also moved swiftly to address the concerns of the state's teachers by announcing the implementation of the Fifth Pay Commission report for almost 400,000 teachers and notified the filling up of 30,000 vacant posts of teachers. Nearly all the steps taken by Singh revealed a plan to boost the confidence of the people not just in the government but also in themselves to push the state out of the quagmire it found itself in.

Many of the reforms initiated by Singh were indeed path-breaking where the thrust for an overall development of Uttar Pradesh was at the forefront such as the special package for the Bundelkhand region. One of the most neglected areas of the state, Bundelkhand was to get Rs 125 crore dedicated to the development of electricity, irrigation, drinking water, roads, bridges and tourism. The state's first-ever university for people with special needs was also a part of the package, and the region would also get its maiden information technology university.

With a view to reaching out to the people, and providing a more accessible face of the state machinery, Singh also celebrated festivals and events by opening the doors of his residence for the general public on days such as Makar Sankranti. Also known as Khichri Parv, since it was a day where the traditional Indian dish made from rice and lentils—khichri—was cooked, the CM's house saw the city celebrate Samta Parv or equality day by welcoming people from all walks of life to enjoy the humble dish.

One of the primary focus of the Singh-led BJP government was to redress the issue of poverty, lack of education and unemployment amongst the state's minority population and ensure that the benefits he announced reached them. Singh's critics had already begun to comment on the populist nature of the schemes and suggested that everything was being done with an eye on the elections. It's the tragedy of Indian politics that anyone who wants to push reforms at a pace faster than the norm and also tries to put in place a mechanism to ensure their delivery is often accused of indulging in populism.

This is not to say that it's not true in most cases. It has been the bane of Indian politics. How else does one explain certain regions never managing to even come close to delivering on their potential while some others continue to thrive? Unfortunately, one of Rajnath Singh's steps aimed at correcting a long-standing wrong was also gauged from the same prism. Singh set up a Social Justice Committee headed by Hukum Singh—which included Ramapati Shastri, the health minister, and Daya Ram Pal, member of the UP Legislative Council—to look into existing government schemes, programmes and facilities for the welfare of Schedule Castes (SC)/Schedule Tribes (ST) and OBCs and suggest, within a period of two months, improvements to achieve the goal of social justice in UP. That such a step was long overdue is clear from the fact that despite five decades of reservations for the SCs and STs and a decade-old reservation system for OBCs in public services and posts, the condition of Dalits and backward classes continued to be miserable, with one single group in each category monopolizing the benefits of reservations.

The committee studied existing reports on the issue, examined what states such as Punjab, Haryana, Bihar, Andhra Pradesh, Tamil Nadu, Karnataka and Kerala had done in this area, and organized 'Social Justice Week' across the state. More than 50,000 families were screened and surveys conducted by nearly 85,000 government servants to analyse the share of various SC/ST and OBC groups across 1,127,311 government posts in UP.[14]

The 200-page report submitted by the committee revealed that the Yadav community, which then constituted 19 per cent of the population of the OBCs, had 33 per cent representation in jobs and the Chamar/Jatava community had the lion's share amongst the SCs. The UP cabinet accepted the report and amended the existing Uttar Pradesh Public Service (Reservation for Scheduled Castes, Scheduled Tribes and Other Backward Classes) Act, 1994, with the Uttar Pradesh Public Service (Reservation for Scheduled Castes, Scheduled Tribes and Other Backward Classes [Amendment]) Ordinance, 2001. The Legislative Assembly approved the ordinance on 27 September 2001.

What this ordinance did was to split the quota into three categories as backward, most backward and extremely backward. Even its most vocal critics found the philosophy behind the move convincing and lauded the political will of the Rajnath Singh government to rationalize reservation in a manner that would see the benefits percolate down the SC and OBC hierarchies.[15]

The years that Singh had been away from the state's affairs while he was in Delhi or the party was out of power had not impacted his natural astuteness when it came to overcoming policy paralysis. In fact, Singh's stint in Rajya Sabha and as a

Union minister had only made his acumen sharper. He could not only look at the missing pieces but also what was needed in the bigger scheme of things. The Hukum Singh Committee's recommendations no doubt promised an equitable system of job reservation, but politically too the move was nothing less than a masterstroke. In a system where caste identity had come to dominate elections, Singh, in some way, levelled the playing field by questioning appeasement politics on the part of many of the BJP's rivals. The OBCs and the Dalits had for long been considered traditional SP and BSP supporters respectively. By segregating the groups more on the basis of economic disparity, Singh seemed to be telling the electorate to vote beyond caste identity. The new quota would also see direct recruitment for nearly 40,000 government posts that would directly benefit the unemployed youth who, up until now, were treated as a vote bank but had never really benefited from such dole-outs.

Throughout his political career, Rajnath Singh had felt inhibited by the system. But his method of dealing with the challenges—persisting with what is right till the objective is achieved—had held him in good stead. On many occasions in the past, the environment made it nearly impossible for him to do what was needed. Indian politicians operate under a number of constraints and compulsions. At the same time, timing too is significant. Irrespective of the situation or the opposition he faced, Singh's conviction guided his path and also conveyed to the electorate his belief in himself. Much like the time he went against the grain to introduce the Anti-Copying Act, 1992, which cost him his seat in the State Legislative Assembly, some of Singh's actions as CM ruffled enough feathers. The eighty-five-member cabinet threw up one challenge after another without enough time for Singh to assess the road ahead, but he remained focused on ensuring that both the party and his image remained strong. Singh dismissed his energy minister, Naresh Agarwal, of the Loktantrik Congress, for making public statements against the BJP, a move that revealed the decisive man in the CM's seat.[16] It could have been considered a folly in the run-up to the assembly elections but not only did it reaffirm Singh's credibility but also marked a departure from the please-all nature of politics in India. There had been rumblings against Singh, but the move sent the clear message that the BJP was in charge and the fact that fifteen of Agarwal's nineteen-member party supported the CM only emboldened Singh. The action prompted state party president Mishra to make it clear, 'Those who do not have a good reputation will not be fielded again.'[17]

Up until a few years ago, Singh as the state BJP president had succumbed to prevailing political constraints when it came to including some 'criminals' in the Kalyan Singh cabinet in 1997.[18] Singh had not been alone in the decision-making process and had not wielded any influence on the CM to either retain or fire anyone with a questionable reputation. He had, however, managed to present an image of being personally committed to cleansing his government of criminalization and corruption, and his decision to dismiss a three-time MLA, Amarmani Tripathi, on 12 December 2001, for his involvement in the kidnapping of a boy, Rahul Gupta from Basti, cemented his stature. A minister in Rajnath Singh's cabinet, Tripathi was a history-sheeter and would later be arrested in the Madhumita Shukla murder case on 9 May 2003.[19]

While in charge, Singh never let political arithmetic dictate his unshakable will. He had no qualms about firing his tourism minister, Ashok Yadav, for filing a petition in the Supreme Court against the state government's Most Backward Class policy. The trouble with Yadav had been brewing for a while. Yadav had been routinely absent from the assembly and was trying to create a caste-based schism in the party by attacking Brahmin and Thakur leaders. When his brother moved the Supreme Court against the landmark Uttar Pradesh Public Services Act, Singh had had enough.[20] The SC stayed its execution following Yadav's petition and in the years to come, Mayawati as the CM would repeal the act.[21]

The pundits labelled most of Rajnath Singh government's schemes populist and aimed at countering anti-incumbency, yet Singh continued to go full-steam ahead with business. There was a concerted effort to go beyond the state's convention of fixing vote bank on caste lines. Before Singh took over the reins, the BJP was losing out to almost all sections of the electorate except the Muslims where its support in western UP increased from 7.3 per cent in 1996 to 9.0 per cent in 2002.[22] The one thing that Singh did for Muslims that could be a game-changer was to make their poverty, lack of education and unemployment an election issue.[23] Moreover, the manner in which Singh's government went about its business would affect people across a cross section beyond religious identity. In many ways, under Singh, the BJP seemed to be pushing for an entirely new electoral, political and social strategy beyond issues such as the Ram Mandir. Not everyone knew how to react and this rattled the Opposition.

As a matter of fact, SP chief Mulayam Singh Yadav had decided to make all his MLAs resign on 11 September 2001 to put pressure on the government to go for early polls. However, the Al Qaeda's attacks on the World Trade Center in New York on the same day took the sting out of the move.[24] Singh had in any case anticipated the opposition and took the political battle to his opponents, declaring that all BJP MLAs and ministers of his cabinet would not take their salaries from the day the Opposition argued that the incumbent assembly was to expire, 17 October 2001. Singh refused to recommend the dissolution of the assembly on the grounds that term was counted from the day it held its first sitting, 26 March 1997, and accordingly would end on 27 March, 2002. On 13 October, the then Chief Election Commissioner J.M. Lyngdoh told media persons in Dehradun that the term of the UP assembly expired in March 2002 and elections would only be held on that basis.[25]

As the elections came closer and the battle lines were drawn, it became apparent that not only Singh's local and state-level initiatives but national as well as global issues would also influence the voter. Singh's out-of-the-box thinking had already pushed the old school to the edge. As a result, the state's petty politicking came to the fore and internal feuds began to be fanned. A big challenge for Singh emerged from within his own party as supporters of Kalraj Mishra, who had been given a Rajya Sabha seat keeping his seniority in mind, began to highlight the state BJP president and not Singh as the visionary behind the government's efforts. The tussle between the one-time contenders for the CM's seat was intense enough to become the main topic of discussion at the party headquarters in Lucknow.

Despite Singh's Herculean efforts, the open scuffle between the two pillars of the party threatened to undo all the good work done by the government. There were rumours of how the Brahmin faction in the state BJP had been speaking ill of the CM, claiming they could 'finish off the upstart Rajnath Singh in no time' if it were not for the elections.[26] The Mishra camp alleged that it was at the behest of Rajnath Singh that the former Samajwadi Party legislator from Karhal, the late Baburam Yadav, had raised the issue of corruption against Kalraj Mishra in the assembly. An inquiry was instituted and nothing came of it. Mishra's supporters were not willing to let go and took the battle to the people. Booklets on the government's initiatives such as Kisan Panchayats with pictures of Mishra were distributed amongst the people to project him and not Singh, who was mentioned in passing, as the 'real people's leader'. The government communique had details and photos of meetings organized by Singh in his official capacity while the party literature seemed to focus on Mishra and the two different types of publicity material hinted at dissension.[27]

Even though state elections were often fought on local issues, the 2002 Uttar Pradesh assembly elections felt the reverberations of certain national as well as international events. The 11 September attacks on the World Trade Center brought to the fore the ugly truth about the terror propagated by Al Qaeda, and one of its repercussions in India was the Central government's decision to ban the Students' Islamic Movement of India (SIMI).

An Islamist organization that was formed in Aligarh, Uttar Pradesh, in April 1977, the SIMI's stated mission was the 'liberation of India' from Western materialistic cultural influence. It had openly celebrated the demolition of the Bamiyan Buddhas by the Taliban regime in Afghanistan. In the aftermath of the 9/11 attacks, SIMI activists hailed Osama bin Laden as a 'true mujahid' and organized demonstrations to that effect as well.[28] Despite a clear affiliation to an international act of terrorism, some political observers felt that the ban on SIMI was aimed at polarizing votes on communal lines.

A few months later, in December 2001, the Parliament was attacked by Pakistan-based terrorist outfits Lashkar-e-Taiba (LeT) and Jaish-e-Mohammed (JeM), which yet again underscored the threat to India whereby external forces could use local help. In retaliation, India mobilized troops to the border and a military stand-off ensued for nearly a month. Later it was said that the 13 December attack on Parliament was carried out on the instructions of the ISI that wanted India to retaliate with troop movement that would provide the Pakistan army an excuse to reciprocate, thus making the Afghan–Pakistan border porous enough for Osama bin Laden to escape from Tora Bora into Pakistan.[29]

When it came to Uttar Pradesh, the BJP's election manifesto promised to eradicate corruption from public office and the removal of Agarwal, Tripathi, besides a few more, validated the claim. The party also assured the electorate about bringing the office of the chief minister within the ambit of the Lok Ayukta and hammered away at making the executive, the legislature, the police and the judiciary taint-free. The manifesto also presented the party's schemes to create 150,000 jobs over the next five years and resolved to construct one million houses in rural areas and connect villages with a population of over 5000 people by roads before the end of its next term.

While the focus of the manifesto was development and good governance, the issue of Ram Mandir was not avoided. The party remained committed to resolving it within the legal framework. Mentioned in the last paragraph of the thirty-two-page manifesto, the Ram Mandir came into prominence with the BJP reaffirming its emotional connection with the matter of faith. In a rally, Singh asked the SP and Congress to clarify their stand on the issue and whether the latter would still want to construct a masjid at the disputed site as it had once promised.[30] On 6 December 2002, Prime Minister Vajpayee asserted that the Ram temple agitation was a 'nationalist movement' and said, *'Kaam adhura reh gaya hai'* (the work remains unfinished), suggesting that the dispute had not been resolved due to a lack of consensus.[31]

The party's central leadership also made terrorism a part of its manifesto, thus connecting global events to local debates. Following an increase in the number of terror attacks and in the wake of the attack on Parliament, the NDA government presented The Prevention of Terrorism Act, 2002 (POTA), to strengthen anti-terrorism operations. The act was passed in a joint session of Parliament, up until then only the third such instance in the history of India, and defined what constituted a 'terrorist act' and who a 'terrorist' was, besides granting special powers to investigating authorities. It replaced the Prevention of Terrorism Ordinance (POTO) of 2001 and the Terrorist and Disruptive Activities (Prevention) Act (TADA) (1985–95) and was opposed by nearly all Opposition parties including the Congress which was certain the government would misuse the 'black law' against political opponents and minorities.[32]

The implementation of the Act was in accordance with the United Nations Security Council's Resolution 1373 as per which, after the 9/11 attacks, the Counter-Terrorism Committee in September 2001 asked member states to prevent terrorist acts both within their borders and across regions.[33] In Paragraph 2(a), the resolution states individuals or organizations should 'refrain from providing any form of support, active or passive, to entities or persons involved in terrorist acts, including by suppressing recruitment of members of terrorist groups . . .' It was perhaps such a definition that widened the ambit of POTA. There was huge criticism following the number of arrests, over 900 within eight months of the enactment, including high-profile ones like S.A.R. Geelani, a lecturer at Delhi University, for his alleged role in the 2001 attack on Parliament and, Vaiko, a Tamil politician, for his support to the Liberation Tigers of Tamil Eelam.[34]

The NDA government established a review committee to hear individual cases related to this Act and the then home minister of India and BJP stalwart, L.K. Advani, underlined the role of the average citizen in the fight against terror.[35] In 2004, the Congress-led United Progressive Alliance (UPA), in its first term, repealed the act.[36]

The 2002 Uttar Pradesh Legislative Assembly election was a watershed for both the state BJP unit as well as Rajnath Singh.

In a pre-poll survey conducted by the Centre for the Study of Developing Societies (CSDS), Delhi, in collaboration with NDTV, a leading private English news channel, across 10 per cent of the state's 403 constituencies, 4800 respondents voted for Singh as the second best choice for chief minister. Singh scored 20.5 per cent after Mulayam Singh Yadav, who seemed to be on a comeback trail, garnering 26.8 per cent in the approval ratings.[37] In the survey that asked people their political preferences for leaders and parties, evaluation of the CM, assessment of the Central government and views on issues relating to general political culture, nearly 41.4 per cent agreed that Rajnath Singh had sought the development of all sections of the society while 55.1 per cent were convinced that Mayawati cared only for the Dalits. Singh was also voted the better option when compared to Kalyan Singh and Ram Prakash Gupta. Intriguingly enough, a large number of the respondents were completely unaware of 'communally sensitive' issues such as SIMI, VHP and POTA but were aware of the demolition of the Babri Masjid and 43.7 per cent wanted a temple to be built there.

If such surveys were any indication, the most ominous sign for the party was that despite the monumental reservation policy or a large number of appointments made in the 'Group C' category of government posts by Rajnath Singh, nearly 74 per cent of the respondents had not even heard of these developments.[38] The fact that 57.8 per cent of the respondents were unaware of the existence of Uttaranchal, a state carved out of UP, even after a year of its creation, hinted at how disconnected the electorate could be from everyday events. As the CM, Singh had announced nearly 700 schemes and in the fourteen months that he held office, nearly 692 of them had been implemented in various stages.[39]

Could this be the outcome of the infighting within the cadre as a result of which the work done by the government was not spoken about by the party in its campaign?

Traditionally, politics at the national level have always been seen as UP-centric and electoral outcomes in the state have often ended up impacting political developments across India. Pundits began to hedge their bets and, in a rare turn of events, a national event ended up influencing the 2002 UP state election.

On 27 February 2002, the Sabarmati Express returning from Ayodhya to Ahmedabad with a few kar sevaks on board was stopped near Godhra railway station and set on fire by a mob following an alleged altercation. The mob was armed with petrol bombs and kerosene and, according to some witnesses, explosives were also used.[40] Four bogies of the train were gutted and at least fifty-eight[41] people, including over a dozen children, were burnt alive. On 28 February 2002, retaliatory attacks on the Muslim community broke out. Numerous accounts over the years have presented different pictures of the communal riots. The BJP-led state under Chief Minister Narendra Modi declared curfew across twenty-seven towns and cities in the state by the end of 28 February 2002 and the army was deployed in the early hours of 1 March 2002.[42]

The events in Gujarat were the first instance of communal riots reported in the age of twenty-four-hour news coverage and most of the reportage described the attacks as having some kind of state patronage. For nearly a decade, there would be a series of national investigations in the form of commissions and special investigation teams appointed by the state government and Supreme Court respectively along with scores of social agencies, non-government organizations and civil groups but the immediate impact of the 2002 Gujarat riots were felt in the UP elections.

For the third time in a single decade, the Uttar Pradesh electorate gave a fractured mandate. The BJP had anticipated a drop in seats but the clear anti-BJP swing was somewhat unexpected. The BJP won only eighty-eight seats, a drop of sixty-eight seats. The SP got 143 seats whereas the BSP managed ninety-eight. Besides the SP and BSP gaining thirty-six and thirty-two seats respectively, the BJP's loss could also be attributed to erstwhile CM Kalyan Singh forming his own outfit, the Rashtriya Kranti Party (RKP), and other heavyweights such as D.P. Yadav who performed better. The poor voter turnout in urban areas, which was always seen as the BJP's stronghold, also led to a drop in the seats it won. Singh won his Haidergarh seat for the second time in as many years but the overall outcome was far from what he would have liked. For two months, the future of the assembly lay suspended as there was no single party with the numbers to form a government on its own and the state was put under President's Rule.

Many changes took place in the two months of inactivity with the main one being Vinay Katiyar's appointment as the state BJP president. After fifty-six days of President's Rule, the BJP and the BSP once again reached an understanding whereby the former would support the latter. Mayawati became the chief minister of Uttar Pradesh for the third time on 3 May 2002.

Rajnath Singh opposed the alliance tooth and nail but with the partnership now in place, it was only natural for him to shift his focus towards the Centre. For Singh, the election marked the end of the road in terms of state-level politics but as one of the most recognizable faces of the young stars in the BJP, his journey at the national level was only beginning.

He had already proved his mettle in the Rajya Sabha. Even during the 2000 elections, where factionalism within the party led to some cross-voting which resulted in three of five BJP members (Balbir Punj, Ram Bux Singh and the future president of India, Ramnath Kovind, who incidentally entered the Rajya Sabha for the first time along with Rajnath Singh in

1996) waiting for the third, fourth and fifth rounds of voting respectively to get through, Singh along with Sushma Swaraj won in the first round itself.[43]

Singh will go down in history books as the last chief minister of undivided Uttar Pradesh. As national politics beckoned him yet again, he embarked on a journey that would see him scale greater heights and reach the pinnacle of his party.

8

His Father's Son

After the Uttar Pradesh assembly elections in 2002, Rajnath Singh was appointed general secretary of the Bharatiya Janata Party. The national-level position entailed extra responsibilities, including having to attend to the niggling issues in his home state where the BJP cadre and the central leadership seemed to be on opposing sides. The delicate nature of the BSP–BJP alliance, with the former refusing to yield any ground—either politically or ideologically—and the legislators of the latter wanting to support the government from outside, had all the ingredients required to trigger a political explosion at a moment's notice.

The BJP's state unit had indicated on many occasions that the party ought to pull out ministers from the UP government and share the same relationship that the BSP had with the National Democratic Alliance at the Centre. Mayawati had already reversed Singh's much-talked-about job reservation policy and, despite the state's precarious financial condition, had ordered the construction of an Ambedkar memorial.[1] As the CM went about empowering the Dalits through a 'presence in space' and a 'presence in time', a cabinet reshuffle by Mayawati, where only those close to senior state BJP leader Lalji Tandon got berths, brought the friction between the two parties out in the open.[2]

Even though he was not involved in the functioning of UP, Singh's emotional proximity to his home state was reason enough for the media to make a beeline for him every time there was a tremor in Uttar Pradesh. On a few occasions Singh even spoke in defence of some of the decisions taken by the Mayawati government that had helped assuage the situation. In fact, on one such instance, Kanshi Ram acknowledged Singh's statesmanship whereby, despite being opposed to the alliance, he found it within him to support Mayawati. The leadership might have asked him to act as the elder brother to steer the flock in the light of how things were playing out in Lucknow. The BJP took pride in being one of the most dedicated cadre-based political outfits in India with a governing structure where leaders and workers had the same amount of say in decision making. As a man committed to the organization, Singh often played the part of the troubleshooter but it was a difficult job, especially when disgruntled party personnel chose to speak to the media rather than speaking to the leadership.

When Mayawati used the Prevention of Terrorism Act (POTA) against MLA Raghuraj Pratap Singh, alias Raja Bhaiya, and his father Uday Pratap Singh, there was strong criticism from state BJP leaders. There were rumours of Singh opposing the investigation against Raja Bhaiya, who was said to be close to Rajnath Singh. However, as the general secretary of the BJP, there were enough things for Singh to worry about in Uttar Pradesh on a daily basis. Both Singh as well as the BJP high command went on record to say that as the chief minister, Mayawati was free to do anything and that there was no evidence to suggest that the POTA had been misused in the case of Raja Bhaiya, who was an independent MLA and not a member of the BJP.[3]

As he went about discharging his responsibilities as the party's general secretary it became apparent that his appeal could not be limited to a single state. Every time the media grilled Singh on events unfolding around the political spectrum of the nation, Singh not only addressed the queries but also displayed the acumen needed to be a national-level leader. For example, consider the manner in which Singh fielded the controversy being stirred by both the Opposition as well as some quarters of the media when, in September 2002, Gujarat chief minister Narendra Modi undertook his Gujarat gaurav yatra to lift the spirits of party workers and connect with the electorate that was poised to go to the polls. Singh pointed out to the time-tested practice of political parties in India reaching out to the masses via media, meetings or, in the case of his party, a yatra. The immensely successful Gujarat gaurav yatra indicated the public mood in Gujarat where the voter connected with Modi who was, at the time, urging the people of his state to repose their faith in him and the BJP in the elections that were called after he dissolved the assembly by resigning in July of the year.[4] Singh also highlighted that the ouster of leaders like Shankarsinh Vaghela from the BJP, and his joining the Congress, did not in any way indicate that the party's chances of winning in the state were slim.[5]

Similarly, Singh did not mince his words when it came to deciphering the drubbing the BJP had got in the Jammu and Kashmir assembly elections. He did not shy away from saying that the people in the state voted against the BJP as it could have perceived they were a part of the incumbent National Conference (NC) even though they fought the elections separately. The BJP was in alliance with the RSS-led Jammu State Morcha and were critical of Farooq Abdullah's government. However, because the NC was a coalition partner at the Centre, it might have ended up confusing the voter.[6]

In the first signs of the 'Rajnath Singh Effect', which was known in the circles of UP politics, Singh also showed his acuity when it came to understanding the aspirations of the average Indian during the 2003 Union budget. The Ministry of Finance grapevine was abuzz with Finance Minister Jaswant Singh considering the removal of some exemptions, including one on housing loans, for computing taxable incomes for income tax purposes, but Rajnath Singh prevailed over the finance minister. The budget retained the housing loan exemptions and Rajnath Singh also managed to convince Jaswant Singh to provide a similar exemption on the money spent on children's education.

In a cabinet reshuffle that took place in July 2002, L.K. Advani had been elevated to the post of deputy prime minister, which according to most, was the first concrete sign of the end of the Atal Bihari Vajpayee era. Later, the January 2003 shuffle saw the swapping of some portfolios between key BJP members such as Arun Jaitley and Pramod Mahajan, but in what would become his last reshuffle as prime minister, Vajpayee, in 2003, had to walk a tightrope given the demands of coalition politics. Vajpayee was looking to relieve some of the ministers who had been 'overburdened' with the responsibility of more than one ministry, and wanted to use the ministerial change to cement a more permanent relationship between the BJP and its allies in the NDA. There were murmurs about him trying to induct Farooq Abdullah, but there was no portfolio important enough for such a senior leader to ease into. He also wanted to get the DMK stalwart Murasoli Maran back after his recovery from illness, but the party prevailed and his one-time replacement, Arun Jaitely, continued as the commerce minister. Some juggling was necessitated with the portfolios offered to the Trinamool Congress as well where Sudip Bandyopadhyay was offered a post much to the chagrin of party chief Mamata Banerjee, who apparently had not given her go-ahead.

In the middle of all the high drama, Rajnath Singh was appointed the Union agriculture minister replacing Ajit Singh, the Jat leader and Rashtriya Lok Dal (RLD) chief, who had resigned just days before the reshuffle. Ajit Singh was his party's lone MP in the Lok Sabha but had offered support of fourteen MLAs in the Uttar Pradesh assembly that had enabled the BSP–BJP alliance in the state.

In the time between the UP assembly elections and the May 2003 Vajpayee government cabinet reshuffle, a lot of changes had taken place and these undermined Ajit Singh's importance. The perilous BSP–BJP partnership had been boosted by a split in the Congress, and it could manage without the RLD. But more than the change in the dynamics of the state, Ajit Singh himself had trouble continuing as the agriculture minister. In a drought-ridden year, Ajit Singh's ministry was besieged with demands for relief from a number of states, and the Centre had announced a relief package of over Rs 1600 crore. Singh, however, had refused to accede to the demands of Andhra Pradesh for a greater quantum.[7] The chief minister of Andhra Pradesh, Chandrababu Naidu, was one of the most important partners in the NDA and due to the coalition's fragility managed to pressure the Centre for more.[8] Ajit Singh had also lost the plot when it came to dealing with the issue of statutory minimum prices (SMP) for the sugar cane farmers of Maharashtra and Uttar Pradesh. Things became untenable after Ajit Singh, instead of ensuring the operation of support prices and the SMP in the capacity of agriculture minister, advised farmers to file suits against sugar factories to secure SMP.[9]

If Ajit Singh—son of Chaudhary Charan Singh, the great kisan leader referred to as the champion of India's peasants, who had also served as the prime minister of India between July 1979 and January 1980—could claim pedigree to position himself as the custodian of Indian farmers, Rajnath Singh too possessed the necessary lineage to identify himself with the millions of hard-working men and women who toiled endlessly to feed the nation. He was born into a family of farmers and, having witnessed their trials, could empathize and also do what was needed to get things right. The pressure was palpable. The task was cut out and Singh took on the challenge. He had inherited one of the most important ministries in any government at the worst time possible. It had been a year of drought marked by a shortage of even drinking water let alone water for irrigation. His predecessor had been unable to decide on the minimum prices for a crop that demanded maximum water—sugar cane—and that too across two states, Maharashtra and Uttar Pradesh, which were different in nature and would require different solutions. Then there were issues related to the Genetic Engineering Approval Committee (GEAC), the Government of India body under the Ministry of Environment, Forest and Climate Change, which appraised proposals relating to genetically engineered organisms and products, including experimental field trials, refusing to approve genetically modified (GM) cotton and mustard seeds.[10] Moreover, the country was to go to polls in a matter of months and some of the decisions that Singh took as agriculture minister could have a far-reaching impact.

Singh dug his heels in and took matters head-on. In a short period of time it was clear that if there was someone who could manage to not just wade through but also perform a minor miracle of sorts it was Singh. At the time Rajnath Singh took charge as agriculture minister, the Vajpayee government had in place a system to uplift the humble farmer; at least on paper the intent was clear. The government had issued the Kisan Credit Card and had allocated over Rs 13,000 crore for rural development.[11] It was perhaps the only government in the last few decades to focus on rural development as a policy and not an afterthought or a reaction to electoral outcomes or as sops for ensuing elections. Most ministries in the government were assiduous in the overall commitment to providing schemes and benefits to the lowest rung of the population that often gets left out. One of the first things Singh did on assuming duty was to push Jaswant Singh, the finance minister, for a separate agriculture lending rate (ALR) on the pattern of the prime lending rate (PLR) available for the weaker sections and other such categories. In a letter to Jaswant Singh, he pointed out that till 1994, when the interest rates were deregulated, the interest on agricultural loans used to be much lower than that on other sectoral loans, such as industrial and housing; but by 2003 the former had an interest rate in the range of 11 per cent to 14 per cent while the housing loan interest rate was mostly under 10 per cent.

Rajnath Singh was aware that once quantity restrictions as per the requirements of the World Trade Organization (WTO) were lifted, the productivity of the average Indian agricultural holding would have to increase in keeping with the standards of developed countries, if Indian exports wanted to compete in the global markets.[12] For this value addition, he urged the finance ministry that it was imperative that it provide enough capital to the farmer at a reasonable rate of interest. In the wake of some cooperative banks levying nearly 14 per cent interest, Singh also asked the finance minister that the ALR should not only be lower than the PLR but also followed to the letter by all commercial banks and regional rural banks.

If the agriculture sector was close to Rajnath Singh's heart because of the emotional bond he shared with the farmer, Vajpayee too had been invested in the betterment of their situation. At a function where a group of farmers felicitated the PM and Singh for pushing for low interest rates, Vajpayee, reiterating their commitment to the cause of the farmer, shared how the government had spent Rs 2400 crore on subsidies to deal with the drought in 2002. Singh reaffirmed Vajpayee's suggestion to set up a monitoring system to ensure that farmers get the direct benefits of the lower interest rates.[13] In order to make farmers across the length and breadth of India aware of the benefits that were theirs for the taking, Rajnath Singh proposed a 'Kisan Channel' to disseminate information about various government schemes to farmers countrywide. The free-to-air television channel would be managed by the Indian Council of Agricultural Research (ICAR) under the agriculture ministry and would also be used to educate farmers about the latest farming technology. Despite the government's massive foray into the rural and farming sectors, many farmers were unaware of ventures such as the Kisan Credit Cards, rural housing, gas and telephone connections and the building of roads to connect villages. During the drought of 2002, the NDA released over 8.8 million tonnes of grain free of cost for farmers and even that remained under-reported, depriving many of the much-needed relief. Moreover, political opponents were also questioning the government's agenda and these included former agriculture minister Ajit Singh, who, since, quitting the government, had labelled it anti-farmer.[14] In short, Rajnath Singh was expected to deliver the near-impossible.

Replacing Ajit Singh with a man who hailed from the same state, Uttar Pradesh, might have worked on multiple fronts for Vajpayee. As someone who was aware of the woes of the sugar-cane farmers of the state, Rajnath Singh ticked the first box. But Singh's bigger challenge was to win the battle of perception. Traditionally, there was a belief that the performance of ministers from the north was less impactful when compared with those from the west and the south, such as Panjabrao Shamrao Deshmukh, the first agriculture minister of India who laid the foundation of India's foodgrain resilience and, later, Annasaheb Shinde and C. Subramaniam, who were behind the country's green and white revolutions.

Rajnath Singh had his ear to the ground and worked on multiple fronts to make the sector robust and undo the damage done over decades of policy decisions pertaining to negative subsidies. Erratic monsoons notwithstanding, experts had raised enough concerns about the Indian farmer being stymied by the almost zero advantage coming their way even after the opening up of world trade in agriculture. In the wake of the failure of rich countries to abide by the commitments under the 1994 Marrakesh Agreement of the WTO and the disputes between the United States on one side and Japan and Europe on the other at the Doha Round, 2001, it was apparent that India could lose out in the aggressive policy war between the rich nations. One of Singh's biggest challenges as agriculture minister came knocking barely three months after he took over, in the form of the fifth WTO ministerial conference to be held in Cancún, Mexico, in September 2003.

In the run-up to Cancún, the commerce ministry prepared a list of 842 agricultural products and items that would be a part of the negotiations amongst member countries but the agriculture ministry was not completely in the know of the range of taxes and duties of the items. Sources within the agriculture ministry were quoted in newspaper reports speaking about the lack of coordination between them and the commerce ministry and the administrative ministries handling specific issues related to the WTO. Unlike the commerce ministry that treated the matter as a trade issue, Singh realized this was not just an economic issue. The situation was dire with farmer suicides and the high interest rates besides the delayed monsoon after a drought-ridden year. Ideally, the ministry ought to have been consulted about the proposal on tax reductions, standardization or restructuring of the percentage of taxes in Cancún. Singh's primary concern was as much about the consequences the farmer would face as it was about the political ramifications. Farmers across the country, ranging from the tobacco growers in Andhra Pradesh and Karnataka, the small onion cultivators in Maharashtra to the groundnut growers in Gujarat, were concerned about the repercussions of the Indian government giving in to the demands of the WTO to reduce customs duties on such produce by half or making it zero.

At the time, when preparations were on for Cancún, India's agricultural produce was in surplus and given its vast market, it ought to have enjoyed more clout as opposed to buckling under pressure from developed countries. Singh knew the significance of agriculture at the Cancún talks, for it was one of the five areas the conference would be centred on. He stood his ground in his deliberations with the commerce ministry. As the date approached, it was Vajpayee's intervention and his instructions to Jaswant Singh to mediate that saw both the agriculture and commerce ministries attempt to end the stalemate.

The Cancún round of the WTO was a failure and all talks collapsed after a walkout by African countries protesting at the West's failure to open its markets to the poor. The five-day-long talks were yet again dominated by a struggle between the so-called traditional power brokers, the European Union (EU) and the United States. But for the first time, developing countries such as Brazil, India and China flexed their negotiating muscles enough to be labelled the new group of 'militant developing countries', which put them in a stronger position when negotiations would eventually restart.[15] Right at the onset of the first round of one-to-one bilateral talks with the US trade representative Robert Zoellick and European Union trade commissioner Pascal Lamy, Arun Jaitley went on the offensive and told them that heavy domestic support and export subsidies in the US and the EU were hurting Indian farmers.[16] Protecting the rights of 650 million farmers of India was of paramount importance and India let the developed countries know that any tariff reduction would only be possible after they agreed to steep cuts in export subsidies.

Despite the failure at Cancún, Singh was optimistic that India was a big enough market and the WTO talks would have no impact. The manner in which developing countries and especially India stood up to the developed counties was a sign of the changing times, but the time had come to enable the Indian farmer to withstand global pressure. The time had come for developing countries to stand united and India could lead the world. Addressing a round-table meeting on WTO-related agricultural issues in Rome in December 2003, Rajnath Singh called upon the international community to not allow advanced economies to undermine the livelihood security of farmers in developing countries under the guise of self-serving trade reforms. With representatives of sixty countries in the audience, Singh stressed the need to mete out special treatment to developing countries to address their legitimate development needs that included food and livelihood security as well as rural development. In discussions with his counterparts from New Zealand, Sweden, Finland and Japan as well as the agriculture commissioner of the European Union, Singh created a consensus that a level playing field for future negotiations can only be created by developing countries having more leverage and flexibility.

Back in India, Singh understood the need to make information reach the farmer that could help them make the most of the opening up of global trade and the world recession. They needed to know of facilities that would allow them to take advantage of technological breakthroughs to take on the world. There were regular panchayats organized for farmers across the country. Singh also announced the launch of a call centre scheme for farmers after the Kisan channel was launched.[17] Under the new scheme, any farmer would be able to obtain agriculture-related information required from a toll-free number.

The NDA government in 2000 had also announced India's first-ever National Agriculture Policy (NAP) that sought to transform the vast untapped potential of Indian agriculture and aimed to achieve a growth rate in excess of 4 per cent per annum in the sector that would be spread across regions and farmers. It had put in place a mechanism to bring agriculture in India to the twenty-first century. This included endeavours such as technology missions on cotton, integrated development of horticulture in the north-eastern states, a national policy on cooperatives, personal insurance against accidental death and permanent disability to Kisan Credit Card holders, a national seeds policy for the development of new and improved varieties of plants, timely availability of quality seeds, compulsory registration of seeds, an act to protect plant varieties and farmers' rights and much more. But one of its most significant achievements in the agriculture sector remained largely unnoticed.

For a country that prided itself in being identified with agriculture, India, oddly enough, never set up a body that looked into what was ailing the farmer and farming as a sector beyond what met the eye. In the middle of subsidies, farmer suicides, low-interest loans and fighting to improve the crisis of irrigation or being too dependent on the rains, nearly every single minister for agriculture overlooked the installation of some mechanism that could help get to the core of the problems of the farmer. Most people continue to remain unaware that one of Singh's greatest contribution as agriculture minister was to set up the National Commission on Farmers (NCF), a pioneering body that would look into the problems of farmer families and suggest solutions to improve farm income, standard of living of farm households and also make farming not only more remunerative but also attractive to the younger generation. Unlike a fact-finding commission, the emphasis of the NCF was on farmers rather than agriculture. In what was his final Independence Day speech as prime minister from the ramparts of the Red Fort, Vajpayee had expressed his desire to create the NCF. It was to help prepare the road map for sustainable development of agriculture, optimize its contribution to growth and development of the economy and make Indian agriculture globally competitive. The seriousness could be gauged from the fact that despite the proclamation from the PM himself, the setting up of the commission took nearly six months as there had been a suggestion to make NCF a constitutional commission at par with the Election Commission with overriding authority on matters that concerned the farmers.[18]

With the NCF, Singh wanted suggestions for not just the advancement of agriculture but also the economic well-being of farming families by putting in place a social security system and support services for farmers that would become a road map and make both future policy formation and execution cohesive. The commission was to be headed by Sompal Singh Shastri, a much-respected expert in agriculture, who had also been a minister for agriculture and a member of the Finance Commission.

As the work on the formation of the NCF began, Singh continued to fire on all cylinders, be it pushing for policy reforms that would give outfits such as the National Federation of State Cooperative Banks (NFSCB)—which provided agriculture and rural credit to state and district cooperative banks and farmer societies across India—the power to recapitalize cooperative societies and lend up to 85 per cent of agricultural loan requirements of bodies and individuals supported by them or initiate a pilot project of the Farm Income Insurance Programme.[19] Covering two critical components of the farmer's income, namely yield and price, through a single policy instrument, the Farm Income Insurance Programme was launched during the 2003–04 Rabi season and guaranteed a minimum income based on the average yield of the last seven years and the minimum support price.[20]

When Rajnath Singh took over the agriculture ministry he had only a few months to not just perform well but probably turn around the fortunes of both the BJP and the NDA as the Lok Sabha elections were only a year away. Even in mid-2003, when Singh assumed office, there were talks about the NDA holding the general elections within six months. Considering the pressure that accompanied him to Krishi Bhawan—the building housing the Ministry of Agriculture—Singh had delivered and also shown enough astuteness to look at things in the long term. Things were always going to be uphill in the short run but in the long run, Singh, like the time he was the minister for surface transport, put into place an apparatus that would work on its own. The farming community was under stress when Singh took charge and although many of their concerns were acknowledged, would it be enough when the government went to polls?

With eight more months left in the thirteenth Lok Sabha, Vajpayee, in February 2004, decided to call for early elections. The BJP-led National Democratic Alliance had won three assembly elections in November 2003 in Madhya Pradesh, Chhattisgarh and Rajasthan and felt it was the right time to go to the people for a fresh mandate. This was only the fourth time in the history of India that a government in a majority would choose to dissolve the Lok Sabha before its scheduled time. Those outside of the government were convinced that the NDA wanted to cash in on the so-called 'India Shining' campaign and the feel-good factor before the claims of development went bust. But truth be told, there had been a great surge in nearly all the indices that indicated growth in terms of the quality of life.

To tackle the polls, the BJP would focus on development and stability that it had offered and there were two people who spearheaded the campaign—Arun Jaitley and Pramod Mahajan. The former was to work on a vision document and the latter was to oversee the campaign and poll management.[21]

The Opposition tried and, perhaps, even succeeded in denting the image of the NDA's feel-good factor. In terms of the agriculture sector, the rising number of suicides in rural areas in states such as Madhya Pradesh, Rajasthan, Karnataka and Uttar Pradesh were cited as glaring examples of the government's failure. In hindsight, the electorate's decision to vote the way it did in the 2004 Lok Sabha elections would be pondered over for years to come, but even till voting day, there was no reason to believe that the Congress or any Congress-led alliance could make a significant impact. If insiders were to be believed, even the Congress high command itself was far from confident of making any headway in the elections. The NDA's decision call for early polls had caught the Congress on the wrong foot. With months to go before elections had to be called, the Congress was not only confused about its political agenda but also had no real road map to offer the voters except criticizing the BJP for pushing the 'feel good' or 'India Shining' hype. The one big factor that could have made a silent contribution to the way things eventually shaped up was Atal Bihari Vajpayee's public declaration that the NDA would fight the 2004 elections under the leadership of L.K. Advani.

The elections for the fourteenth Lok Sabha were held in four phases between 20 April and 10 May 2004. After eight years in political wilderness, the Congress returned to power, managing to put together a comfortable majority of more than 335 members with the help of its allies. Pre-poll alliances and surveys had confirmed the BJP/NDA's internal assessment of an overwhelming majority for the BJP but the end result was something else. The BJP had worked on the resurgence of India in terms of its foreign policy and making it economically robust.

It was Vajpayee's foreign policy which made China change its stance on Sikkim and since his 2003 visit, the Chinese ceased to stake any claim. The Bombay Stock Exchange fell a week before counting as the clouds of instability loomed and even though it regained when it became evident that Congress would form the government, it plummeted again when the the left parties announced their support to Congress and hinted at doing away with Vajpayee's disinvestment ministry.

The Vajpayee government had tried to make entrepreneurship a virtue and promoted free-market economy, but was something amiss for it to lose the 2004 elections? According to political commentators on both sides of the spectrum, the BJP managed to change India but had not been able to change itself.[22] A few even went to the extent of suggesting that the reaction was also against a leadership that stubbornly refused to give up hierarchies based on age.

Irrespective of the analyses, the results meant only one thing: BJP was out. For Rajnath Singh, the loss meant trying, all over again, to make an effort to understand the unpredictable pulse of the Indian voter. If a victory called for a celebration, a loss demanded a relook at the organization that could pave the path for corrective measures. It was time for the BJP to make some changes and shed the past but it would take a long time for the old order to make way for the new guard. Singh's contribution as agriculture minister would be overshadowed by nearly a decade of inactivity and a misplaced sense of direction.

Following the change in the government, the National Commission on Farmers too underwent a significant change. The new government replaced Shastri and appointed M.S. Swaminathan, the well-known geneticist, renowned for his role in India's green revolution, as the chairman of NCF.[23] The National Commission on Farmers would present its report in 2006 and make suggestions for the advancement of agriculture by setting an important goal for farmers' welfare in the form of ensuring a 'minimum net income' to improve the economic viability, besides suggesting that the human and gender dimensions in all farm policies be mainstreamed. It would suggest giving explicit attention to sustainable rural livelihoods, completion of unfinished land reforms and much more. Unfortunately, most of these recommendations would not be put into place in the decade that followed. In the meantime, Rajnath Singh was set to assume greater responsibilities and prepare his party for new political dynamics in India that would take many by surprise.

9

The Party President Years

A political mandate delivered by the people needs to be assessed for a variety of reasons. One, it is the only thing offering an insight into how the voter thinks and although learning something in hindsight rarely has a bearing on the present, it nonetheless warrants a re-examination of what any political party offers the voter. In the case of the 2004 Lok Sabha elections, even for political pundits, the victory of the Congress-led UPA was not as shocking as the rout suffered by the BJP and the NDA. Although the BJP's internal evaluation took a while, mainly because of the political drama unfolding in the corridors of power in Delhi, analysts had begun to put the onus of the loss to factors such as 'India Shining', a campaign that underscored the feeling of economic optimism across segments in India. For the Congress, there was little doubt about party president Sonia Gandhi being their prime ministerial candidate and with Congress being the single largest party within the UPA, the allies too would not pose any threat. This foregone conclusion faced legal and constitutional obstacles that surfaced as efforts to pitch Sonia Gandhi as the PM gained momentum.

Television channels, the Internet and newspapers were having a field day with conspiracy theories and the many permutations and combinations evolving, while the Indian citizen was avidly following every move of the party in Delhi. There were rumours about President A.P.J. Abdul Kalam being told that the Indian armed forces might have a problem with Sonia Gandhi at the helm. In the end, it was perhaps a letter written by the then Janata Party president Subramanian Swamy that seemed to seal the fate. Swamy informed President Kalam that a 'reciprocity' proviso to Section 5 of the Citizenship Act put a 'clear legal bar' on Sonia Gandhi becoming the prime minister of India.[1] In a press conference, Swamy told media persons that the proviso stated that an Indian citizenship, conferred under this section to an Italian, shall be subject to the same conditions and restrictions that apply to Indians who sought Italian citizenship, and because a naturalized citizen could not hold a high public office like the prime minister of the country in Italy, Sonia Gandhi too could not do that in India.

While Congress workers refused to take no for an answer, Swamy threatened to approach the Supreme Court if Deputy Prime Minister L.K. Advani, to whom he had already written a similar letter, did not issue a government order to make India's official position clear. At this juncture, Sonia Gandhi, in a dramatic turnaround, sacrificed the PM's post after listening to her 'inner voice'.[2] She chose senior Congress leader and former finance minister Dr Manmohan Singh as the prime minister of India. Sonia Gandhi's 'sacrifice' would become an issue of debate for years to come.

In his 2012 memoir, *Turning Points: A Journey Through Challenges*, Kalam wrote that he would have appointed Sonia Gandhi the prime minister had she staked a claim but that was never the case.[3] According to media reports, sources close to the president claimed that Kalam had raised legal issues over the appointment of Mrs Gandhi as prime minister. They were never officially denied.[4] In 2014, veteran Congress leader K. Natwar Singh mentioned in his book *One Life Is Not Enough:*

Over the years

Younger days: By the mid-1980s, Rajnath Singh was a recognized face across his home state of Uttar Pradesh and beyond.

Rajnath Singh welcoming Atal Bihari Vajpayee in Lucknow with chief minister Kalyan Singh looking on.

At a public rally with Atal Bihari Vajpayee.

Prime Minister Atal Bihari Vajpayee and Sushma Swaraj during a visit to Uttar Pradesh with Rajnath Singh and Uttar Pradesh chief minister Kalyan Singh.

Rajnath Singh accompanying Atal Bihari Vajpayee as he files his nomination papers from Lucknow along with Kalyan Singh and Kalraj Mishra.

Rajnath Singh's hands-on approach as the minister for surface transport saw him take epoch-making decisions, 1999.

Under Rajnath Singh, the ministry of surface transport laid the ground work for the ambitious Golden Quadrilateral project besides ushering in reforms in the sector.

Surface Transport Minister Rajnath Singh at a demonstration, 2000.

Rajnath Singh addressing the students of Lal Bahadur Shastri College of Advanced Maritime Studies and Research, Mumbai, 2000.

Rajnath Singh inspects a guard of honour at Lal Bahadur Shastri College of Advanced Maritime Studies and Research, Mumbai.

Arriveth the hour, arriveth the man: The decision to make Rajnath Singh
the chief minister of Uttar Pradesh saw the party regain much of
the electorate's confidence.

All ears: Rajnath Singh in conversation with Kalraj Mishra, the then general
secretary of the BJP, Narendra Modi and the then chief minister of
Uttar Pradesh, Ram Prakash Gupta, 2000.

People's chief minister: Besides helping his party regain some of the ground it had lost with the voter, Rajnath Singh was also the last chief minister of undivided Uttar Pradesh.

All the CM's men: Rajnath Singh at the swearing-in ceremony of his cabinet, 2000.

BJP General Scretary Narendra Modi accompanies the new Uttar Pradesh Chief Minister Rajnath Singh, Lucknow, 2000.

From left to right:
Governor of Uttar Pradesh
Vishnu Kanth Shastri,
Chief Minister Rajnath
Singh, Lalji Tandon
and Kalraj Mishra at a
function, 2001.

The chief minister and the prime
minister: Rajnath Singh with the prime
minister and senior BJP leader Atal
Bihari Vajpayee at the Uttar Pradesh
chief minister's official residence,
5 Kalidas Marg, Lucknow, 2001.

The governor, the prime
minister and the chief
minister: Vishnu Kanth
Shastri and Atal Bihari
Vajpayee with
Rajnath Singh at an event
in Lucknow, 2001.

The chief and the chief minister: CM Rajnath Singh with long-time associate and state BJP Chief Kalraj Mishra, 2002.

Taking it to the people: CM Rajnath Singh and Kalraj Mishra, 2002.

Team BJP: CM Rajnath Singh along with Kalraj Mishra and other party members on the campaign trail, 2002.

Rajnath Singh with Jagadguru Sri Jayendra Saraswathi
Shankaracharya of the Kanchi Kamakoti Peetham.

President A.P.J. Abdul Kalam administering the oath of
office and secrecy to Rajnath Singh as he joins Atal Bihari
Vajpayee's cabinet as the minister for agriculture, 2003.

In a meeting with functionaries of the agriculture ministry, 2003.

The right mix: Aware of an average farmer's trials, Singh's ministry introduced schemes to making farming financially viable.

As agriculture minister, Rajnath Singh travelled across India to see how things stood in order to provide all necessary help to the sector.

Under Rajnath Singh, the agriculture ministry made use of technology to not only aide the Indian farmer but applied it to make farming easy.

Front row (from left to right): George Fernandes, Atal Bihari Vajpayee and Rajnath Singh; second row (from left to right): Uma Bharti, Kalraj Mishra and Murli Manohar Joshi, 2004.

Rajnath Singh as the Union minister of agriculture with Prime Minister Atal Bihari Vajpayee at the launch of the Kisan channel along with Hukmdev Narayan Yadav, the Union minister of state, agriculture, 2004.

In the driver's seat: Hailing from a farmer's family, Rajnath Singh knew what ailed the humble farmer.

In the company of stalwarts: Flanked by senior leaders L.K. Advani, A.B. Vajpayee and Jaswant Singh, Rajnath Singh assumes charge as BJP's national president, 2005.

'Rajnath *aage, aage, hum peechhe*': Rajnath Singh's idol Atal Bihari Vajpayee offering sweets to the new national president, 2005.

Change of guard: L.K. Advani felicitates BJP national president Rajnath Singh.

A meeting of National Democratic Alliance members: (From left to right): Parkash Singh Badal, Atal Bihari Vajpayee, BJP national president Rajnath Singh, Nitish Kumar and Sharad Yadav, 2006.

BJP national president Rajnath Singh along with Gujarat Chief Minister Narendra Modi and senior leaders L.K. Advani, Jaswant Singh and Murli Manohar Joshi at an election rally in Gujarat, 2007.

Meeting Shiv Sena supremo Balasaheb Thackeray at Matoshree in Mumbai, 2007. Also present are Shiv Sena's senior leader Manohar Joshi, Uddhav Thackeray and the BJP's Gopinath Munde.

During the first term as the party's national president, Rajnath Singh traversed the country to boost the morale of the cadre and strengthen the party at the grass roots. Seen here with Nitin Gadkari and Gopinath Munde, 2008.

At the 65th Session of the General Assembly of the United Nations in 2010, Rajnath Singh raised the issue of global terrorism in his speech as a member of the Indian Parliament. After Atal Bihari Vajpayee, Singh became the second leader to deliver a speech in Hindi at the UN.

Celebrating Holi with L.K. Advani, 2013.

Two in a wave: Narendra Modi and Rajnath Singh at NDA's oath-taking ceremony in May 2014.

We are the champions: In his second term as the BJP national president, Rajnath Singh delivered the best-ever victory the party had witnessed until 2014. Seen here with Narendra Modi, whom Singh championed as the NDA's prime ministerial candidate, Sushma Swaraj and Arun Jaitley.

Rajnath Singh takes oath as the Union minister of home affairs, 2014.

At the seventh home/interior ministers meeting of
SAARC nations, Islamabad, 2016.

Clicked: As home minister with a newly inducted all-women
batch of Central Industrial Security Forces at the CISF
Regional Training Centre (RTC), Arrakonam, 2017.

Taking aim: Rajnath Singh in Ulaanbaatar, Mongolia, 2018.

On the campaign trail: Rajnath Singh addressed over 100 public rallies during the 2019 Lok Sabha elections. Seen here in Lucknow during the filing of his nomination papers.

As the new defence minister of India, Rajnath Singh visited Siachen to pay his tribute to the martyred soldiers who sacrificed their lives while serving at the world's highest battlefield. Seen here with Army chief General Bipin Rawat and Northern Army Commander Lt General Ranbir Singh, 2019.

On top of the world: Defence Minister Rajnath Singh meets the 'rakshaks', the bravehearts of the Indian Army, Siachen, 2019.

An Autobiography that it was not Sonia Gandhi's inner voice but Rahul Gandhi, her son, who was the reason behind her not becoming the prime minister. Rahul Gandhi was 'vehemently opposed to his mother becoming prime minister, fearing that she would lose her life, much like his grandmother and his father'.[5] Swamy had questioned Kalam and asked him to make public his letter to Sonia Gandhi and, around the time of Kalam's revelation, in a reply to a Right to Information (RTI) query, the president's secretariat indirectly confirmed that it was, in fact, Swamy's letter that led Kalam to finally accept Manmohan Singh as the PM.[6]

If the Congress had turned to the old guard to lead, the change of guard in the BJP also reflected the same. Following the loss in the general elections, M. Venkaiah Naidu resigned from the post of party president and L.K. Advani was appointed for the third time.[7] Naidu had opted to quit for personal reasons as he wanted to devote time to his ailing wife. With Naidu leading the BJP's election campaign and Advani as the prime ministerial candidate, the party had sought the mandate of the people based on their performance, but for most of the party members there seemed to be a 'mismatch between development, performance and the verdict'. There were a few silver linings, with its performance in Arunachal Pradesh—where it had opened its account bagging nine assembly seats without allying with anyone—being the highlight. Besides taking over the reins of the party, Advani also continued to be the leader of the Opposition in the Lok Sabha. As he passed on the baton, Naidu had hoped that under Atal Bihari Vajpayee's 'guidance' and Advani's leadership the party would surge forward.

As one of the founding members of the party, Advani faced a great challenge: to not only understand why the nation had voted against them but also, and more importantly, initiate the process of rebuilding the party both nationally as well as provincially. Advani expressed his view that the catchphrase 'India Shining' might not have been wrong but it was not appropriate.[8] He believed self-criticism was needed but, despite the unexpected result, there was no need for self-flagellation. He was more than hopeful that the BJP had a bright future and it was only a matter of time before it bounced back.

Did the BJP lose because of campaigns such as 'India Shining', or was the 2004 mandate somewhere a judgement about what the party had pitched for the future? For the party to be able to make a comeback, there was a dire need to send a message that things were going to change. Revered as he might be within the party, Advani as the party chief did not really suggest a revamp. Some of the most successful ministries under Vajpayee had been headed by the next generation of leaders and, perhaps, there was a need to invest more in the future than the past. Individuals such as Rajnath Singh, Sushma Swaraj, Pramod Mahajan and Arun Jaitley being given a great role would have also been a sign to both the cadre as well as the electorate that the party was looking ahead.

Rajnath Singh had been elected to the Rajya Sabha for a second term in 2003 and was reappointed national general secretary of the BJP in 2004. During his first stint as the party's general secretary, he was in charge of two states— Chhattisgarh and Jharkhand—and it was his organizational skills that played a significant role in the creation of the first-ever BJP government in the former in 2003. The party's stunning victory in the states of Madhya Pradesh, Rajasthan and Chhattisgarh in the 2003 assembly elections was one of the reasons why Vajpayee had confidently called for early elections in 2004. The three elections were textbook studies in the manner in which various quarters of the BJP approached the elections. The charge of coordination in each state was given to a young leader: Madhya Pradesh to Arun Jaitley,

Rajasthan to Pramod Mahajan and Chhattisgarh to Rajnath Singh, and Vajpayee had decided to fight the elections on issues of development and governance. In what seemed to be a gamble for traditional BJP observers, the party chose to avoid mentioning Ayodhya and kept the leaders of the VHP from campaigning. The issue of bijli (electricity), sadak (roads) and paani (water) was raked up and the voter reposed its faith in the BJP.[9] Advani had appointed candidates for the chief minister's position for each state as well and it was clear that when people voted, they did do for Vasundhara Raje Scindia in Rajasthan, Uma Bharti in Madhya Pradesh and Dilip Singh Judeo in Chhattisgarh. Following a video accusing Judeo of accepting a bribe for mining rights in Chhattisgarh, the state BJP head, Raman Singh, was appointed the first BJP chief minister of the state and would go on to remain in office for three terms.[10] The success in the assembly elections in Rajasthan, Madhya Pradesh and Chhattisgarh gave the BJP the belief about performing better in the Lok Sabha elections. But much of it could be attributed to the presence of younger leaders who ensured smoothness of operations and emerged as the face of the future. If that be the case, how long before the writing on the wall became clear to the old guard within the party?

The first major crisis that the BJP faced after the 2004 debacle was the unfolding of the 2005 assembly polls in Jharkhand. Despite the BJP being the single largest party, the governor, Syed Sibtey Razi, invited Shibu Soren to form the government on 2 March 2005. The elections had thrown up a hung mandate and the NDA, with forty-one MLAs, had staked its claim, but the governor chose to call Soren's Jharkhand Mukti Morcha (JMM) to form the government. This was despite the fact that the party had submitted a list of only thirty-six MLAs. As the state in charge, Rajnath Singh felt that the governor, in a display of abject misuse of power, had throttled democracy.[11] The BJP called the decision a 'constitutional outrage' and the former chief minister of Jharkhand, Arjun Munda, moved the Supreme Court.[12]

While the Court deliberated, the NDA presented all its forty-one MLAs to President Kalam on the evening of 3 March but not before executing an intricate cat-and-mouse hunt dubbed 'Operation Decoy'. The Congress headquarters had pushed for a patch-up between Soren and Lalu Prasad Yadav, who was miffed at the pre-poll alliance the Congress had had with JMM and even dispatched the then water resources minister Priya Ranjan Dasmunshi and Ajit Jogi to Ranchi to oversee things.[13] The BJP spread the news of all forty-one MLAs flying to Delhi but replaced five independent MLAs with party activists and decided to take the five independents by road to the neighbouring state of West Bengal from where they would be flown to Delhi. Soren got wind of it and put up check posts at the borders. This forced the MLAs to change their plans and head towards Kharagpur in Midnapore district of West Bengal.

Later that night, the independents caught a train for Bhubaneswar, arriving in the capital of Odisha at 5 a.m. and there they rested for a while.[14] During the course of the day, the Congress and the Jharkhand Mukti Morcha mounted a desperate hunt for these independent legislators in Ranchi and Delhi and even in Ahmedabad as rumours that the MLAs could have been taken to the BJP-ruled state of Gujarat began to circulate. In the afternoon the MLAs flew to Delhi where they were kept in Gujarat Bhawan and taken to the Rashtrapati Bhawan at the appointed hour.

A three-member bench of the apex court, headed by Justice R.C. Lahoti, called Soren's government a 'total fraud on the Constitution' and asked for the Soren vote of confidence to be advanced.[15] The entire episode left the Manmohan Singh government visibly embarrassed and, ultimately, he ordered Soren to give up the post.[16] Ten days later, Arjun Munda was sworn in as the chief minister after Soren was unable to even begin his floor test.

A few months later the party came face-to-face with an unexpected challenge that brought Rajnath Singh squarely under the spotlight. In June 2005, during a visit to Pakistan, Advani found himself on the wrong side of the tracks when he praised the founder of Pakistan, Muhammad Ali Jinnah, by calling him a secular ambassador of Hindu–Muslim unity. Born in undivided India, Advani's association with the RSS had begun in Karachi where he was a pracharak in Sind. His visit to Jinnah's mausoleum was the most high-profile by an Indian leader in recent times and he was the first mass leader to mention Jinnah as a great man. The general secretaries of the CPI and CPI (M), A.B. Bardhan and Harkishan Singh Surjeet, respectively, had visited Islamabad in 2004 on the invitation of the communist parties in Pakistan, but unlike their trip, Advani's trip was much publicized; he was given a guard of honour by the Pakistan navy and his visit to Jinnah's mausoleum was covered live on local TV channels.[17] The manner in which Advani was treated was befitting a visiting head of state and his comments sparked off a controversy in India.

The BJP found itself in a tight spot as Advani refused to withdraw his statement and the RSS publicly expressed its disagreement with the party president's statements. Advani's controversial comments were seen as an effort on his part to portray either a 'softer' image towards the minorities, or do away with the 'Hindutva hardliner' identity that had become inseparable with him after the 1992 Babri Masjid demolition.[18] Upon his return to India, Advani offered to quit as the BJP

president. He was asked to continue after a unanimous resolution
was passed within the party. Although Advani withdrew his
resignation, which he would later term as a mistake, the cracks
had become permanent and it was only a matter of time before
a change was imminent.[19]

The first indication of the generational shift in the BJP's
leadership and the signalling of the end of the Advani–Vajpayee
era presented itself in a roundabout way. On 29 November 2005,
Krishnanand Rai, a sitting MLA from the Mohammadabad
assembly seat in Uttar Pradesh's Ghazipur district, was gunned
down along with six others in what was said to be gang-based
rivalry between the groups of Mukhtar Ansari and one Brajesh
Singh. Rai had started off as a contractor and later forayed into
politics on the behest of his close friend and BJP member Manoj
Sinha and was said to be close to Ansari's rivals.[20] But more
than anything else, Rai probably earned the wrath of Ansari
when he contested the Mohammadabad assembly seat in the
2002 elections and ended Ansari's brother and the Samajwadi
Party candidate Afzal Ansari's run of five victories.[21] Starting
on a CPI ticket in 1985, Afzal Ansari went on to win the next
three assembly elections in 1989, 1991, and 1993 and then
won the Mohammadabad seat for the fifth consecutive time in
1996 but on a Samajwadi Party ticket. Rai's victory could also
be seen as symptomatic of and end of religion-based politics as
Mohammadabad had a numerically significant and politically
influential Muslim population.[22]

The brutal manner in which Rai was killed, allegedly by
contract killer Munna Bajrangi, who is also believed to be the
one who introduced the Kalashnikov to gangs in Uttar Pradesh,
sent shockwaves across the region.[23] There was outrage amongst
Rai's supporters and much of it was focused on Mukhtar
Ansari, who was also an independent MLA. Although the
first information report (FIR) filed at the Ghazipur police

station named Mukhtar Ansari, Afzal Ansari, who by then
was a Lok Sabha MP representing Ghazipur that he had won
on the Samajwadi Party ticket in 2004, and Munna Bajrangi,
there was a clamour for the Central Bureau of Investigation to
investigate the killing.

The Mulayam Singh Yadav-led state government refused
to give in to the demand and, beginning 30 November 2005,
Rajnath Singh sat on an indefinite dharna at the Varanasi
district headquarters. The protest gathered momentum and,
over the course of the next few days, several BJP MLAs from
across the state, including Ajay Rai, Lallu Singh and Ram
Ekbal Singh, as well as former state BJP president, Om Prakash
Singh, joined in. Later, a few MLAs from Bihar too reached.
Several senior leaders from the party including Advani, Kalyan
Singh and Pramod Mahajan also marked their presence. As the
dharna was completing its second week, Vajpayee dropped in to
meet Singh. In the evening, Singh joined Vajpayee for dinner
in his room at the Circuit House, which was at a stone's throw
from the nerve centre of the protest. Vajpayee told Singh, *'Kab
tak dharna karoge . . . ab janta tak le jao'* (How long will you be
on dharna, it's time to take it to the people). Singh responded,
'Jaisa aap kahe' (As you wish).

The next morning, on 14 December 2005, Atal Bihari
Vajpayee flagged off the 'Nyay Yatra' or March for Justice
under the leadership of Rajnath Singh to highlight the
'criminalization of politics' under the Samajwadi Party's
rule.[24] The veteran leader had not been keeping well for the
past few days, and although Singh was happy that his idol
had travelled all the way, he noticed that Vajpayee looked
somewhat under the weather as he took to the podium to
address the crowds. The yatra was scheduled to pass through
different parts of Uttar Pradesh and end with a massive rally
in Lucknow on 22 December.

It was in the course of his speech that the veteran leader proclaimed, 'Rajnath *aage aage, hum peeche!*', which was met with approval from the gathering. Singh found the statement out of context and without making much of it attributed it to the senior leader's fondness for him. As the yatra made its way through eastern UP, Singh began to hear murmurs about his name being in the fray for the post of the BJP's national president. He did not think much about it then as older leaders like Advani and Vajpayee were very much around and for someone like Rajnath Singh to believe that he could even be a contender for the party's top post was beyond the realm of his imagination.

The yatra came to an abrupt end just days before it could reach Lucknow. The party's two-day national executive meeting scheduled to take place in Mumbai during 26–27 December and the three-day-long silver jubilee national convention that was to follow overshadowed the yatra and Singh was summoned to New Delhi. Moments after Rajnath Singh and Savitri landed in the capital, he got a call from Jaswant Singh congratulating him and informing him that he would be the party's next national president.

At Mumbai's Shivaji Park, during BJP's silver jubilee celebrations, two of the tallest leaders in the party handed over the reins. Two days before Advani was expected to resign as the BJP president, Atal Bihari Vajpayee announced his retirement from active politics. Vajpayee's surprise announcement was accompanied by a cryptic message where he announced the duo of Advani and Pramod Mahajan as the 'Ram' and 'Lakshman' of the party.[25] What set the party aflutter was not as much as his decision to retire but his conspicuous refusal to acknowledge the man who was all set to replace Advani as the new party president. Perhaps Vajpayee was hinting at the fissure in the party or maybe it could just be that he did not want undue spotlight to fall on the issue. In any case, there was no opposition to the next president and on 31 December 2005, Rajnath Singh was elected the BJP national president.

Although there was just a two-year age gap between Singh and Naidu, the former was seen as more contemporary. Also, as the first Bharatiya Janata Yuva Morcha president to head the BJP, besides being actively involved with both the RSS and the ABVP, Singh had the widest support base amongst the recent BJP chiefs. His appointment also sent out the first signal that the party was indeed ready for a metamorphosis and if there was anyone who was aware of the need that the party needed an overhaul, it was Singh.

Singh's elevation as the BJP's chief brought in its wake Herculean responsibilities and impossible expectations. Realist that he is, Rajnath Singh assessed that his primary objective lay in reclaiming the space the BJP had lost both in terms of the narrative of Indian politics as well as with the electorate. He had the challenge of treading a fine line between the tradition of the party that would make him reiterate the familiar and the need to come up with new ideas to set the foundation for the future. Singh's personal style of seeking a common ground with rivals and the steadfast belief in principles that did not change with changing circumstances made him the ideal person to usher in the new phase of the BJP. He was known to rarely push a decision down anyone's throat. At a time when all was not well with the party, Singh's approach of arriving at a resolution through consultation allowed fresh ideas and new thoughts to flow.

The beginning of Singh's tenure also highlighted the role of the younger Turks—Arun Jaitley, Sushma Swaraj and Pramod Mahajan—in the greater scheme of things. Singh had begun to look at Mahajan in the same light that Vajpayee had defined him, and as the *jagat* or everyone's 'Lakshman', Mahajan was poised to play a significant part in taking the party to new heights. For many in the BJP it was Mahajan's acumen as a tireless strategist that made him a fast-rising leader of his generation, but, for Singh, Mahajan offered the right mix of a traditionalist and a modernizer. Unlike most politicians, he did not shy away from owning up to failures and took the blame for the way the 'India Shining' campaign, which was his idea, had backfired.[26]

If Rajnath Singh was the next generation's Vajpayee, albeit without the latter's verbal lyricism, Mahajan, with his legendary organizational skills mixed with charismatic oratory, was a hybrid of Vajpayee and Advani. As a true party man and team player, Mahajan had underplayed his so-called coronation by Vajpayee during the BJP's December 2005 national convention in Mumbai and enjoyed a great working relationship with Rajnath Singh. Already there were indications of the BJP cadre getting back into the groove for the civic polls in Uttar Pradesh followed by assembly elections in Goa, Himachal Pradesh, Punjab, Uttaranchal and Singh's own home state, Uttar Pradesh. For the press and political commentators, this was being seen as Singh's acid test following his elevation to the post of BJP's national president. Singh, however, could not be bothered with the intricacies and focused on recovering lost ground. He held fast to the belief that the 2004 verdict was more of a defeat of the BJP than a decisive victory of Congress.[27]

As the UPA inched towards the middle of its term, Singh undertook the mission of connecting with the electorate and bringing to the attention of the voter the state of the nation. There was a sense that certain policies of the Central government had led to the creation of political, economic and social problems that posed a threat to national security and sovereignty. In July 2005 there had been two terror incidents—an attack on Ram Janmabhoomi in Ayodhya and the Jaunpur train bombing—

and later in October and December, three powerful blasts in New Delhi and a shootout at the Indian Institute of Science in Bangalore. Following a series of bombings in the city of Varanasi on 7 March 2006 where the crowded Sankat Mochan Hanuman Temple and the Varanasi Cantonment Railway Station were targeted by a little-known Islamic terror outfit Lashkar-e-Qahab, Singh planned the Bharat Suraksha Yatra to create an awareness among the people of the country about the threat to its internal security.[28] With Singh starting from Puri, Odisha, and Advani from Rajkot in Gujarat, the two decided to cover nearly 12,000 km between themselves across ten states including Uttar Pradesh, Rajasthan, Punjab and Haryana to highlight the 'appeasement' of Muslims by the Congress-led United Progressive Alliance government at the Centre.

While the perpetrators of the Jaunpur bombings were unknown, and the Lashkar-e-Qahab had owned up to the bombings in Varanasi, the other attacks could be directly linked to the Lashkar-e-Taiba. The security agencies had arrested persons with links to Bangladesh and, in a scathing judgment, the Supreme Court repealed the Illegal Migrants (Determination by Tribunals) (IMDT) Act in Assam where large-scale infiltration by Bangladeshi nationals had also been reported. A July 2005 WikiLeaks cable release seemed to suggest that the Congress government used the Act as a 'clever sham to build a voting block' and 'pay lip service to expulsions for electoral gain while allowing illegal immigration to continue unabated'.[29] Rajnath Singh charged the UPA government with being soft towards terrorists and asked if this was just for the sake of vote-bank politics. What prompted many people to question the UPA government were developments such as the commissioning of the Sachar Committee shortly after assuming office in 2004 to highlight the issues faced by the Muslim community and their representation in Indian society.

As a party considered right-wing and pro-Hindutva, the BJP remains the only Indian political party to put its weight behind implementing the Uniform Civil Code that would replace personal laws based on the scriptures and customs of each major religious community in India with a common set of rules governing every citizen. For the BJP, political overtures such as the formation of the Sachar Committee, reservations based on religion coupled with the delay in dealing with terrorists amounted to minority appeasement and also posed a threat to internal security and the social fabric of the country.

The Bharat Suraksha Yatra was successful in creating public awareness and, in under twenty days, Rajnath Singh traversed 3738 kilometres across eight states and held seventy-two public rallies and over 130 meetings while the old pro of yatras, L.K. Advani, managed to cover nearly 4700 km across six states with 170 big and small meetings.[30]

The yatra hit an unexpected bump on 22 April 2006, when Pramod Mahajan was shot four times with a .32 Browning pistol by his estranged younger brother, Pravin, inside the former's apartment in Mumbai. The news sent shockwaves through the BJP and senior functionaries rushed to Mumbai's Hinduja Hospital. The first shot fired by Pravin had missed but the remaining three were lodged in Pramod Mahajan's liver and pancreas. Despite flying in doctors such as Mohamed Rela, one of the world's foremost liver transplant specialists, who also headed King's College Hospital, London, Mahajan succumbed to his injuries and died following a cardiac arrest thirteen days later, on 3 May 2006.[31] Following Mahajan's death, the BJP formally cancelled the last leg of the Bharat Suraksha Yatra.

The death of Pramod Mahajan left a great void in the BJP and there was a general feeling that it would probably take three people to do what Mahajan could do single-handedly. For a man considered to be an integral part of nearly all major future plans to be taken out in such a way, was nothing short of a crippling blow for a party seeking to rejuvenate itself. After Mahajan, the only other leaders amongst the so-called GenNext of the BJP who possessed the right blend of mass appeal and organizational skills were Rajnath Singh and Narendra Modi.[32] Mahajan's importance to the party lay in the manner in which he could imbibe the RSS's teachings and still be in touch with the times. After Mahajan's death, both Modi and Singh understood the importance of blending the best of both worlds and took on the challenge of filling up the void left behind by one of their trusted colleagues.

In December 2006, at the BJP's national convention in Lucknow, Rajnath Singh was officially appointed the president in the presence of his long-time idol Atal Bihari Vajpayee, who openly expressed his wholehearted support for Singh. For most of the party cadre present, Singh's elevation was not a fortuitous accident but something that was inevitable. Singh was expected to restore the glory and energize the party, and the faith the old guard—including Atal Bihari Vajpayee, L.K. Advani, Jaswant Singh and Murli Manohar Joshi—reposed in him was as visible as the hope of brighter days within the cadre. Singh's hard-boiled realism was far from the rootless idealism often attributed to the BJP by detractors.[33] He was known for his ability to take along a wide cross section and, in the period that he had been the interim president, he brought back the culture of internal democracy. In his presidential address, Singh highlighted how his appointment proved beyond doubt that in the BJP, even the most ordinary worker could be called upon to take up the highest responsibility. The BJP's confidence in Singh got a boost with the party winning eight out of the twelve municipal corporation seats in the civic elections held in November 2006 in Uttar Pradesh and Singh hoped that they would perform as well in the upcoming state elections. Even though Advani was

officially the leader of the Opposition in the Lok Sabha, Singh
as the president assumed the responsibility of leading the party
in the road ahead.

In the course of his speech he also spoke at length about
the failures of the Manmohan Singh government and expressed
the party's view on a host of subjects ranging from internal
security and the delay in the efforts to modernize the army to
farmer suicides, the government's non-implementation of the
recommendations of the National Commission for Farmers—a
body that had been constituted by Singh when he was the
agriculture minister—and the UPA's debacle on the economic
front. Singh took the fight to the next level, questioning the
Congress's intentions that appeared to have created a divide
between Muslims and the rest of India by keeping the former
apart from the national mainstream.[34]

A few days before the BJP's national convention, while
addressing the National Development Council, Prime
Minister Manmohan Singh had made a statement that seemed
to suggest Muslims should have the first claim on resources.[35]
Coming in the wake of the Justice Sachar Committee report
that had numerous statistics to prove that Muslims were
extremely backward with regard to all social indicators, this
statement by the prime minister hinted at the manner in which
the Congress and the UPA appeared to be making a case for a
different kind of social reform. Singh reminded the Congress
and the government that the state's primary objective ought
to be to ensure equality and that the basic structure of the
Constitution did not permit religion-based reservation.[36]
Singh asked the question which was on the minds of millions
of Indians: if the Muslims were in the situation they were in
even after fifty-nine years of independence, weren't those who
had governed this country for fifty-three out of those fifty-nine
years responsible?

With terror strikes in the country's national capital, Delhi, the financial capital, Mumbai, and cultural centres like Varanasi, and the Israeli government issuing a rare terrorism alert by Al Qaeda on tourists during the new year in Goa, Singh questioned if the UPA had a policy to secure Indians from the looming shadow of terror.[37]

Within a few months of Singh's official appointment, the BJP won state assembly elections in Himachal Pradesh, Punjab and Uttarakhand (as Uttaranchal was named by then) in February 2007. The results boosted the party's morale and acted as the shot in the arm it desperately needed to prepare for bigger challenges that were to come before the year ended. As the BJP president, Singh proposed that in the states where the party was in power, it should provide loans to farmers at 1 per cent interest. Singh also extended the party's support for the statehood of Telangana and reiterated the BJP's stance right from the Jana Sangh days when it supported the concept of smaller states.[38]

The assembly elections in Uttar Pradesh was being seen as a litmus test for Rajnath Singh. With the electoral success in the three states behind him, he put in place a new organization team. He struck a near-perfect balance between the old and the new and also worked to get some prominence at the grass roots. He got in Rajiv Pratap Rudy as the spokesperson in place of Jaitley, who was made the secretary of the Central Parliamentary Board (CPB), made Ravi Shankar Prasad the head of the media cell and also included first-time MPs Dharmendra Pradhan from Odisha and Kiren Rijiju from Arunachal Pradesh. The Central Election Committee (CEC), which had the veto on the distribution of tickets, also saw changes with Ananth Kumar being made secretary. Before his death, Pramod Mahajan had held the posts of secretary of the CPB and of the CEC, but Singh divided the duties. The seventy-year-old Yashwant Sinha was made a vice-president and Balbir Punj became a secretary.

The one development that raised eyebrows among both party members as well as the media was the dropping of Gujarat chief minister Narendra Modi from both the CEC and the CPB. There were murmurs that Modi's run-ins with the RSS in his state was the reason behind his removal, but the move actually freed him from party organizational duties to concentrate on assembly elections and fight anti-incumbency. Although Uttar Pradesh was the biggest state-level elections in India, Gujarat too would go to the polls later in the year, in December, and much like winning UP, retaining Gujarat was also paramount to the BJP. In some way, Singh's statesmanship unencumbered Modi to seek the electorate's mandate and return with an impressive victory.

The victories in Punjab and Uttarakhand were seen as the beginning of the upswing for the BJP and winning the largest state elections in the country, Uttar Pradesh, would put the party's resurgence beyond doubt. It was Rajnath Singh's home state and was important from a prestige point of view; it was imperative for him to better the previous outing that saw the party lose the 2002 elections under him. Despite not being the kind of politician who put too much weight on personal image, he knew that winning handsomely in the state had its own benefits as Uttar Pradesh played a great role in determining a party's fortunes at the Centre. In 1991, when the BJP became the main Opposition party it had 119 seats across India with fifty-four of them from UP. When it formed the government in Delhi for the first time, it had 182 seats nationwide and sixty of them were UP's contribution. Moreover, the presidential elections were also due in 2007, and UP had the largest number of votes.

All through the campaign in the state, Singh pitched for Kalyan Singh, who was back in the BJP, and in keeping with his approach of 'never letting the past influence the future',

Rajnath Singh gave Kalyan Singh a free hand. Rajnath Singh proclaimed that Kalyan Singh had been the best chief minister of the state, better than not just Mulayam Singh or Mayawati, but someone who also outdid him.

The BJP made governance and development the core agendas and when Singh was asked in a television interview if Ram Mandir would be included in the party manifesto, he replied that it was a matter of faith and belief and the party did not want to make it a political issue.[39] The pundits were already beginning to see a victory in UP as the surest sign of the BJP returning. Yet, even after opinion polls gave it a slight edge over the others, the BJP lost in the state.

Despite the impressive victories in Punjab and Uttarakhand, the loss in UP was labelled as a personal drubbing for Rajnath Singh even though winning or losing UP was not dependent on a single factor. Singh had always taken victory and defeat with equanimity and his long journey from being an RSS shakha member to a student leader, an MLA, the chief minister of India's biggest state and to the head of the party was a testimony to his approach. Singh continued to build the party ground upwards and his unhurried presence at the Centre, at a time when electoral defeat could prompt any party to usher in drastic changes, was much needed. In his interaction with the press and also the regular party worker, Singh kept reaffirming that the BJP was the only national party that did not change its identity and also gave Indian politics an ideological concept. At the same time, Singh questioned the basic policy of the UPA towards the common citizen who was suffering from a massive price rise in basic commodities in the three years that the UPA had been in power. Singh wrote a twenty-one-page letter to Prime Minister Manmohan Singh asking for immediate action on price rise among other issues affecting the aam aadmi.[40]

What Rajnath Singh was doing was giving the BJP a space in contemporary Indian political narrative without losing its core. He articulated equality for one and all in the form of a Universal Civil Code and equal status for all Indian states by abolishing Article 370 that provided the state of Jammu and Kashmir with a special status. Even on Hindutva, he often told journalists that it needed to be defined as a geographical concept or a way of life and not seen through a religious prism.[41] At the same time, Singh was clear of not letting the mindset of how things were in the past mar the chances of the future. In this aspect, Modi's term as the longest-serving chief minister of Gujarat and the achievements of his government were an affirmation of the path that Singh had envisioned for the BJP.

Singh formed a committee led by Sushma Swaraj that also included Najma Heptullah, Kiren Rijiju and Sumitra Mahajan— the last named would go on to become the Speaker of the sixteenth Lok Sabha—to propose changes within the BJP's constitution to ensure that the party had 33 per cent representation for women at an organizational level.[42] Most political parties had opposed the Women's Reservation Bill that proposed to reserve 33 per cent of all seats in the Lok Sabha and in all state legislative assemblies for women. Leaders like Mulayam Singh Yadav and Lalu Prasad Yadav were of the opinion that such a reservation along with the already existing 22.5 per cent for Scheduled Castes and Tribes would lead to nearly 55 per cent of the seats in Parliament being reserved and would amount to overlooking the case of Dalits, backward classes and Muslims and other religious minorities.[43]

No change of mindset is ever easy. In the case of the BJP, where organizational structure is one of its core identities, cultural cognition, a theory that suggests individuals shape opinions to conform to the views of the groups with which they strongly identify, came into play more than anything else. In the run-up to the 2009 general elections it was clear that the BJP was in the middle of shifting from a 'leader-driven' to a 'leadership-enabled' mindset. This shift threw up challenges where Singh's role as the national president of the BJP transcended formal hierarchies.

There was no question of the BJP putting up a challenger to L.K. Advani as its prime ministerial choice but the process of leadership somehow could not fructify in the shadow of the leader's persona. In response to a time of disruptive change in the BJP and the political discourse of the country, Advani, the leader, reverted to a more classicist approach where the people's desire for a 'strong' leader saw him providing answers replete with a compelling vision and an unambiguous implementation plan. As the leader of the Opposition in the Lok Sabha, Advani juxtaposed India to the British system of a shadow cabinet where members of the Opposition mirror the cabinet. However, instead of particular members questioning or challenging their counterpart in the cabinets by way of which the Opposition sought to present itself as an alternative government-in-waiting, Advani referred to himself as the 'PM-in-waiting', which, needless to say, sent a signal that all was still not well in the BJP.[44] The Opposition and the people on the outside began to question the party's structure. The press too began to read 'motives' in Advani's statements such as how, despite being the leader of the Opposition, he was more of a 'consultant' when it came to the party's organizational matters.[45] The manner in which Advani's stance on issues appeared to differ from the party's stand was too conspicuous to be ignored. Unsurprisingly, the question, 'Why does Advani periodically surface at the oddest of places to put his party in the oddest of situations?' came to the fore.[46]

With Vajpayee shifting to the elder statesman mode who offered advice when it was sought, Advani was the leader with

the highest stature in the BJP. As a result, some of his statements
such as on the Indo-US nuclear agreement—where he openly
deviated from the party stand to say 'there is no problem with
the 123 Agreement' if the Manmohan Singh government could
bring an amendment in the Atomic Energy Act to protect
India's strategic independence—revealed a schism within the
party. Some of Advani's actions such as statements on the 123
Agreement, asking Lok Sabha members such as V.K. Malhotra,
who represented Delhi and was also the BJP's deputy leader in the
lower house, to resign in December 2008 in order to concentrate
more on state-level work undermined the authority of the party
president.[47, 48] It also made clear that he was not keen to limit
himself to just being a hands-off patriarch. Most of Advani's
statements and actions were attributed to the stalwart's ultimate
ambition that remained unfulfilled—the prime ministership.

The party was yet to formally announce its prime ministerial
candidate but Advani's eagerness was evident in a television
interview in which he mused that while he had always backed
Vajpayee for the prime ministership, 'there is no question
of anyone returning any favour of this kind'.[49] The hint of
dissonance persisted for months and undermined Singh's
presidency in a manner that it became necessary to take a call.
The shadow of the party leadership question loomed over the
thumping victory that Modi and the BJP got in the December
2007 Gujarat assembly elections, the wins in Madhya Pradesh
and Chhattisgarh and the triumph in Karnataka in May 2008,
the first time that the BJP had formed a government in south
India. The issue of leadership and the manner in which the
party appeared to be pulled in two opposing directions came to
a head in July 2008 when the UPA faced a vote of confidence
on the floor of the Lok Sabha.

The Left Front led by the CPI (M) withdrew support to
the UPA over India approaching the International Atomic

Energy Agency (IAEA) for the Indo-US nuclear deal. Under the agreement, India had consented to separate its civil and military nuclear facilities and had agreed to an inspection of its nuclear programme by the United Nations in exchange for the United States of America supplying nuclear technology. With the Left Front walking out of the government, the Samajwadi Party stepped in with its thirty-seven MPs to support the government.

During the vote, which the UPA ultimately won with 275 votes against the Opposition's 256, with eleven members abstaining, three BJP MPs—Ashok Argal, Faggan Singh Kulaste and Mahaveer Bhagora—waved bundles of cash, alleging that they were given money by the UPA floor managers to secure their support during the trust motion. The BJP demanded the resignation of Prime Minister Manmohan Singh over the allegations and claimed that they had video evidence of the deals being made. The party also criticized CNN-IBN, a television news channel which had collaborated with the BJP MPs to record the sting operation, for opting to not broadcast it. The channel said that it did not telecast the story as they felt it was incomplete.[50]

The Manmohan Singh government surviving the confidence vote became a big scandal, and it would be years before multiple investigations came out with their findings. By 2011, the allegations of the then Samajwadi Party member Amar Singh offering a bribe to the three BJP MPs would lead to the arrest of Sudheendra Kulkarni, an aide of L.K. Advani during the time of the confidence vote. According to media reports, the Delhi Police alleged that Kulkarni had approached Amar Singh to offer the bribe to the BJP MPs and then got a television channel, CNN-IBN, to secretly film the episode to nail the government.[51] In March 2011, a cable released by WikiLeaks claimed that Nachiketa Kapur, an aide of Congress

Rajya Sabha MP Captain Satish Sharma, was working on the
Opposition's allies such as the Shiromani Akali Dal and the
Shiv Sena through financier Sant Singh Chatwal to abstain
from voting and also reported that Ajit Singh's RLD had been
paid INR 10 crore (about US $2.5 million) for each of their
four MPs to support the government.[52]

The manner in which the confidence vote and, subsequently,
the cash-for-vote scandal played out defined the immediate
path ahead for both Congress and the BJP. For the BJP, it was
the sign to get into election mode. The sly attacks on the party
leadership were pushed to the background and Rajnath Singh's
clarion call got all hands on deck. Beginning around September
2008, things began to take shape for the Lok Sabha elections
with Singh and Advani starting Vijay Sankalp (determination
of victory) rallies across the country.

For nearly a year before the rallies that took the party to
the voter, Rajnath Singh had been criss-crossing the country,
addressing workers at the grass roots. This was around the
same period that Advani had begun interacting with the media
and projecting the leadership role he was slated to play. The
rallies also saw Narendra Modi make appearances and tell the
electorate about the failures of the UPA government, especially
when it came to the security of the country.[53] The 26/11 attacks
in Mumbai and the security failure only reinforced the BJP's
claim, but before the party could take any advantage, its internal
dissensions messed things up.

Advani's PM-in-waiting attitude, members such as
Arun Shourie and Arun Jaitley endorsing Narendra Modi as
the future PM, and Jaitley reportedly sparring with Rajnath
Singh over the appointment of Sudhanshu Mittal as one
of the co-conveners of the north-eastern states showed the
party in a bad light.[54] Developments such as former UP chief
minister Kalyan Singh, who had returned to the BJP in 2004

after being expelled, deciding to leave the party again also did not help.[55]

Under Rajnath Singh, the BJP tried to present itself as a party with a difference. Its manifesto showed its resolve to rise above contentious issues. It decided to focus on three goals: good governance, development and security. The terror attacks witnessed in late 2008, primarily the Malegaon Blasts in September and the Mumbai attacks in November, had made the threat to life a burning issue of the day. The usage of the term 'saffron terror', which was first heard in the early 2000s, too, became prominent, especially on the part of members of the Congress party. Despite international agencies such as the United States Department of the Treasury issuing statements and executive orders about certain operatives connected with terror outfits like Lashkar-e-Taiba and Al Qaeda providing direct support as well as facilitating terrorist attacks such as the attack on the Indian Parliament in December 2001, the commuter train blast in Mumbai in July 2006, the Samjhauta Express bombing in Panipat in February 2007 and the attacks in Mumbai in November 2008, Indian investigators continued to pin the blame for the Samjhauta blasts on local outfits such as Abhinav Bharat.[56] Some local Hindus that were arrested for their suspected involvement in the October 2007 Ajmer Sharif blast were also suspected to be behind the May 2007 Mecca mosque blast in Hyderabad. However, on 6 August 2010, the US State Department publically notified that the Harkat-ul-Jihad-al-Islami (HUJI) of Pakistan was responsible for the Mecca mosque attack.[57] According to the same notification, HUJI was also responsible for the March 2006 suicide bombing of the US Consulate in Karachi, Pakistan, which killed four people and injured 48 others and also the March 2007 Varanasi attack, which killed 25 and injured 100.[58] The issue was lent further credence when a major part of print and electronic

media disregarded information that was in the public domain
to question the existence of 'saffron terror' in the manner it was
pitched. Some analysts also pointed out that by politicizing,
and communalizing the investigation into incidents such as the
Malegaon blasts, the government of the day was vitiating the
relationship between Hindus and Muslims.[59]

At a public rally held in Panipat in November 2008, Singh
urged the nation to be careful of a situation where the incumbent
government continued to coin phrases like 'Hindu terrorism'
and 'Muslim terrorism' while actual acts of terrorism were not
contained, it could take the country towards a civil-war-like
scenario.[60] If elected, the BJP planned to revive, within the first
hundred days, the anti-terror mechanism that the Congress
had dismantled; strengthen the operational role of the National
Investigating Agency; launch a massive programme to detect,
detain and deport illegal immigrants; completely revamp the
internal and external intelligence agencies, including the setting
up of a digital security agency to deal with cyber warfare,
cyber counter-terrorism and cyber security of national digital
assets; facilitate better interstate coordination and real-time
intelligence sharing apart from helping states to raise anti-
insurgency forces to face the threat posed by Maoists; expedite
the long-pending acquisition of military hardware through
absolutely transparent means in a time-bound manner; and
also resolve all pending issues of pay and privileges of the
defence forces, including the One Rank One Pension (OROP)
scheme.[61] The manifesto also laid out a detailed road map to
revive the economy, implement the Goods and Services Tax
(GST). However, more than anything else what made media
headlines was the way Advani addressed issues like Ram
Mandir, Article 370, and the Uniform Civil Code, which was
reminiscent of the Vajpayee era. At the onset of the Ayodhya
Movement, Vajpayee had expressed his reservations about

the BJP's direct involvement with the cause but accepted the majority decision of the party and, nearly three decades later, Advani was ready to walk the same line.[62]

Despite the BJP losing momentum on the economy and the terrorism front as the elections approached, there was hardly anyone who did not believe the campaign had been mounted on right ideas that were universally acknowledged. The factors that contributed to the possible change in the minds of the voter included the manner in which the party persisted with Varun Gandhi, the son of late Congress leader Sanjay Gandhi and Maneka Gandhi, even after an inflammatory speech against Muslims. The BJP candidate from Pilibhit, Varun Gandhi, allegedly threatened to cut off the hands of those who harm Hindus and crudely compared a rival Muslim candidate to Osama Bin Laden.[63] In an era when the battle of perception made a huge difference, the Congress dropped Jagdish Tytler and Sajjan Kumar, two accused in the 1984 anti-Sikh pogrom in Delhi after a Sikh protestor flung a shoe at home minister P. Chidambaram to protest against the accused going unpunished. The BJP's refusal to discard Varun Gandhi, who eventually went on to win the Lok Sabha seat, probably sent the wrong message.[64]

Advani's scathing indictment of Manmohan Singh being the 'weakest PM ever' backfired when the Congress brought up the issue of him claiming that, as the home minister in 1999, he was unaware of his government's decision to swap terrorists for hostages of the Indian Airlines plane that was hijacked on 24 December 1999.[65] Between 2004 and 2009, Manmohan Singh had transformed, albeit momentarily, from the 'accidental prime minister' to an authoritative figure with the success of the Indo-US Nuclear Deal. As a result, UPA had little difficulty in getting home. Manmohan Singh became the first prime minister since Jawaharlal Nehru in 1962 to be re-elected after completing a full five-year term and the UPA formed the government once again.

Most post-poll analysis pointed out Advani's apparent eagerness to become the prime minister as the major reason for spoiling the BJP's chances. At eighty-two, Advani also failed to connect with a populace where 60 per cent were below the age of thirty.[66] The manner in which Advani targeted Prime Minister Manmohan Singh rather than Congress party president Sonia Gandhi, who also headed the National Advisory Council (NAC), a non-constitutional body formed in 2004 that came to be seen as an alternative cabinet, also did not work with the electorate. A mix of activists, bureaucrats, economists and politicians, the NAC was responsible for the drafting of several key bills passed by the UPA government and was criticized for being a body with no constitutional legitimacy created solely to allow Sonia Gandhi to have a direct say in government policy.[67] The average Indian youth, irrespective of religion, caste and background, seeks a better life and the BJP's messaging that front failed to go beyond its manifesto.

Internally too, the BJP had begun to raise questions. In a letter written to the leadership, veteran leader Jaswant Singh asked why those responsible for election strategizing were being rewarded with plum posts while mentioning that the party was making the same mistakes it had in 2004.[68] The letter was widely circulated as some media outlets managed to access a copy. Some strategists like Sudheendra Kulkarni had already written articles in a magazine blaming the second generation for the party's debacle, which was criticized by party members like Arun Shourie, who charged him with exceeding his brief. Kulkarni had been dismissed from the party but made a comeback during the general elections and become one of its main spokespersons besides being the key strategist for Advani.[69] At a meeting of senior leaders held at Advani's residence, Jaswant Singh also questioned Arun Jaitley for writing a column in a newspaper outlining the reasons for the party's defeat in the elections.[70] In his article, Jaitley noted that the BJP failed to read the voter's desire for stability free of roadblocks and obstructions.[71] The manner in which the Left Front had freed the UPA by walking out made the voter reaffirm their mandate in Manmohan Singh's favour. In the same piece, Jaitley wrote that with the change in the profile of the Indian voter, both the Indian politician and the political parties also needed to change.

Two months after UPA-II took oath, the ghost of Muhammad Ali Jinnah came back to haunt the BJP. In his book on the founder of Pakistan, *Jinnah: India, Partition, Independence*, Jaswant Singh took a divergent stand from most and blamed the partition of the country as well as the creation of Pakistan on the Congress and Nehru rather than Jinnah. Calling the Quaid-i-Azam of Pakistan a great man, Jaswant Singh felt that not only had India misunderstood Jinnah but also demonized him as we [India] needed to create a demon.[72] After Advani's 2005 comments, this was the second instance when a senior BJP leader had showered lavish praise on the person who played a leading role in pushing the demand for a separate state for Muslims. The BJP expelled Singh and a few days later the ousted leader spoke at length about Advani being 'at the centre' of the cash-for-votes scam in the Lok Sabha in July 2008. He remarked that Advani was consumed by his ambition to be the prime minister, and that desire made him commit so many mistakes.[73]

Whether directly or indirectly, nearly every disgruntled senior party member pinned the 2009 loss on Rajnath Singh. Arun Shourie dared Singh to sack him for indiscipline after calling Singh 'Alice in Blunderland', while Jaswant Singh called him a provincial leader who should never have been pushed up.[74] Unlike the old guard that rarely contested Lok Sabha elections, Rajnath Singh won his parliamentary seat from Ghaziabad that was not only an unlikely choice for him but also far from being a safe seat. Typically for him, he wasn't bothered about his own image but was more interested in seeking answers to the basic question of what the BJP needed to do in order to learn from 2009 that went beyond basic psephology and opinion pieces.

With time enough evidence emerged to substantiate that elements beyond Rajnath Singh were responsible for the defeat, but Singh took the responsibility. For him the debacle was a sign that it was time to hand over the mantle. At the BJP's national executive held in Delhi in June 2009, Singh asked the party to introspect. He also highlighted that the difference between the BJP, the second largest party, and the next largest parties was more than twenty seats. For him, this was a sign that the voter was looking for a two-party system. In the years to come, if the BJP took effective steps to win the people's mandate, the party could form the next government. In his final address, Singh also reminded the cadre that a rejection of the BJP was not a rejection of the ideology of Hindutva by the people of India. Hindutva for the BJP was not an election issue but a geocultural concept that would not be discarded because the party had faced a second consecutive loss. Mentioning the 1995 Supreme Court judgment that ruled that Hindutva was a way of life, Singh told everyone present that if anyone asked the BJP about Hindutva, the answer was clear: it was and would always be the national essence of India.[75]

In December 2009, the future appeared unclear as Rajnath Singh gave up the post of the BJP's national president. After the loss of the 2002 UP state elections, this was Singh's biggest defeat and everything about him was being questioned. If at that time someone had told Singh what lay in store for him in the next Lok Sabha elections, he would never have believed it.

10

Take It to the Voter

The years between 2010 and 2013 will perhaps go down in history as one of the most significant periods in the contemporary socio-political history of India. Following the 2008 US presidential elections, where nearly 75 per cent of the adult voter population, which translated to 55 per cent of the entire adult population of the United States of America, went online to either take part in or get news and information, the Internet emerged as a significant tool for the politician to connect with the electorate and the manner in which the voter responded.[1] This was a phenomenon waiting to be replicated in India. While 2009 did not see the Internet play a major role, the combination of a burgeoning young voter base and the advent of social and news media was rewriting the rules of the game. Social media platforms like Facebook and Twitter were not only bringing the world closer, they were giving the average Indian a peek into what was happening in the world by relaying global events such as the Arab Spring or the devastating earthquake in Haiti in real time.

There was a tectonic shift inside the mind of the politically active Internet user. Although, with 2.5 million Facebook users in June 2009, social media was not the 'battleground' for the 2009 Lok Sabha elections, the rate at which it was growing—17 million by December 2010 and 28 million by June 2011—was a portent of things to come.[2] Beginning in 2009–10, the situation in India mirrored the United States where the politically aware Internet user, especially the younger voter, switched away from news sites as they barely offered anything that matched their political views and headed towards social media.

What makes social media potentially capable of making a big difference in an election is the demography of its user base. In October 2010, nearly 53 per cent of Facebook users were in the 18–25 age group which, in a country where the median age in the same period was 25.1 years, meant this was a big constituency waiting to be addressed.[3]

After taking over as the BJP's national president, Nitin Gadkari continued with the agenda of keeping the party's focus on development, socio-economic reform and nationalism. Gadkari always regarded politics as an instrument of socio-economic reform and, for him, good governance was an essential prerequisite. The BJP constituted a good governance cell under Manohar Parikkar to study all government schemes and address the issue of development across not just the nine states in which the BJP was in power but also states such as West Bengal, where the Left had been in power for nearly three decades, as well as states like Tamil Nadu.[4] In order to prepare the cadre to be able to deliver better, Gadkari understood the significance of laying a foundation on which it could be brought up to speed with the changing world and started a training programme to train 10,000 party workers annually. Unlike the Congress or most other political parties in India, the BJP fostered the growth of strong regional leaders from states who would go on to play an all-important role at the Centre. The emergence of Shivraj Singh Chouhan, Vasundhara Raje Scindia, Raman Singh and Narendra Modi as voices that mattered in the way national politics would play out was not accidental, nor did it happen overnight. The state leaders ensured that the pulse of the common people across states in India was conveyed to the National Executive Committee, thus playing a vital role in framing the policy for the road ahead.

Growing concerns around rampant corruption as well as a threat to both internal and external security reached a point where pundits who had questioned 'India Shining' now began to notice a mood of 'India whining'. A 2012 Pew Research Center study indicated deepening economic doubts amongst Indians with only 38 per cent of the respondents satisfied with the direction in which the country seemed to be headed. More than the number, it was the trend that it indicated that conveyed the troubling state of affairs. Only a year earlier, in 2011, 51 per cent Indians were satisfied with the state of the economy and the course of the nation. This decline was the largest in countries that were surveyed, which included Brazil, China, the United States and the European Union that included Britain, France, Germany, Spain and Poland.[5] Internal security too appeared to be in disarray. In just 2010, there were over 150 deaths in Naxal and Maoists attacks. In one of the biggest strikes since the launch of a large-scale offensive against the rebels, ultras killed over seventy soldiers in Dantewada in April 2010. Radical terror continued to target innocent lives in civilian areas such as Pune's German Bakery in February 2010 where seventeen lives were lost and nearly sixty injured. The attack was considered to be a part of the 'The Karachi Project', a new wave of proxy wars targeting urban centres in India. David Coleman Headley, a Pakistani–American, who played a key role in the 2008 Mumbai terrorist attacks, revealed that the project had allegedly mobilized militant and criminal syndicates—Pakistani and fugitive Indian nationals—to deploy disaffected Indian youth to carry out terror attacks in India using locally available explosive material so that the attacks could not be traced back to Pakistan.[6] Indians seemed to be under a threat not just within the nation but also internationally. In March 2010, the global menace of Somali pirates struck India, as they hijacked eight Indian vessels and abducted 120 sailors off the coast of Kismayo, Somalia.[7]

If on one hand, the Congress and the UPA seemed to be at sea about governance, on the other, the BJP under Gadkari was trying to find its place in the new India where it could actually manifest itself as the national party best suited to address growing concerns over not only the economy and security but also the basic dignity of the common man.

As someone whose success was as much a result of his own efforts and perseverance as it was a product of the BJP's organization structure, Rajnath Singh went back to the basics in order to get a better understanding of the situation on the ground. Through 2010 and 2011, Singh connected both with the cadre at the grass roots as well as the people across states and cities. As one of the senior leaders in the party, Singh was expected to set the tone for the cadre to follow in a period when the party was in Opposition. Singh addressed the issues of the people both with state governments as well as the central dispensation. In Pratapgarh, Uttar Pradesh, Singh attacked Chief Minister Mayawati for putting the blame of the deaths of sixty-three devotees, including women and children in a stampede, on Kripalu Maharaj, the head of an ashram, and questioned her for not visiting the site of the accident. Mayawati had held the organizers responsible for the deaths and issued a statement that the state government would provide financial assistance to the kin of the victims only if the Centre failed to respond.[8] It was clear to Rajnath Singh that the Centre's inability to curb spiralling prices of basic commodities was a major reason why massive crowds often gathered at ashrams and other charitable events for the 'bhandara' (community kitchen) and gifts.

The UPA government had announced major social programmes such as the National Rural Employment Guarantee Act 2005 (NREGA), which was later renamed the Mahatma Gandhi National Rural Employment Guarantee Act (MGNREGA), with a lot of fanfare. It aimed to enhance livelihood security in rural areas by providing at least 100 days of wage employment in a financial year to every household whose adult members volunteer to do unskilled manual work. The Act was celebrated as a 'people's Act' as it focused on labourers' rights to employment, minimum wages and timely payments; and the manner in which several people's groups were involved in its drafting and the transparency provisions only enhanced its reputation. The UPA also believed that the Act had played a great role in its re-election in 2009 but by 2010 there were numerous instances of serious delays, of up to six months, in the payment of NREGA wages. Additionally, there were cases of massive pilferage of money, thanks to middlemen and the failure of vigilance at any of the stipulated eleven stages of implementation.[9] In most cases, there was enough evidence of the significant influence of the sarpanches in deciding work allocation to the extent of their rationing in favour of the village where the sarpanches resided. The non-timely payment of wages resulted in people being forced to take up jobs with lower wages or even exploitative employment and also distress migration leading to a diminished interest of labourers in employment under the Act.[10] A member of the Central Employment Guarantee Council (CEGC) claimed a massive scam amounting to over Rs 10,000 crore in Uttar Pradesh that included payment of wages against fake job card holders and fake construction work; creating fictitious purchase invoices; payment to ghost firms against the procurement of various items including hybrid seeds, calendars and publicity material; purchase of instruments used by labourers for construction works and purchase of photocopy machines and computers.[11]

One of the means to overcome delay and pilferage lay in using technology as in the case of the state of Andhra Pradesh that adopted a computerized method of payment using biometrics. Fears regarding the theft of funds in the NREGA at every level or improving access to state benefits were allayed to an extent with the launch of the national identity scheme, Aadhaar, in September 2010. The scheme was initially conceived in the aftermath of the 1999 Kargil war, when the Kargil War Committee headed by security analyst K. Subrahmanyam submitted its report to the then prime minister Atal Bihari Vajpayee in January 2000. The committee recommended that citizens in villages in border regions be issued identity cards. The national identity scheme underwent many transformations over the years. In 2001, the Government of India accepted a recommendation for a multipurpose national identity card after reports of some people obtaining multiple passports with different details came out. Besides providing the Indian citizen with a unique identification number, the project would also aim to provide various rights to persons of Indian origin. After much discussion, the Unique Identification Authority of India (UIDAI), a statutory authority, came into existence in January 2009. It provided a twelve-digit unique identity number for residents of India based on biometric and demographic data. At the launch of 'Aadhaar' (Foundation), the name given to the initiative, then prime minister Manmohan Singh noted that it would not only provide the poor with an identity to open bank accounts or get ration cards and avail benefits of government schemes but also help in national integration.[12] In November 2012, Manmohan Singh would launch an Aadhaar-linked direct benefit transfer scheme to eliminate leakages in the system by directly transferring the money to the bank account of the recipient.[13] Despite the potential that it displayed at the onset and the results it produced between 2014 and 2018, the revolutionary idea would continue to be at the centre of many right-to-privacy issues.[14]

Be it raising questions on inflation and security issues, Rajnath Singh continued his journey both as a parliamentarian and an important member of the main Opposition party. In many ways, fate was recasting Singh in the same mould as his long-time hero Atal Bihari Vajpayee. In October 2010, destiny bound them together when Singh became only the second person in the history of the United Nations to address the General Assembly in Hindi after Vajpayee. As an MP from India, Singh reminded the world body about the memories of the 2008 Mumbai terror attacks and urged the General Assembly to declare Pakistan and other states aiding international terrorism as rogue states.[15] Even in the midst of launching a full frontal attack on the UPA government, the BJP continued to contribute to the national cause by standing alongside the prime minister in issues that directly benefited the nation. The BJP supported the heavily debated Nuclear Liability Bill, offered suggestions to the government that were included in the contentious Bill and, in a rare instance of bonhomie, members of the two parties were seen patting each other for enabling the proposed legislation to come into effect.[16]

With each passing quarter, it was becoming clear that the Congress and the UPA would not be able to win the voter's trust for a third term. The level of corruption at the highest ranks manifested itself in the 2G and coal allocation scams. In the former, the UPA government was accused of undercharging mobile telephone companies for frequency allocation licences, which they used to create 2G spectrum subscriptions for cellphones. In the latter it was charged with allocating coal blocks in an inefficient manner between 2004 and 2009. High-profile individuals were allegedly involved in many of these scams. These included A. Raja, the Union minister for communication and information technology in the Manmohan Singh government, M.K. Kanimozhi of the DMK, and Suresh Kalmadi, the president of the Indian Olympic Committee, whose alleged involvement in corrupt practices in the 2010 Commonwealth Games held in New Delhi made India a laughing stock in international sporting circles.

Every morning newspaper headlines would splash new exposés. Every evening, prime-time news channels raised hell while questioning the government. But nothing hurt the government more than the manner in which the common Indian took to new media such as blogs, streaming audio and video, advertising on the Web, mobile apps and other online communities to not only highlight issues but also comment on it. Personal blogs, YouTube posts, Facebook feeds and Twitter timelines were replete with the average citizen expressing their anger towards the system. These comments, not limited to individuals, spread like wildfire with thousands watching, sharing the comments or forwarding them, making them more potent in the process. Social and new media were changing the rules of engagement between political leaders, journalists and the public. It was a matter of time before the disaffection shifted from the virtual online space to manifest itself in the real world. Nothing exemplified this better than the manner in which social activist Anna Hazare's movement took the nation by storm.

In April 2011, Hazare started an indefinite hunger strike in New Delhi to demand drafting of a bill with more stringent penal provisions, giving more independence to the Lokpal (ombudsman) by a committee that would feature both the government and a civil society representative.[17] The fast was a reaction to the rejection of his demand by Manmohan Singh and it caught the attention of not just the media but also thousands of supporters, some of whom also joined Hazare in his protest. Social activists from across the country who supported Hazare included Magsaysay Award winners Kiran Bedi, the former IPS officer known for her no-nonsense attitude and her jail reforms; Arvind Kejriwal, who is recognized for his involvement in the grass-roots movement Parivartan using the right to information legislation in a campaign against corruption; and Medha Patkar, the founder member of the thirty-two-year-long Narmada Bachao Andolan (NBA) movement that opposed the construction of dams across the Narmada. The movement was also supported by spiritual leaders Sri Sri Ravi Shankar, Swami Ramdev and Swami Agnivesh. Hazare's decision to not allow any politician to sit with him attracted the common citizen in droves and the mass movement spread to Bangalore, Mumbai, Chennai, Ahmedabad, Guwahati, Shillong, Aizawl and other Indian cities.[18]

On 9 April, the government constituted a Joint Drafting Committee that included five ministers—Pranab Mukherjee (finance minister), P. Chidambaram (home minister), Dr Veerappa Moily (law minister), Kapil Sibal (HRD minister and minister of communication and information technology) and Salman Khursheed (water resources and minority affairs minister)—and five nominees of Anna Hazare (including himself)—Justice N. Santosh Hegde, senior advocate Shanti Bhushan and his son and advocate Prashant Bhushan, and Arvind Kejriwal.[19] The drafting committee was tasked with preparing a draft Lokpal Bill by 30 June. However, both parties never agreed on the ambit of the Lokpal and differed on bringing the prime minister, higher judiciary and MPs under its purview. Not surprisingly, the government was not in favour of including the PM and higher judiciary while Hazare and his team demanded that they had to be.

Around 5 June, when yet another round of talks between Hazare and the ministers failed, the Delhi Police swooped down on Baba Ramdev, who along with his supporters were protesting against black money stashed in foreign tax havens.[20] A little after midnight, the police resorted to a lathi charge on Ramdev and his followers and fired tear gas shells at the gathering, resulting in serious injuries to some of them, including a fifty-one-year old woman, Rajbala Malik, who suffered a crippling spinal injury that left her paralysed. She succumbed to her injuries in September 2011.[21]

The BJP opposed the police action against Ramdev and sat on a day-long protest at Rajghat, the memorial of Mahatma Gandhi. Senior leaders, including Nitin Gadkari, Arun Jaitley and Sushma Swaraj were present at the spot from the very beginning. Sushma Swaraj, the leader of the Opposition in the Lok Sabha, called the police brutality 'pre-planned' and asserted that one does not resort to such an act merely at the police level; the manner in which the police came down on Baba Ramdev and the protesters more than hinted at the consent of UPA chief Sonia Gandhi, the prime minister and the home minister P. Chidambaram. In his address, Rajnath Singh took strong exception to the government's stance that people such as yoga guru Ramdev should not be commenting on political issues.[22] Singh noted that social as well as cultural leaders in India had never shied away from leading people every time there was a threat to the nation. Singh made it clear that for the BJP politics was not a means to form governments but to contribute to nation building and a protest such as the one Ramdev had undertaken should not be viewed from a political perspective.

Traditional and new media did not fail to pounce upon a single misstep on the part of the government or the people who wielded power. The new medium opened up wider avenues for political discourse and, although social media often got ugly with trolls, the collective influence was pushing political leaders to be more accountable. Millions now had a tool to express themselves across a barrage of issues and become watchdogs of any government in power. Its ability to influence the mainstream narrative, to some extent, gave it more bite. There had been governments in the past, such as the 1991 Congress government led by P.V. Narasimha Rao that was besieged by corruption charges, but thanks to the new media, the UPA-II government came to be labelled as possibly the most corrupt government seen by the country in its seventy-year history.

Although the 24/7 television news cycle barely left anything out of the debate, there was still a section of the society whose troubles went unnoticed. The BJP chose Rajnath Singh to address some of these issues such as the irregularities in land allocation to the Rajiv Gandhi Charitable Trust, a trust promoted by the Nehru-Gandhi family for the construction of an eye care hospital around Gurgaon.[23] Singh undertook a padyatra across Ullahawas, Baharampur and Ghata, all in Gurgaon district, to get a first-hand account from the farmers on how the Haryana government was indulging in open loot of farmers' land in connivance with builders. At kisan panchayats organized during his visit, Singh expressed shock on the state-sponsored racket of issuing notifications under Sections 4, 6 and 9 of the Land Acquisition Act to acquire farmers' land and, subsequently, releasing it from acquisition proceedings after big builders had purchased land in a panic sale from hapless farmers.[24] In Singh's home state of Uttar Pradesh, corruption became the fulcrum of the BJP's attack on the Mayawati government. The period preceding the 2012 state assembly elections saw the BJP undertake two Jan Swabhiman Yatras to raise the issue of poor law and order and loot of public money. Covering sixty-one districts and 370 assembly constituencies, the two yatras were led by Rajnath Singh and Kalraj Mishra, the latter now a national vice-president of the party. Nearly the entire BJP top brass, including leaders of the Opposition in both the Lok Sabha as well as the Rajya Sabha, Sushma Swaraj and Arun Jaitley, respectively, along with L.K. Advani, Vinay Katiyar and Ramapati Ram Tripathi and also the NDA convenor, Sharad Yadav, were present as the two yatras were flagged off from Mathura and Varanasi to mobilize support to bring about a political change in the state.[25]

The year 2012 did not begin on a good note for Rajnath Singh. The appointment of Singh's son, Pankaj Singh, as the general secretary of the BJP's UP unit led to three senior state-level functionaries tendering their resignation in protest. The three state-level party secretaries—Daya Shankar Singh, Santosh Singh and Ashwini Tyagi—were of the opinion that the only reason why Pankaj Singh was promoted to the post of general secretary was that he was Rajnath Singh's son.[26] Pankaj's foray into politics began in 2002 when he campaigned for his father in Haidergarh in the Barabanki district of Uttar Pradesh, and even though Rajnath Singh won his seat, the party lost the mandate. Post-2002, Pankaj worked around Varanasi and familiarized himself with politics at the grass roots; and in 2004 his efforts saw him get into the executive committee of the BJYM in the state.[27] A little before the 2007 assembly elections, Pankaj was elevated to the BJP's state executive committee but the moment his name was considered for the Chiraigaon seat in Varanasi, Pankaj had to suffer widespread vilification. There were rumours of Pankaj getting the ticket because he was the then BJP national president's son. Rajnath Singh's personal image had been clean through the course of his career and stories about his uprightness abounded. In fact, the legend of his personal car, a broken-down Fiat, was often quoted by both the party cadre and the public. When aspersions were cast, suggesting that Singh junior probably got the attention due to his father's position, Rajnath Singh asked his son to step down. Pankaj was denied a ticket again, for the third time, on similar grounds for the 2012 assembly elections from both Lucknow (East) and Varanasi. In a country notorious for dynastic politics, Pankaj was an exception considering that his father had headed nearly every post in the party hierarchy. According to a BJP spokesman, Mukhtar Abbas Naqvi, Pankaj's elevation was probably an alternative responsibility assigned to Singh by the party after Pankaj was denied a ticket.[28]

At the time Uttar Pradesh was getting ready for the elections, an event that would shake the foundation of not only the UPA government but also the way the media engaged with both the political dispensation as well as the general masses supposedly took place and went unnoticed till a few months later. On 4 April 2012, a leading national daily, the *Indian Express*, reported how the then chief of army staff, General V.K. Singh, allegedly attempted a 'coup' after two key army units moved towards Delhi without notifying the government.[29] The paper suggested that General Singh had attempted or given the hint of a coup by moving two army units from Hisar in Haryana and Agra in Uttar Pradesh on the night of 16 January 2012, when he had approached the Supreme Court regarding the issue of his date of birth.[30] The issue of when General Singh retired, either in 2012 or 2013, appeared to be of great significance to the UPA government.[31] There had been many run-ins between the UPA-II government and General Singh. A top-secret letter written by the latter to the prime minister, warning him of the perilous state of the army's defence preparedness, was even made public. But instead of addressing the letter's contents the media's attention was directed at trying to find out who had leaked the information.

The government vehemently denied the newspaper's claims of deep distrust. The prime minister said the 'alarmist' report 'should not be taken at face value' and then defence minister A.K. Antony called the movement a routine exercise and termed the report as 'absolutely baseless'.[32] However, the manner in which the whole episode was reported marked the beginning of an epochal change. The criticism of the mainstream media by the average person at the click of a button on social media platforms revealed to the people the power they wielded when it came to setting the narrative. Traditional media such as newspapers, television, and radio would continue to play a role, but the ability to set the narrative and steer the discourse was shifting to new media. Journalists working for legacy organizations would continue to engage in serious news gathering and investigative reporting but mainstream journalists would come to rely heavily on new media content as a source of news.[33] The day's headlines would invariably be influenced by the prime-time television news debate the night before, which, in turn, was dictated by the new media through the course of the day by social media timelines. With each passing day, the new media began to influence the quality and nature of news content as well as the style of political reporting.

If mainstream media was coming to terms with new media making it appear as a bunch of disconnected elites who did not understand the dynamics of public opinion, political parties too were pushed to a corner when it came to engaging with the electorate. The complexities of social media and new media were alien to most political parties in India. The BJP was one of the first political parties in India to understand the power of social media. Unlike other parties, who would rather keep it at an arm's length, the BJP began to look at ways to engage with the electorate. Since its defeats in 2004 and 2009, the BJP realized that a change in the way the party approached the voter was essential. The question was one of right timing. Some of its leaders had begun to comprehend the changing nature of the electorate and most noticeably it was Gujarat chief minister Narendra Modi who took the lead. Modi started narendramodi.in in 2005 and by 2009 he was active on Facebook and Twitter, positioning him as a politician who was in step with the times.[34]

As the next general elections approached, the talk about the potential prime ministerial candidate for the BJP was set in motion. Once again, there were murmurs about Advani and the senior BJP leader himself commented on the matter on his eighty-fifth birthday in November 2012. When asked what his party had gifted him, Advani said, 'The party has given me so much all my life that when somebody says you have to become the prime minister, I say becoming prime minister is not more than what I have got from the party.'[35] Exactly a year earlier, in October 2011, during the campaigning for the Uttar Pradesh assembly elections, Uma Bharati publicly claimed how Advani was the most suitable candidate for the prime minister's post.[36] If in 2009 Advani's inability to connect with the younger electorate on account of his age stood out like a sore thumb, in 2014 there would be nearly 160 million first-time voters, who would have felt disenchanted with an eighty-seven-year-old leading them.[37]

Up until 2009, most political parties focused on more traditional segments to win votes but in order to have the edge in the 2014 elections, parties would need to win over the first-time voter. For this, political parties would need to present a leader who could connect with the electorate both on a one-to-one basis as well as a mass leader but, more importantly, display an aptitude for delivering on voter expectations. Like most elections in India, the general elections of 2014 were about the same promises about a better future, but, at the same time, there was a clamour to overhaul the system in whatever way possible. In other words, the voter demanded someone beyond the usual suspects.

Before the BJP could name someone who could do that, it was hit by an unforeseen crisis. In October 2012, Nitin Gadkari found himself in the centre of a corruption scandal. It was alleged that as the public works department (PWD) minister in the Maharashtra government between 1995 and 1999, the BJP national president had entered into a quid pro quo financial arrangement with a construction firm that won contracts worth Rs 194 crore.[38] Further, when Gadkari was out of power, he had launched the Purti Group in April 2010 and there were reports in the media that the same construction firm, Ideal Road Builders, which won the contracts from the ministry headed by Gadkari between 1995 and 1999, had made major investments in and advanced large loans to Purti.[39]

The allegations raised questions about whether Gadkari would get a second term as the national president. Senior leader Ram Jethmalani asked him to step down; Yashwant Sinha suggested Gadkari step down as the president after the corruption scandal broke and even hinted at contesting against him. Owing to Gadkari's proximity with the Sangh, the media speculated that, ultimately, the RSS would decide on Gadkari's future. However, RSS chief Mohan Bhagwat refused to comment on the matter, calling it an internal matter of the BJP.[40]

For weeks the grapevine was rife with rumours about who would become the next president of the BJP. Many conjectured that the choice would boil down to either Arun Jaitley, who was said to have the backing of the RSS, or Sushma Swaraj, who, as the story went, had the blessings of Advani and Narendra Modi.[41] Some even said the chief ministers of Madhya Pradesh and Goa, Shivraj Singh Chouhan and Manohar Parrikar, respectively, could also get the call. With less than a year to the elections, the BJP found itself caught between a rock and a hard place.

Gadkari was allowed time to clear his name given speculations that there could have been someone within the BJP who had fuelled the entire campaign.[42] But at a time when the party was mounting an anti-corruption offensive against the UPA and focused on assembly elections in Himachal Pradesh and Gujarat, graft charges against its national president was the last thing it needed. As the year ended, it was certain that the party would appoint a new president and, in January 2013, the party once again turned to Rajnath Singh to guide it out of the doldrums. In a little over three years since he had resigned, Singh found himself in the driving seat once again. The heavens were giving him another shot at leading the BJP in the Lok Sabha elections.

11

Two in a Wave

The timing of and manner in which Rajnath Singh took over the reins of the BJP as the national president for the second time were far from ideal. There might have been some lack of exactness in the way the post came to him or what lay ahead for the party, but there was complete clarity in what he was expected to do.

A day before the official announcement, Singh received a frantic call from Muralidhar Rao, who asked him about his whereabouts. A former RSS pracharak known for his exceptional organizational skills as a student leader while he was with the ABVP, Rao had joined the BJP in 2009 and was part of Singh's team during his first term as the national president. Unaware that he was even being considered to lead the party, Singh told Rao that he was on his way to his constituency, Ghaziabad, to pay homage to the former mayor of the city who had passed away. Thanks to the Singh's fondness of him, Rao could speak his heart to Singh and asked him how, with so many developments taking place at such a pace, he could even think of driving to Ghaziabad. Singh was aware that Nitin Gadkari was to file his nomination papers the next day and had made up his mind to return the same evening. He conveyed the same to Rao. Up until the evening before the day of filing the nominations, there was little doubt in anyone's mind about Gadkari's second term. The consensus was that irrespective of what the media was speculating, Gadkari was bound to get re-elected. Rao, however, informed Singh to return right away to file his nomination as the party was set to unanimously choose him as the next national president.

By the time Singh returned to his residence, word had spread and a few more people had dropped in. Balbir Punj, a former columnist who joined the BJP and was first elected to the Rajya Sabha in April 2008, joined Singh and Muralidhar Rao. Pensive, Rajnath Singh went through the motions of acknowledging the congratulatory calls and messages pouring in. He could feel the anguish of the person he was poised to replace and that wore him down. He knew the emotional trauma that Gadkari might have been going through at the same moment and that clouded any joy he might have felt at his own elevation.

The next day, in his first address to the press after assuming charge as the BJP's national president, Singh expressed how the circumstances under which he was stepping into Gadkari's shoes were far from ideal.[1] Singh underscored the dedicated party worker Gadkari was known to be and publicly assured Gadkari that the entire party was with him in his fight for justice to clear the alleged charges of impropriety.

In nearly the decade that the UPA had been in power, an entire generation had come of age without any idea of what the BJP or the NDA had done during their tenure under Vajpayee. Singh had to present the party as an acceptable alternative to the Congress and resurrect the almost non-functioning National Democratic Alliance as a worthy substitute to the United Progressive Alliance. Moreover, the legacy of two successive losses, particularly the burden of the debacle of 2009, made the task more arduous.

Looking back at how things had played out after 2009, it would not be incorrect to say that Singh perhaps paid a greater price than any other member. The BJP's loss in 2009 was not solely the result of a decision taken by the party's national president. Even in the demand for a change or some kind of rejig, no matter how minor, for a long time the same voices emerged and the same names kept popping up. L.K. Advani continued to be seen as the BJP's 'go-to' prime ministerial candidate for years to come. Arun Jaitley, the then general secretary of the party and the chief campaign manager, became the leader of the Opposition in the Rajya Sabha. Jaitley had resigned as the general secretary once he was named the leader of the Opposition, which was in synch with the party's tradition of 'one-man, one-post', but criticism from members such as Jaswant Singh on the 'disconnect between parinaam and puraskar' (results and rewards) more than hinted at how, despite failures, some functionaries of the party continued to be rewarded with plum posts.[2] Besides Rajnath Singh, Yashwant Sinha resigned from all his posts that included party vice-president and the national executive member and asked for not only responsibility to be fixed but also a reconstitution of the party.

Those critical of Singh's appointment as party president in 2013 termed it as a compromise between the party and the RSS. They even suggested how 2014 might be a rerun of 2009, but the first indication of how it would be different came when Singh named his core team. In election mode, most political parties opt for a mix of the old guard and the young Turks in setting up teams. For Singh, however, the team had to reflect not just the party's potential but also the expectations of the billion people who would decide the course of the biggest elections known to humanity.

Singh's new team had twelve vice-presidents, ten general secretaries, fifteen secretaries and seven spokespersons, besides a twelve-member Central Parliamentary Board, a nineteen-member Central Election Committee and a five-member Central Disciplinary Committee. With more than seventy names in various capacities, Singh's team included veterans such as the Bihar strongman C.P. Thakur, Balbir Punj, Mukhtar Abbas Naqvi, Kiran Maheshwari and Smriti Irani as vice-presidents, and Amit Shah, Dharmendra Pradhan, Varun Gandhi, Muralidhar Rao and Rajiv Pratap Rudy as general secretaries. He made Poonam Mahajan, daughter of late party leader Pramod Mahajan, secretary. Saroj Pande succeeded Smriti Irani as the Mahila Morcha chief and Anurag Thakur was given another term as the head of the BJYM. The team also included numerous *prabhari*s, 'handlers', who were in charge of various states.

The one appointment that made the headlines was Narendra Modi's in the BJP Central Parliamentary Board, the highest decision-making organ of the party. During Singh's first tenure, Modi was excluded from the same body as he would have been the only chief minister on the CPB, which seemed unfair to the other serving CMs. It was the death of veteran leader Balasaheb Apte that led to one vacant seat on the CPB. In the midst of calls for Narendra Modi's name to be announced as the party's prime ministerial candidate, the appointment was seen as a sign of things to come. Unlike the old guard, Singh was not unaware of ground realities. For the sceptics, it was the clout of Modi speaking but Singh was no pushover. He knew that to win the people's mandate necessitated all hands on deck. The nomination of Amit Shah as in-charge for Uttar Pradesh, Singh's own home turf and one of the most important states in the grand scheme of things, hinted at how Singh was thinking. Shah was known to be a great organizational man and entrusting him with UP showed that Singh meant business.

For most political commentators and journalists in India, politics meant a silent competition between members of a party who could barely see eye to eye on most things. They were always on the lookout for the 'bad vibes' between the so-called chosen ones. This myopic view could have originated from the manner in which Indira Gandhi handled the Opposition, but to reverse-engineer the same explanation to a party such as the BJP revealed more about the commentators. Most newspapers and television reports focused on reading between the lines and commented on how Singh had, in fact, picked a 'Modi' team. However, the reality is that both Singh and Modi are quintessential organization men who put the party before everything else. Both had taken up the responsibility they were given through the course of their public life and focused on doing what was right, which, at times, could come at the cost of what others in the party felt. From the outside, it was convenient to see things in terms of seniority or experience but unlike most political outfits, the BJP operated on different principles. Irrespective of how the media projected the nomination of the prime ministerial candidate as a race between feuding satraps, Singh made it clear that there was no race and that the decision would be taken by the CPB in consultation with all senior leaders.

In addition to putting together a team that would inspire the cadre, Singh also cleared the decks when it came to the working relationship between the leaders. Right at the onset of his second term, Singh's message was clear: it was time that the second generation of the BJP took charge. A few days after Singh's new team was announced there were signs of the message going across loud and clear. While addressing the audience at the BJP's thirty-third foundation day celebrations in New Delhi, L.K. Advani mused how the BJP of the day was different from his idea of the party. Singh was present on

the dais when Advani spoke his mind. He had also heard the
Delhi BJP chief Vijay Goel comment that the next government
at the Centre would be formed under the leadership of
L.K. Advani and 'nobody else'. But when the media put the
'leadership' question to Singh, he reiterated the BJP's style of
functioning where the party president consulted the CPB and
proposed a name. He added how, during his previous tenure,
he had proposed Advani's name and this time too the Central
Parliamentary Board would decide whether to project him
or not.[3]

The challenge that Rajnath Singh faced was more than
formulating a strategy to rejuvenate the BJP. As one of
the senior leaders of the BJP who had relentlessly travelled
across the country in the recent past, be it to interact with
the voter or to manage troubles within the party like the one
the state unit was facing in Karnataka after chief minister
B.S. Yeddyurappa resigned in 2010,[4] Singh had his ear to the
ground throughout.[5] He was aware of how, sitting in Delhi,
one could make mistakes in assuming certain realities about
different parts of the country and he was not going to let his
learnings go waste.

Since he had taken over, nearly everything else about the
party had paled in comparison to the question of who would be
the BJP's prime ministerial candidate. For all practical purposes,
the media and a large chunk of the political dispensation within
the country had assumed Narendra Modi would be the one.
Based on the rumours, the BJP's allies within the NDA had
also begun to voice their opinion. Some of them, such as the
Shiromani Akali Dal (SAD), were on the same page as the
BJP. The Akali Dal's Sukhbir Badal pitched Modi's name in
January 2013 and came out in support of the then Gujarat
CM's developmental track record.[6] Others like the Shiv Sena
were problematic. Party leader Uddhav Thackeray and the party

seemed to have different opinions. In an editorial in the party mouthpiece *Saamana*, Uddhav Thackeray urged the BJP to let Modi remain Gujarat CM till 2017 given the latter's statement about not having any prime ministerial ambitions. The Shiv Sena had in the past rooted for Sushma Swaraj as the prime ministerial nominee but a week after Thackeray's statement, party spokesperson Sanjay Raut declared that the Shiv Sena has decided to support Modi or any other person its ally, the BJP, puts forth as the PM nominee.[7] Ironically enough, Uddhav Thackeray's cousin, Raj Thackeray, who broke away from the Shiv Sena to form his own party, the Maharashtra Navnirman Sena (MNS) and differed on most things with his cousin, had no qualms about openly supporting Modi.[8] If a few of the other allies were playing their cards close to the chest, some like the Janata Dal United (JD[U]) indicated that Modi might not be acceptable, citing his communal credentials in the wake of the 2002 Gujarat riots.[9]

Despite the Special Investigation Team (SIT) appointed by the Supreme Court having given Narendra Modi a clean chit in the Gulbarg massacre case, a large section of the press continued to cast aspersions over the three-time Gujarat chief minister. It was alleged that Narendra Modi had colluded with senior ministers, bureaucrats and the police to fan the communal violence in 2002. But after four years of investigations, the SIT, in February 2012, filed a closure report indicating that its inquiry found no prosecutable evidence against Modi and fifty-nine others in the particular case.[10] In the course of the SIT's investigation, Modi was interrogated for over nine hours in 2010; in 2011 allegations were levelled by a senior police officer that as chief minister Modi had asked him and other cops to allow Hindus in the state to avenge the killing of fifty-nine karsevaks on the Sabarmati Express near Godhra, but the SIT concluded that the testimony of the officer, Sanjiv Bhatt, was not reliable because he nursed a grudge against the Modi administration after being sidelined by it.[11]

For Singh, the question, 'who was it going to be', quickly transformed into 'how can Modi be the one'—at least from the media. The decade-long intense contempt for Modi continued unabated. As late as August 2013, a TV news anchor, while interviewing a British MP, went on to call Modi 'an extremely controversial figure' in India as well as around the world and asked the MP if he was aware that the invitation extended to the Gujarat CM would create controversy.[12] Singh continued to maintain there was no doubt about Modi being a popular leader and had projected a successful model for development in Gujarat but added that it was CPB that would take the final call.

In a matter of weeks since taking over, Rajnath Singh could see that the thought of Narendra Modi leading the BJP was taking a concrete shape among the party cadre. As a realist, however, Singh also got the sense that pitching Modi would not be easy as more than allies on the outside, there appeared to be enough opposition inside the BJP. Yet Singh was confident that when the hour comes, the cadre, as well as the leadership, would speak in unison. Singh's ability to get people with opposing ideas on the same page and his steadfast dedication to not letting disagreements fester for long was put through the toughest of tests.

The first indication Singh got that all was not hunky-dory was when some senior leaders, including L.K. Advani, decided to skip the party's June 2013 national executive in Panaji, Goa.[13] The possibility of Narendra Modi being given a greater responsibility for the 2014 elections, if not being named as the party's prime ministerial candidate, was, apparently, enough to make Advani, Yashwant Sinha, Jaswant Singh, B.C. Khanduri and a few more, including Uma Bharti, Ravi Shankar

Prasad and Varun Gandhi, give the event a miss. This made it abundantly clear what an uphill task it would be to get the leadership to jointly put their weight behind a single candidate.[14] While Prasad, who was the deputy leader of the Opposition in the Rajya Sabha, was in Sri Lanka with a delegation, newly appointed general secretary Varun Gandhi was in Paris due to some personal reasons. Senior leaders were hoping that Advani would make it to Goa on the second day but no one knew for sure if that would come about.

Despite the lack of a clear agenda, the cadre was expecting the national president to give a clear message to the party. The rousing welcome that Modi received upon his arrival, which also included a public announcement of support by Goa chief minister Manohar Parrikar, set the tone for the meeting.[15] Singh had been in constant consultations with the top brass but some of the opposition to any formal announcement regarding Modi was too conspicuous to disregard. If on the one hand, before arriving in Goa, Singh heard about BJP members hinting at possible names to the media, on the other, he got calls from allies who wanted to know what was on his mind. Nitish Kumar of the JD (U) had made his reservations about Modi being projected as the BJP's prime ministerial candidate quite clear and asked Singh if the party was going to make it public in Goa. Singh told Kumar that the CPB would assign some extra responsibilities to Modi, but no final call had been taken yet. Kumar was not convinced and attempted to dissuade Singh from declaring Modi as the party's candidate.

During the two-day national executive, there were whispers about a clear opposition towards Modi emanating from, primarily, what the press had dubbed 'Team Advani'. This was the first time in over five decades that Advani had not attended a key meeting of the political outfit that he had been a part of, but he was consulted by the PCB as well as Singh on the final decision. There were reports about the grand old man of the party not too keen on announcing Modi's name as the head of the campaign for the general elections right away. Some say there were suggestions to give Modi charge of upcoming assembly elections in states such as Madhya Pradesh and Chhattisgarh.

It was inevitable that the absence of some of the key members of the CPB would lead to a delay in arriving at a consensus for the 'bigger' announcement—Modi as the BJP's prime ministerial candidate—but going back from Goa without any conclusion would send out the wrong message. The press had a field day reading into every development such as the delayed arrival of Sushma Swaraj, which was interpreted as her being against Modi's elevation.[16] Looking at the manner in which some quarters were opposed to his name and privy to the constant back-room chatter about moves to scuttle his appointment, Narendra Modi thought of opting out.[17]

Having worked alongside for many years, both Singh and Modi had found in each other the perfect sounding boards. In September 2012, as Modi undertook his month-long Vivekanand Yuva Vikas Yatra, Singh was present to extend his support for his colleague's journey through 182 assembly constituencies of Gujarat.[18] Starting at Bahucharaji, a temple town near which a massive Maruti car plant was to come up, and ending at Sanand, where industrialist Ratan Tata had set up the Tata Nano plant after the Mamata Banerjee government in West Bengal practically pushed Tata Motors out of Singur, the journey was a showcase of what Modi had achieved in terms of development in Gujarat.[19] Singh had been witness to Modi's work as the chief minister of Gujarat and was also aware of his immense popularity amongst the cadre. It was around the same time that, in the course of a television interview, Singh, unaware of how fate would make him the BJP's national president in a few months, mentioned Narendra Modi when asked to name the one face amongst his generation of party leaders as the ideal PM candidate for the BJP/NDA for the 2014 elections. In the interview to ETV's Hari Shankar Vyas for his show *Central Hall*, Singh spoke about Modi's mass appeal as well as a solid track record of delivering on all parameters as three-term Gujarat chief minister.

During the final discussions at Panaji, Singh's resolve only strengthened. Even in the face of overwhelming opposition, he dug his heels in. As Singh reasoned with the entire gamut of the leadership, irrespective of age and experience, he underlined how any deferring of an announcement would take away the tactical advantage that the party would have over others. But more than anything else, the lack of clarity could dampen the spirits of the cadre. Personally, Singh always adhered to the voice of what he considered his dharma and, as party president, his first and foremost responsibility was to pick a candidate who could deliver victory.

Singh was the last person to speak on the final day of the executive meet and, as he rose to address the gathering, there was nothing on the agenda that indicated any 'major' announcement. In his twenty-five-minute-long address, Singh sounded the clarion call. He expressed his desire to start a central booth management committee to facilitate better coordination with the electorate across every single booth in the country. He also asked the party to connect with the voter on the Internet, use social media platforms to their optimum and, if they did not understand the medium, to get people who did, especially the younger generation to join in. As his address drew to an end, Singh repeated that the leaders of the party might have differences of opinions but it would be impossible to find such large-hearted leaders elsewhere. Keeping in mind the challenge of the biggest elections known to man, Singh proposed the creation of a central campaign committee and then, without much ado, announced Narendra Modi as its chairman. In the midst of thunderous applause that took a while to die, Singh said that people would inevitably ask, '*Kyon kar diya aap ne*' (Why did you do it?), '*Kya hai?*' (What was that?). The answer to that was clear. There was no dearth of able leaders in the party. However, the manner in which Modi had not only won the elections three times in a row but also established a new parameter of development in the state which was acknowledged globally had led the party to repose its faith and hope in Modi. Ending his address, Singh repeated the announcement of Narendra Modi as the chairman of the central campaign committee and asked him to join the others on the podium. The announcement was so unexpected that there was no bouquet to felicitate Modi with. So Singh picked up one lying next to the lectern, which had been given to someone else before, and handed it to him.

The next day, at a meeting where Singh, along with Arun Jaitley, Manohar Parrikar and Narendra Modi were interacting with party workers from Goa, Singh broke protocol and opted to speak before the others. He told the gathered workers that the reason he had got up to speak before Modi, who had been invited to deliver his address by Jaitley, was simply that he did not want to come between them and the *yuva neta* (young leader) whom they had come to hear. He asked them to get ready for a decisive election up ahead and welcomed Modi to address them.

Rajnath Singh's unexpected and terse announcement was signal enough of what lay ahead. The manner in which one of the most significant developments of the 2014 Lok Sabha elections—that could possibly change its course—was handled also indicated the massive opposition he faced. Singh's last-moment announcement was seen as bringing Narendra Modi one step closer to being made the party's prime ministerial candidate.

The announcement had its repercussions. Nitish Kumar called Rajnath Singh to inform him that the JD (U) had made up its mind to leave the NDA after a seventeen-year-old alliance.[20] Singh mentioned that nothing had been announced barring Modi given the charge of managing the elections, but for Nitish Kumar, everything was crystal clear the moment Singh had called Modi the leader.

It was nearly three months before Narendra Modi was finally announced the BJP's prime ministerial candidate. On 13 September 2013, the party's CPB in New Delhi unanimously elected the Gujarat CM as the one to lead them in the Lok Sabha elections.[21] Barring L.K. Advani, who skipped it expressing anguish about the way the party was functioning, the meeting was attended by every other member of the twelve-member board. It is to Singh's credit that nearly all the opposition towards Modi just a few months ago was a thing of the past.

The press was following each and every development, right from the back-to-back meetings between senior party leaders such as Nitin Gadkari and Ananth Kumar who were endeavouring to get Advani to attend the CPB meeting, as well as statements from nearly every single BJP member who had put their weight behind Modi.[22] Following the Goa session, the grapevine in Delhi had been abuzz with suppositions and conjectures. Advani's letter to Rajnath Singh outlining his disappointment with the way things had shaped up fuelled these further.

Through the course of the day, there were multiple meetings between Advani and Rajnath Singh, Nitin Gadkari and Sushma Swaraj, besides others, to try to convince one of the founder fathers of the party to support Modi. There were talks about the other senior leader Murli Manohar Joshi opposing Modi's candidature, but just as the meeting was to start, Joshi made a statement supporting Modi's candidacy as every member of the CPB was behind it. With Advani finally choosing not to come to the meeting, the CPB named Modi its prime ministerial candidate.

For over nine months, Lutyens's Delhi was talking about how Modi's candidature was a given as he had the RSS's backing. But ever since he became the chief minister of Gujarat, Modi was far from being the Sangh Parivar's blue-eyed boy. It's true that the RSS is the ideological fount of the BJP, but the equation had changed over the years. Although it still remained the moral compass for the BJP, the Sangh functioned as an independent entity as did the BJP. As swayamsevaks, Singh as well as Modi were proud of the Sangh's influence on their thought process and their careers but that was where the influence ended. The same media that had assumed that Rajnath Singh had ousted Modi from the party's Central Parliamentary Board bowing to the diktat of K.S. Sudarshan, the then sarsanghchalak of the RSS, now conveniently believed that Singh took his cue from Mohan Bhagwat, the incumbent RSS chief, and pushed Modi as the BJP's prime ministerial face. Despite the Sangh's keenness, Modi's selection also had to do with the single logic of him being the most likely candidate to deliver a decisive victory.

Running in nine phases from 7 April to 14 May 2014, the longest-ever elections in the history of independent India saw the BJP win 282 seats. The National Democratic Alliance tallied 336 seats, thus accounting for the largest majority government since the 1984 general elections. With over 814 million people voting, this was the largest election in the world. Although statistically one could argue that the BJP and the NDA won only 31 per cent and 38.5 per cent of the vote share respectively, the lowest in the case of a single party forming a majority government, the reality of the elections for the sixteenth Lok Sabha lay elsewhere. The most astounding aspect of the mandate was that the Indian Parliament would remain without an official Opposition party for the next five years. The Congress, the second largest party, had garnered only forty-four seats or 8.1 per cent of the votes, which was less than the mandatory 10 per cent of the seats (fifty-five seats) needed to be the main Opposition party.[23]

Rajnath Singh had contested the election from Lucknow, a constituency fondly associated with his long-time idol Atal Bihari Vajpayee, and won by a record margin of 2.72 lakh votes, the highest in the electoral history of the city.[24] It was a sweet victory for the man who, just five years ago, in 2009, was held responsible for losing an election that was considered a no-contest.

In a rare gesture, the United States' flag was flown at Capitol Hill in Washington DC in the honour of Singh on 30 April 2014, the day Lucknow voted. Such an honour is usually extended by the Architect of the Capitol, a federal agency responsible to the United States Congress and the Supreme Court for the maintenance, operation, development and preservation of 17.4 million square feet (1.62 million square metre) of buildings and more than 553 acres (223.8 hectares) of land throughout Capitol Hill. Requested by American Samoan Congressman Eni Faleomavaega, this was the first time that such a gesture was extended towards an Indian political leader. Saluting Singh's endeavours, the certificate issued by the then Architect of the Capitol, Stephen T. Ayers, highlighted how 'the president of BJP, born into a farmer's family, educated in a village, a brilliant student who completed his MSc Physics, entered politics in 1974, and together with Shri Narendra Modi and the love and affection of the people of Lucknow, is taking forward the historic work of transforming India'.[25]

For Rajnath Singh, winning the 2014 Lok Sabha election
meant delivering on a promise that he had made to himself
half a decade ago. The best part of the victory was the NDA
winning seventy-three—seventy-one for the BJP and two for its
allies—out of the eighty seats in his home state, Uttar Pradesh.
It was the party's best performance in the parliamentary
electoral history of Uttar Pradesh. The thumping victory would
become a part of Rajnath Singh's political legacy as would his
unwavering dedication to push Narendra Modi as his party's
prime ministerial candidate. True to his persona, Singh moved
away from the spotlight as soon as the job was done. On 26
May 2014, Narendra Modi took oath as the prime minister and
Rajnath Singh was sworn in as home minister of the republic
of India.

12

Set It Right

As prime minister, Narendra Modi began the uphill task of getting things in order. Overhauling India's internal security was one of the top priorities. The home ministry was not only one of the most important portfolios, but also of great significance for both Modi and the BJP. Modi turned to Rajnath Singh to head the ministry. Apart from being an obvious choice as a popular senior figure, Singh also possessed the acumen and the tenacity needed to withstand the rigours of the job. For nearly a decade since the NDA was voted out of power in 2004, Singh had expressed his concerns regarding national security and the failures of the Manmohan Singh government when it came to tackling terror. Having travelled extensively across the country, Singh was well aware of the bleak situation. The danger to average Indian lives from enemies both within and outside was clear and present. A well-oiled Ministry of Home Affairs (MHA) that would be on top of things, be it preventing terror strikes, eliminating or reducing the level of external and internal threats to the people of the country, raising the morale of the security forces and, essentially, creating an atmosphere of peace, was going to be the key for everything that the Modi government envisioned. Most importantly, for India to be a major player in the fast-changing global geopolitics, Modi needed someone who could ensure things would be fine at home.

In January 2014, Singh as the BJP national president, in a television interview, stated that the BJP government would endeavour to have better relations with its neighbours and the rest of the world. In the interview, Singh underscored a complete lack of diplomacy on the part of the UPA government and evoked the first NDA government of Atal Bihari Vajpayee during which, for the first time, India had begun to be equidistant from both Russia and the United States. In a glorious example of how deft the Modi government would be when it came to applying diplomacy to change the way India was viewed on the world stage, Narendra Modi, as prime minister-elect, invited the heads of the governments of all South Asian states to attend his swearing-in. In the past, no world leader had been invited by India for the swearing-in ceremony of a new government, which was traditionally viewed as a domestic event. The unprecedented gesture reportedly caught by surprise not just diplomats, but also the RSS. For most experts and commentators, the real significance of the move was to see how Pakistan would react and could the country's democratically elected prime minister, Nawaz Sharif, be his own boss or buckle under the pressure of the army, which reportedly played a greater role than the elected representatives.[1]

As the head of a ministry whose work was often compared to oxygen, a vital yet often taken-for-granted element on account of being invisible, Rajnath Singh's task was perhaps more significant than one would have imagined. At the time Singh took over the MHA, India was facing insurgency across three regions—Kashmir, the north-east and the Naxalite–Maoist infested 'Red Corridor'. While Kashmir was comparatively known and more visible in terms of media attention, the other two areas had extracted as much a human price. The insurgency in the north-eastern states of India had limited its participation in national endeavours, but the emotional alienation that locals felt was the bigger concern. Similarly, the Naxalite–Maoist insurgency across the Red Corridor, a region in the eastern, central and the southern parts of India, spread across parts of several Indian states—including parts of Andhra Pradesh, Bihar, Chhattisgarh, Jharkhand, Madhya Pradesh, Maharashtra, Odisha, Telangana, West Bengal and eastern Uttar Pradesh—had claimed thousands of lives. The ongoing conflict between the Indian government and Maoist groups, which in their present form came into existence in 2004 with the formation of the Communist Party of India (Maoist) (CPI-Maoists), a rebel group that came into existence through the merger of the People's War Group (PWG) and the Maoist Communist Centre (MCC), is probably the biggest threat to India within its borders.

In 2009, the UPA-II government had initiated the Integrated Action Plan (IAP) that included greater funding for grass-roots economic development projects in Naxalite-affected areas as well as increased special police funding for better containment and reduction of Naxalite influence. The IAP included Central grants schemes aimed at addressing issues of healthcare, drinking water, education and roads and generated a good response. Under this scheme, each district affected by left-wing extremism (LWE) got Rs 25 crore per annum. To speed up the development process, the money was given directly to the district. In 2010, Karnataka was removed from the list of Naxal-infested areas and, by 2011, over 66,000 developmental works costing almost Rs 2732.58 crore were taken up by district authorities.[2] Despite the great response and the successful completion of over 17,000 projects across sixty Maoist-infected districts, in July 2011, the Centre tentatively considered declaring nearly twenty more districts as 'Naxal-hit'.[3]

Besides these three theatres, there were growing reports
that certain swathes along the West Bengal–Bangladesh border
were transforming into a safe haven of sorts for terrorists. For
Singh, intelligence gathering and prevention of terror attacks
was of paramount importance and he was keen for the MHA
to come up with a road map that focused on giving his security
forces more teeth. Developmental and outreach programmes
would also deliver better if the threat levels were reduced. The
arrest of Odisha's most-wanted Naxal leader Sabyasachi Panda
in July 2014 by the police, acting on intelligence information,
was a major achievement. Panda was accused of gunning down
VHP leader Laxmanananda Saraswati and his four disciples at
an ashram in Kandhamal district in August 2008 that led to
large communal violence in the region.[4]

Soon after the Modi government was sworn in, it was faced
with one of its first big challenges. Incessant rain and landslides
had wreaked havoc in Jammu and Kashmir where normal life
was disrupted like never before. The MHA dispatched two
teams of the National Disaster Response Force (NDRF) to aid
in the relief and rescue operations in the flood-affected areas
of the state. The NDRF units were airlifted from Bathinda
in Punjab to Srinagar and worked with the local government
bodies to meet the challenges posed by the unprecedented floods
which had submerged most parts of south Kashmir, including
Pulwama, Anantnag and Kulgam. Singh monitored the rescue
operations and promised all possible help to Omar Abdullah, the
state's chief minister. Assessing the situation, the Centre sent
in eight additional teams of the NDRF and initiated Operation
Megh Rahat. From 2 September 2014, the Indian armed forces
was deployed in large numbers to conduct search, rescue, relief,
relocation, humanitarian assistance and rehabilitation missions.
Singh held meetings with the chief minister and other officials
of the government in Srinagar and undertook an aerial survey

of the flood-hit regions.[5] The entire mission saw the Indian Army, Air Force and Navy commit over 30,000 troops, fifteen engineering task forces, eighty-four Indian Air Force and Army Aviation Corps aircrafts and helicopters, MARCOS (previously known as the Marine Commando Force—MCF) or the special forces unit of the Indian Navy created for conducting special operations and also set up a base hospital, four field hospitals and over 100 medical detachments.[6] By 18 September, over 200,000 people were rescued from various parts of Jammu and Kashmir by the armed forces. Following this the government launched 'Operation Sadbhavna' or the relief and medical assistance support that continued to work in close synergy with the civil administration and the police.

Images of the devastation caused by the flash floods across Jammu and Kashmir were broadcast on news channels. Watching entire cities and townships in the Kashmir Valley underwater and people from all walks of lives navigating the waist-deep water filled everyone with a sense of anguish at the loss. At the same time, images of the Indian armed forces rescuing thousands of victims also warmed hearts. This was perhaps for the first time that many locals, who had a different opinion of the armed forces, saw them putting themselves in harm's way to rescue others. Refusing international aid, Prime Minister Modi announced assistance of Rs 745 crore to the state government, which was in addition to the already earmarked Rs 1100 crore.[7] The torrential rainfall caused damage to Pakistan-occupied Kashmir as well. Offering any assistance that it might need in its relief efforts, Modi wrote to his Pakistani counterpart, 'Our resources are at your disposal wherever you need them.'[8]

The swift manner in which the security forces as well as the government machinery responded to the floods in Jammu and Kashmir suggested a high degree of preparedness. The response time of the agencies, the ability to manage well beyond both capacity and resources convinced Rajnath Singh that if the standard operating procedure (SOP), along with the stock in terms of ammunition and other resources at their disposal were updated, the threat to the country's security could be mitigated to a great extent. There was more than a pressing need to hit the refresh button on the requirements of various agencies across the country that were looking after external as well as internal dangers.

In October 2014, Singh constituted a two-member committee to give inputs to revamp the Central Reserve Police Force (CRPF), the lead force against the Maoists, with the aim of creating a 'newly packaged CRPF'. The home ministry asked two former CRPF directors, General K. Vijay Kumar and General A.S. Gill, to come up with an action plan right from training the force to equipping them with the right kind of weapons and other requirements, including SOPs standard operating procedures to not only work in Maoist areas but also emerge as the principal counter-insurgency force.[9] During one of his initial visits to Maoist-infested areas, where he interacted with troops on the ground, Singh asked the men to tell him their needs and assured that the government would deliver to the best of its capacity. In the course of the interaction, several troops asked Singh to give them more AK-47 rifles instead of the INSAS rifles, and motorcycles for greater mobility when it came to ensuring safety from the weapon of choice of the Maoists—landmines. Singh struck out the INSAS on the file right away and made a note for immediate issuance of the Avtomat Kalashnikova assault rifle for the ground forces. Singh also wanted the committee to address the issue of the physical and psychological well-being of men deployed in sensitive areas for prolonged periods of time.

Despite the urgency in ensuring inter- and intra-agency cohesiveness between the security forces there were bitter reminders at regular intervals. In October 2014, a bomb blast in Burdwan district, West Bengal, demonstrated how hitherto little-known terrorist groups had begun operating from within Indian territory. For some years, India had been concerned about Bangladesh harbouring insurgents and exporting terror to India. The prolonged neglect of the porous India–Bangladesh border, coupled with the use of migrants for electoral gains, had created a conducive environment for Bangladeshi terror outfits to base themselves in India. The Burdwan blast brought to the fore the reach and expanse of Jamaat-ul-Mujahideen Bangladesh (JMB) in West Bengal. The investigations conducted by the National Investigation Agency, National Security Guard (NSG) and the Intelligence Bureau revealed eight terror modules operating from illegal madrasas in West Bengal, which, following further probe, revealed that they had links with extremists in Bangladesh.[10]

The more the investigative agencies explored, the more complex the entire issue turned out to be with many direct and indirect players. The NIA and NSG searched areas of Burdwan and Murshidabad districts and recovered mobile phones, SIM cards, jihadi literature and cables from the residence of one Jamat Sheikh, the father-in-law of absconding terrorist Sheikh Yusuf, the prime terror suspect. Yusuf was a teacher at the Simulia madrasa, believed to be a training centre for terrorists where men and women from the impoverished minority population were introduced to radical philosophy. Sources revealed that the subversive modules, several of whom were members of the JMB, started operations in West Bengal in October 2011 and enjoyed local political support mainly from the ruling party in the rural belts as no one could question their identity.[11] The NIA investigations also uncovered a plot by JMB to assassinate Bangladeshi prime minister Sheikh Hasina. After India handed over a dossier with details, Bangladesh tightened security on the border.[12]

Close on the heels of Burdwan came three more attacks which underlined how bad the situation had become. In separate incidents, all three theatres of trouble came alive. Maoists ambushed and killed fourteen CRPF personnel in Sukma district of south Chhattisgarh. Four terror attacks rocked the Kashmir Valley days before the prime minister was due to visit. Bodo rebels in Assam gunned down more than seventy Adivasis in orchestrated attacks in different parts of the state. Singh categorically ruled out talks with the National Democratic Front of Bodoland (Songbijit) (NDFB-S) and ordered an NIA investigation of the attack, which the government considered an act of terror. Singh assured time-bound action and made it known that the Indian government had also received the assurance of cooperation from 'one of the premiers' of Bhutan and Myanmar for flushing out terrorists from their territories.[13] The attack in Sukma ended an eight-month-long calm while those in Kashmir were aimed at undermining the third and last phase of the state assembly elections that saw heavy voter turnout in the first two even though the separatists had called for a boycott of the elections.[14]

It was not long, however, before Indians got an inkling of what this newly elected government could do when it came to answering its enemies. In the early hours of 1 January 2015, around 356 km from the coast of Gujarat, a Pakistani boat carrying explosives mysteriously blew up near the maritime border between India and Pakistan. The boat, said to have originated from a port near Karachi, was chased by the Indian Coast Guard ships and aircraft. It sped away and set itself on fire, killing all four people on board.[15] There is no denying that had the Indian Coast Guard failed and the vessel reached Gujarat with the cargo, the possibility of an attack similar to the one in Mumbai on 26 November 2008 could not be ruled out.[16] Though the government said the vessel was set on fire by its crew, a deputy inspector general of the Indian Coast Guard, B.K. Loshali, later claimed that he had ordered the blowing up of the Pakistani boat and was dismissed for his comments.[17] Irrespective of how it played out, it was clear that the government would no longer take things lying down.

The visit of US president Barack Obama in January 2015, when he also attended the annual Republic Day parade on 26 January in New Delhi as chief guest, the first ever for a US president, became one of the first signs of the world looking at India with renewed interest. Modi had previously met Obama during his visit to the United States in September 2014 and had extended him an invitation to visit India soon. As the first US president in office to visit India twice within the same term, Obama's visit set the foundation of a new relationship between the two countries. A few days before Obama landed, US Secretary of State John Kerry visited the Vibrant Gujarat summit where he met Modi and set the stage for President Obama's visit. The visit also expedited negotiations between the two countries on issues such as climate change, military purchases, and investment and manufacturing rules, but, most importantly, it reinvigorated talks on finally implementing the Civil Nuclear Agreement, which had been in limbo since it was signed in 2005.

In the course of his presentation at the Vibrant Gujarat summit, Secretary of State Kerry stressed upon the significance of Obama's visit, clearly outlining how the United States wanted to increase trade with India to US $500 billion a year, which was a significant leap from US $97 billion in 2013.[18] Obama's visit produced results both in terms of signed agreements and symbolic gestures that would become significant building blocks for the next phase of the Indo-US ties. The two countries broke the nuclear logjam, making headway on the liability hurdle, signed new initiatives which would see funds worth US $4 billion flow into India to boost trade, and agreed on climate change issues with both countries working towards clean energy.[19] Both countries also renewed their defence framework for a period of ten years to focus on co-development and co-production of defence equipment in India for India and the global market that would boost 'Make in India', the initiative launched by the Indian government in September 2014 to encourage companies across twenty-five sectors to manufacture their products in India and also increase their investment.[20] Both countries also advanced their counter-terrorism dialogue and recommitted to cooperating against Pakistan-based groups such as the Lashkar-e-Taiba.[21]

A few months later the 'new India' showed itself to the world following the successful evacuation of over 4000 Indians stranded in war-torn Yemen. The Middle East is home to nearly seven million Indians and, in March 2015, approximately 4000 of those got caught in the crossfire of a civil war in Yemen. The internationally recognized Yemeni government, led by Abdrabbuh Mansur Hadi, was fighting the Houthi armed movement, and the presence of the likes of Al Qaeda and ISIS did not help. A Saudi Arabia-led Arab Coalition began a military intervention alongside eight other Arab states with the logistical support of the United States against the Houthis. As the situation worsened, the Indian government initiated Operation Rahat under the command of General V.K. Singh, the former army chief and presently the minister of state for external affairs, to evacuate its citizens from the war zone. It was for the first time that a high-ranking Indian minister travelled into an active warzone to conduct such a diplomatic and military operation.

In the past, India had undertaken evacuation missions such as the one during the first Gulf War in 1990, where nearly 500 Air India flights evacuated over 110,000 people in the world's largest civil evacuation and, later, in Iraq in 2003, Lebanon in 2006, and Egypt, Libya and Yemen in 2011. But what made Operation Rahat stand out was the manner in which India managed to negotiate a time-frame whereby the Saudi-led forces ceased bombing the Yemeni capital of Sana'a to enable the Indian aircraft to land and take off.[22] Leading from the front, General Singh orchestrated the meticulously planned and efficiently executed operation from Djibouti, located on the other side of the Gulf of Aden. While, on the one hand, the Indian Navy, the Indian Air Force and Air India got together to begin the rescue operations, on the other, Indian diplomats in Yemen, led by Ambassador Amrit Lugun, worked to get the damaged airport in Sana'a ready for the evacuation.[23]

To help facilitate ground operations, the prime minister of India called King Salman bin Abdulaziz Al Saud of Saudi Arabia, who assured Modi of all possible assistance for the early and safe evacuation of the Indians stranded in Yemen.[24] Over the course of four days, four Air India aircraft and three Indian Air Force's C-17 Globemaster planes operated in and out of Yemen ferrying Indians and foreigners to Djibouti. Three Indian Navy warships, INS *Mumbai*, INS *Tarkash* and INS *Sumitra*, which had been patrolling the Gulf of Aden on an anti-piracy mission, along with two Indian passenger vessels—*Kavaratti* and *Coral*—sailed into a 'barrage of bombs' to bring Indians to safety from Aden, Al Hudaydah and Al Mukalla.[25]

By the time Operation Rahat came to an end, India had safely evacuated over 6710 persons from Yemen, including 4748 Indians and 1962 foreign nationals from twenty-six other countries.[26] Nearly twenty-six countries, including the United States, France, Germany, Hungary, Ireland, Sweden and others approached India to help their citizens stranded in Yemen.[27] Three Pakistani nationals also made it out of Yemen on Indian passports and Prime Minister Modi thanked Nawaz

Sharif for rescuing eleven Indians who were evacuated by a Pakistani ship.[28]

The manner in which the Indian government managed the crisis in Yemen through Operation Rahat, as also its rescue and relief operation in Nepal—Operation Maitri—in the aftermath of the April 2015 earthquake, showed that these were not just humanitarian missions but, in fact, a display of India's military intervention capabilities.[29] Operation Rahat had also seen an inter-ministerial 'Standing Group for Repatriation of Indian Nationals from Abroad' set up by the Ministry of External Affairs, which worked along with the Ministries of Home, Defence, Shipping and Civil Aviation. This hinted at the government's approach in tackling threats to India's national security and foreign policy. Right from the time the Modi government came into office, there was a sustained focus to strengthen the country's defence capabilities. In a span of four months, between January and May 2015, India conducted the third successful test of the Agni-V—an intercontinental surface-to-surface ballistic missile (ICBM) with a range of more than 5000 km with road-mobile launch capability. It also cleared a US $8 billion warships project approving the construction of seven stealth frigates and six nuclear submarines for the Indian Navy besides successfully test-firing Astra, the indigenously developed beyond-visual-range (BVR) air-to-air missile.[30] Although, to the outsider, such expansion might seem a little too much, for the Indian armed forces, whose main focus remained ensuring peace through deterrence, the development of military capability was a key component of the strategy. Years of neglect had put India on the back foot as far as the ability to fight a two-pronged war against China and Pakistan was concerned. With Chinese submarines docked in Sri Lanka, the Indian Navy needed a shot in the arm and, following a cabinet meeting summoned by the prime minister, the cabinet committee decided to press the accelerator on 'Project 17-A' that had been awaiting a clearance since 2012.[31] Similarly, with Agni having a range of more than 5000 km, potentially bringing targets in China within striking distance, defence preparedness attained critical national importance.[32]

While as a senior cabinet minister, Rajnath Singh was very much a part of these crucial initiatives, his first real hour of test as home minister came close to after a year in office when, on 4 June 2015, an Indian Army convoy was attacked in Chandel district of Manipur by the Naga insurgent group, the National Socialist Council of Nagaland (Khaplang) (NSCN-K). The organization aims to establish 'Nagalim', a sovereign Naga state consisting of all areas inhabited by the Naga people in north-east India and north-west Myanmar. The outfit's manifesto proclaims its slogan as 'Nagaland for Christ' and it has been accused of kidnapping, assassination, forced conversion and acts of terror.[33] Upon hearing the news of the attack, which resulted in the death of eighteen jawans of the 6 Dogra Regiment, Singh left for Dimapur to take stock of the situation. Upon reaching Dimapur, he met with army and police officials who briefed him on the ground situation. The home minister was clear—this was an attack on India and a strong message needed to be sent across. He stopped the presentation midway and told the General Officer Commanding (GOC) of the Dimapur-based 3 Corps, Lt Gen. Bipin Rawat, that the government would be more than fine with whatever be the army's response. Later, in a one-on-one meeting with high-ranking officers before leaving for Delhi, Singh once again told them that nothing was off the table and India wanted to give a befitting reply.

In Delhi, Singh chaired a meeting, attended by Defence Minister Manohar Parrikar, National Security Adviser Ajit Doval and Chief of the Army Staff General Dalbir Singh Suhag, which decided to go in hot pursuit of the militants across the border into Myanmar. The army chief was against a retaliatory attack the very next day as it was too short a notice but agreed that the strike would have to be within a seventy-two-hour window as that was the ideal time.[34]

An air strike was ruled out on account of possibilities of high collateral damage and once the plan was put in place, it was approved by the prime minister upon his return from an official visit to Bangladesh between 6–7 June. Doval dropped out of the PM's visit in order to fine-tune the operation and once the PM gave the go-ahead, commandos of 21 Para were airdropped around 3 a.m. near the Myanmar border. Equipped with assault rifles, rocket launchers and grenades, the Para commandos trekked nearly 5 km before reaching the training camps of the NSCN-K and KYKL (Kanglei Yawol Kanna Lup), another militant outfit believed to be involved in the attack on the Indian Army. The seventy-member team of Para commandos was divided into two subgroups with one conducting the direct assault while the second formed an outer ring to prevent insurgents from escaping.[35] The Myanmarese authorities were kept in the loop about the attacks and thermal imagery was used to track the development by the second. The Indian Air Force was also on standby with Mi-17 helicopters ready to evacuate the commandos in case anything went wrong. The actual strike, spread over forty minutes, left the camps completely destroyed with reportedly 150 insurgents dead. The Indian Army suffered no casualties.

What the surgical strike managed to achieve was to send a message across that India would not be pushed around any more and that it was a country that could take care of its national interests.[36] It represented a shift in India's approach to counter-insurgency and showed that the political will to conduct surgical strikes across the border was no longer missing.[37] The decision to undertake such an exercise with such alacrity reposed the faith in the army, and post-Myanmar, the Indian Army routinely began to maintain a level of preparedness to respond to any similar incident.[38] The home ministry also declared the whole of Nagaland as a 'disturbed area' for one more year beginning June 2015 despite the state government seeking to remove the tag since 2005. Since assuming office, the NDA-II government had accorded a high-priority status to the Naga issue, and the prime minister had spelt out his vision of transforming the north-east during the many trips he had undertaken. In fact, the 'Act East' foreign policy of the Modi sarkar was also extended to the north-eastern states of India, emphasizing peace, security, connectivity and economic development.

The Naga insurgency was the oldest insurgency in the country and came to a boil when a group of 140 members from the Naga National Council (NNC), which had come into existence in 1947, refused to accept the Shillong Accord signed between the NNC and the Government of India in 1975, whereby a section of the NNC and NFG (Naga Federal Government, established by Angami Zapu Phizo in 1946) were to lay down arms. The NNC group led by Thuingaleng Muivah, which was in China when the Shillong Accord was signed, joined hands with Isak Chisi Swu and S.S. Khaplang to form the National Socialist Council of Nagaland (NSCN) in 1980. Eight years later, a violent clash saw them split into NSCN (IM) and NSCN (K).

In the early 1990s, Muivah, Swu and a few top leaders of the NSCN (IM) escaped to Thailand and P.V. Narasimha Rao, the prime minister at the time, kept sending feelers for talks without any precondition. Following a positive response to then Nagaland governor M.M. Thomas, Rao met Muivah, Swu and others in Paris in 1995 to negotiate peace. Rao had also sent the then minister of state for home, the late Rajesh

Pilot, to meet the group in Bangkok. Subsequently, then prime minister H.D. Deve Gowda also met them in Zurich in early 1997 and followed up with more meetings in Geneva and Bangkok.[39]

The first positive outcome of the sustained meetings came when the Government of India signed a ceasefire agreement with the NSCN (IM) in 1997 and, later, Prime Minister Atal Bihari Vajpayee met them in 1998. Since then there had been over eighty rounds of talks between the two sides. In 2001, the government entered into a formal ceasefire with the NSCN (K) and in 2007 it was extended indefinitely. In March 2015, S.S. Khaplang abrogated the 2001 ceasefire agreement and, following the June attack by the NSCN (K), the MHA was clear about its mission to crack down upon the outlawed elements. There was a push to reimpose the ban on the outfit under the Unlawful Activities Prevention Act (UAPA). The MHA also sought to freeze the assets and properties of the group's local top leadership.

The deftness with which Singh's ministry addressed the operation showed that while peace was the number one priority, the government would not be a mute spectator to violence against the state. Within a month after declaring Nagaland a 'disturbed area', the MHA managed to bring the two-decade-long peace process that began with P.V. Narasimha Rao in 1995 to a conclusion under Narendra Modi in 2015. On 3 August 2015, the Government of India and the NSCN (IM) signed an agreement that finally addressed the six-decade-old Naga political issue.[40] In addition to the home ministry's efforts, the government managed to achieve the near-impossible due to the presence of experts such as R.N. Ravi, a former IB official with years of experience in the north-east, who was also the government's interlocutor for the Naga peace talks, as well as the governor of Nagaland, P.B. Acharya, an RSS veteran of the north-east.[41] The agreement was signed by Ravi and Isak Chishi Swu and Thuingaleng Muivah, in the presence of

Narendra Modi, Rajnath Singh and Ajit Doval. The prime minister lauded the courage and wisdom of the Naga leaders and civil society in marking not merely the end of a problem but the beginning of a new future.[42]

The government was focused on ending all strife in the north-east and, during his visit to China in November 2015, Rajnath Singh brought up the issue of Chinese arms and ammunition reaching dozens of insurgents in the region.[43] Singh was the first home minister to visit China in a decade and held extensive talks on strengthening cooperation between the two countries on border and counter-terrorism during his six-day visit.

China's reluctance to de-hyphenate Pakistan from India was more than visible from the visit of the vice chairman of China's Military Commission, General Fan Changlong, who arrived in India after visiting Pakistan. But India was not deterred and carried on working on an 'assertive multilateral engagement' and sent the Indian Army chief, General Dalbir Singh Suhag, on a visit to Japan at the same time that General Fan was in India.[44] Rajnath Singh's visit as the second-highest-ranking minister in the Indian government, close on the heels of PM Modi's trip a few months earlier in May 2015 assumed great significance as it was a part of India's new evolving defence diplomacy. During his visit, Singh cemented a high-level-meeting mechanism between the two countries, whereby the home minister of India would meet the minister of public security of China once every two years in Beijing and New Delhi. He also reached a consensus with the Chinese for enhanced cooperation in combating international terrorism through the exchange of information on terrorist activities, terrorist groups, their linkages and other terrorism-related crimes, besides coordinating positions on anti-terrorism endeavours at regional and multilateral levels.[45]

More than anything else, terrorism, both internal and from across the border, remained India's biggest threat. Diplomatic talks between India and Pakistan made little headway largely due to the latter's inability to contain its state and non-state players. There had been a great stress on India maintaining people-to-people contact and other confidence-building measures (CBMs) and, even though most Indian governments kept diplomatic channels open, Pakistan would invariably push things to a point where deterrence became the only option. As home minister, Singh too carried on the Indian official stance of never firing the first bullet, but unlike some of the other governments in the past, this government decided to show its mettle in case of aggression initiated by the other party.

The Modi government regularly approached Pakistan, beginning with the invitation to Nawaz Sharif in May 2014 to attend the swearing-in ceremony, but made it amply clear that India would respond with massive force to any cross-LOC firing or infiltration by terrorists and, irrespective of what the past policy was, it would frown upon any high-profile meeting with the Hurriyat by Pakistanis prior to any bilateral talks. In December 2015, the Indian prime minister made an unannounced visit to Lahore and met Nawaz Sharif in what was seen as yet another effort to engage with the democratically elected government of Pakistan. Many experts such as Vikram Sood, former chief of the Research and Analysis Wing (R&AW), were of the opinion that every time the premiers of India and Pakistan met, it resulted in a terror attack orchestrated by the latter.[46]

It was no different this time too. Less than a week after PM Modi met his counterpart in Lahore, heavily armed terrorists suspected of belonging to Jaish-e-Mohammed attacked the Pathankot airbase in Punjab. The perpetrators were able to penetrate the outer perimeter despite advance intelligence and massive security deployed in anticipation. Although they were unable to attack the main airbase, what was truly alarming was how they commandeered a vehicle and were aware of their destination. The terrorist spoke to two Pakistan-based phone numbers in the course of the attack, and the possibility of sleeper cells based in India was high considering they were able to get to the target, 30 kilometres from the border, in the dead of night.[47]

The January 2016 attack saw a breakdown of Indo-Pak ties. The manner in which Pakistan-based militants had once again tried to sabotage any chance of peaceful relations between India and Pakistan was enough to prove it was the handiwork of the Pakistani Army and its infamous spy service, the ISI. For years, the ISI had been supporting insurgent groups in India. Nearly every effort of the Indian government on the world platform to get Pakistan to refuse safe haven to such outfits and prevent them from operating from within its borders had failed to yield results. During Singh's visit to Beijing, the issue of the Chinese using a 'technical hold' to block India's bid for UN censure of Pakistan for releasing LeT commander Zaki-ur-Rehman Lakhvi, the mastermind behind the 26/11 Mumbai attacks, had come up for discussion.[48] The ostensible aim of militant groups like the LeT, Jaish-e-Mohammed and Hizbul Mujahideen mirror the ISI's motto—bleed India into ceding control over Kashmir—and no platform is too small or no place too insignificant for them to push this agenda.[49]

It was therefore shocking to hear words and slogans echoing the same sentiment in an event organized on the campus of the Jawaharlal Nehru University (JNU) in Delhi a few weeks after the Pathankot attack. There were videos from the event that showed students and protesters chanting '*Bharat tere tukde honge, Inshallah, Inshallah*' (India will be broken to pieces, Inshallah, Inshallah) among other anti-India slogans. A couple of days after the event, when the Delhi Police arrested the university's student union president, Kanhaiya Kumar, on charges of sedition and criminal conspiracy, Rajnath Singh issued a statement that the campus stir had received support from Lashkar-e-Taiba founder Hafiz Saeed. Around the same time a fake Twitter account attributed to Saeed sent out a tweet supporting the JNU protests. The media as well as the public ran with the story that the home minister's statement was based on the fake account's tweet. Some news agencies reported that sources inside the Ministry of Home Affairs said Singh's statement was based on the 'consolidated inputs' from security agencies.[50]

For days after the JNU incident, the general perception doing the rounds was that the government had perhaps come down too heavily on the students. Various quarters, including the US thinker Noam Chomsky, criticized the officials for letting the police enter the university premises four days after the event. Later, when some students who had gone underground after the incident resurfaced on the campus after nearly ten days, they refused to surrender to the Delhi Police and asked the police to come and arrest them. When the vice-chancellor of the university did not permit the Delhi Police to enter the campus, the police camped outside and continued to do so until the students who were charged surrendered.

As days passed, Rajnath Singh could not help but recall the days when different political ideologies saw many of his contemporaries on opposite sides of an argument. But no matter how much one differed from the other, there were never any slogans on dividing India. Singh reminisced about the past when, despite being a swayamsevak, he would attend public rallies of senior Congress leaders like Kamlapati Tripathi and Chaudhary Charan Singh just to hear them speak.

In the case of the JNU students' protest, an inquiry committee of the university claimed that provocative slogans were raised at the 9 February 2016 event but it was done by a group of outsiders. The committee's findings suggested that the event was held without permission, thus amounting to 'wilful defiance', and pointed out that posters with titles such as 'Against the Brahminical collective conscience', 'Against the judicial killing of Afzal Guru and Maqbool Bhat' were prominently displayed at the gathering. The slogans included incendiary ones like 'Kashmir *ke log sangharsh karo hum tumhare saath hain*', 'Manipur *mange azaadi*', 'Kashmir *ke azaadi tak jang rahegi jang rahegi*, Hindustan *ke barbadi tak jang rahegi jang rahegi*', 'Go back India, *Ek* Afzal *maroge, har ghar se* Afzal *niklega*'.[51] According to reports, a lot of Kashmiri students from inside and outside the campus were to attend the event and the university's security staff even noted the presence of outsiders, which was also confirmed by eyewitnesses.[52] The chants heard at JNU appeared to play straight out of an ISI playbook, but in the face of the support and compassion for the students it was unacceptable to even hypothetically question the odd similarities between the actions of those present in an educational institution in the heart of India's capital and the ISI's Joint Intelligence Bureau (JIB), the department responsible for political intelligence that has one of its three subsections devoted to operations against India.

For the home ministry, addressing the ISI's psy-ops had become nearly as important as strengthening the security forces with arms and the attitude to take on the enemy. A report published in the *Pioneer* in June 1999 had enumerated in great detail the three-decade-long plan of the ISI to spread its tentacles across every nook and cranny in India. By the late 1990s, there was probably not a single Indian city where the ISI did not have either an active or a sleeper agent who could spread terror by triggering blasts, fuelling communal riots in peaceful cities and blowing up railway stations anywhere it wished.[53] There is enough empirical research to substantiate the ISI's meddling in the internal affairs of India across Jammu and Kashmir, Punjab and the north-east.[54] It was ISI that planted the first seed of terrorism in Jammu and Kashmir in the early 1980s and began its operations with indoctrination and an 'India-hate' propaganda. The ISI proactively trained frustrated youth, bribed and funded so-called political and social leaders and subverted the law and order system in the state to such an extent that the Indian government had to send in the army. This ploy could be seen at play in the way the Pakistan-based terror outfit Hizbul Mujahideen released a picture of eleven young militants moving in a forest wearing camouflage and holding Kalashnikov rifles. The photo was widely circulated on Facebook, following which it became a recruiting tool. Mainstream newspaper articles with catchy headlines profiled the young men, including Burhan Wani, a native of Tral and a Hizbul commander, all of whom were educated and wealthy, furthering the recruitment drive with more Kashmiri youth entering the folds.[55] Since the image went viral, all of the eleven terrorists including Wani were eliminated one by one by the Indian security agencies.[56]

In July 2016, Rajnath Singh ushered in one of the most comprehensive overhauls of India's Arms Rules in nearly five decades. And in trademark style, he did it without much fanfare. Under the new policy, foreign manufacturers and Indian private sector players were allowed to produce small weapons like automatic pistols, machine guns and assault rifles within the country. Besides meeting the requirement of the Indian armed forces, police and paramilitary forces that the state-owned ordnance factories were failing at, the home ministry's new policy also boosted the government's Make in India drive. It also helped promote export and generate employment by allowing foreign and private sector companies to manufacture locally.

The policy change that would make the country self-sufficient in weapon parts, slings and butts was first proposed in 2001, when a cabinet decision allowed private players to manufacture arms and ammunition with up to 26 per cent foreign direct investment (FDI). Since 2006, the progress was stalled for a decade as the MHA was not okay with the Ministry of Defence and the Foreign Investment Promotion Board (FIPB) as the only two bodies involved in the licensing process.[57] The MHA was made the sole licensing authority in 2010 and with the new 100 per cent FDI policy that came into play in 2014, the Arms Rules 2016 was nothing less than a game changer. The new policy also made it tougher for private citizens to get licences to acquire guns for personal protection while increasing the quota for sports shooters from 15,000 rounds of ammunition per year to 50,000 to boost India's shooting talent. The rules also became stricter for the issuance of new licences (any staff member employed by a shooting club or a manufacturer or dealer now needed to complete the arms and ammunition safety training course) and owning or inheriting multiple weapons. The licencing as well as the renewal fee was also increased from Rs 500 to Rs 5000 per firearm up to 1000 units and from Rs 100 to Rs 3000 per firearm respectively.[58] In order to curb illegal arms licences, the MHA also directed all licensing authorities to generate a unique identification number (UIN) for each licence without which any arms licence would be considered invalid.[59]

India also decided to replace the ageing guns of its artillery by going ahead with the acquisition of 145 M777 ultra-light howitzers (ULH) from BAE Systems, US. It had also come to a conclusion that an indigenously upgraded version of the Swedish Bofors FH77 Field Howitzer would have to be inducted.[60] Being light, the M777 could be deployed in high altitudes and could be easily carried by CH-47 Chinook helicopters that the Indian Air Force was acquiring from the Boeing Company based in the United States. The Defence Acquisition Council (DAC), the highest decision-making body of the ministry headed by Defence Minister Manohar Parrikar, also cleared the production of the indigenous Dhanush gun, which was based on the designs supplied by the Swedish company thirty years ago following trials to the army's satisfaction. Much to Pakistan's chagrin, India also successfully tested the Barak 8, the jointly developed Indian–Israeli air and naval defence missile system within months of the Modi government taking office in November 2014.[61]

Rajnath Singh became the first Indian home minister to visit Israel since 2000 and, during his four-day trip in November 2015, laid the foundation of a new era of India–Israel ties. Close on the heels of Modi's meeting with Benjamin Netanyahu on the sidelines of the United Nations General Assembly meeting in New York, Singh conducted meetings across the board to review existing cooperation and future possibilities of enhancing engagement between the two nations. Besides strengthening defence ties, Singh also discussed the use of social media by jihadi elements for indoctrination and the pressing need to devise ways to curb this. Israel extending the red carpet for Singh and also making several exceptions, which are usually reserved for heads of states, showed their desire for expanding cooperation in all fields and at any level.[62]

Singh was also taken on a helicopter tour of the Jordan Valley and Israel's northern and southern region with National Security Adviser Yossi Cohen to get a sense of the security situation in the region. Watching the working of the comprehensive integrated border management system (CIBMS) programme, a high-tech surveillance system that reduced the dependency on physical patrolling, Singh immediately decided to start working on getting the same for the Indian borders. By 2015, Israel Aerospace Industries (IAI) and the Indian state-owned Defence Research and Development Organization (DRDO) began collaborating on a jointly developed surface-to-air missile system for the Indian Army. The Government of India also approved the purchase of ten armoured Heron TP-armed drone vehicles from Israel to help secure the borders. This brought to a closure a proposal that had been pending since 2012 when the UPA was in power.[63] Rejecting a rival bid from the United States for its Javelin missiles, India also bought 8356 Spike anti-tank missiles and 321 launchers from Israel in a deal worth US $525 million.[64] The Spike missile did not require a lock to launch and had a tiny fibre-optic cable linking the launching vehicle with the missile, as well as a camera in the missile itself, that allowed only the operator to know the rough coordinates of the target for the launch. The Spike acted as precision artillery and the TV guidance allowed the missile to retarget in flight with the operator only needing to steer to a different target.[65]

In the midst of revamping the security apparatus, diplomatic interaction between India and Pakistan did not take a back seat. At least, not from India's side. It was in the shadow of these developments that a scheduled meeting of the home/interior ministers of the South Asian Association for Regional Cooperation (SAARC) member countries in Pakistan came up. It was in 2005 at the thirteenth SAARC summit in Dhaka that the leadership decided that home/interior ministers of member nations should meet annually to strengthen cooperation in the area of counter-terrorism.[66] Before Rajnath Singh left for Islamabad there was a discussion between him and the prime minister if India should even consider attending it. Even though the relations between the two countries were far from cordial, Modi was keen on keeping a channel of discussion open. If India kept away, chances of other member countries that included Afghanistan, Bangladesh, Bhutan, Nepal, the Maldives and Sri Lanka giving the whole thing a miss could be high, but Modi left the decision to Singh's best judgement.

The home ministry had pointed out Pakistan's efforts to stoke unrest in Kashmir following the killing of Burhan Wani in July. The violence that followed had cost nearly fifty lives and left hundreds injured. Nevertheless, Singh decided to attend the summit in Pakistan, primarily to tell Pakistan to stop supporting terrorism in India and control outfits like Lashkar-e-Taiba and Jaish-e-Mohammed operating from within its boundaries. Pakistan was aware that Singh was not someone who could be mollycoddled or distracted. It was also aware that if there was an Indian home minister who could be expected to have a no-holds-barred talk on issues ranging from illegal trafficking in narcotics, cross-border terrorism or raking up the topic of one of the world's most wanted terrorists, Dawood Ibrahim, rumoured to be based in Karachi, it was Rajnath Singh.[67]

From the moment Singh and his delegation, that included officials from his ministry as well as the Ministry of External Affairs, arrived in Islamabad, Pakistan's official attitude towards them was far from diplomatic. The Pakistani home minister Chaudhary Nisar Khan was cold. Protests against the Indian delegation, by the Jamaat-ud-Dawa, a front group of the LeT, appeared to have the support of a section of the establishment. The official Indian media contingent comprising Doordarshan, ANI and PTI accompanying the minister was made to sit out during Singh's speech. Pakistan had denied visas to all Indian media personnel except media owned by the government. Singh made a few changes in his speech and made it clear that there were no good or bad terrorists. He also pointed out that one country's terrorist could not be hailed as another country's freedom fighter. Pakistan's undiplomatic treatment continued when, in a gross breach of diplomatic norms, Nisar Khan skipped the official lunch at the meeting venue. Singh too did not attend the lunch and left Pakistan earlier than scheduled. Once back in India, he told Parliament that he had not gone to Pakistan to have lunch and did what he did, keeping in mind the country's prestige.[68]

Rajnath Singh's visit to Pakistan happened between the time Burhan Wani was killed by security forces and the growing unrest in Kashmir that followed the death of the young Hizbul militant. The strain Wani's killing had had on Indo-Pak relations ruled out any chance of a one-on-one dialogue between Singh and his Pakistani counterpart. Things got worse when Nawaz Sharif not only praised Wani but also remarked that Kashmir would one day belong to Pakistan. The protests in the Kashmir Valley increased exponentially and two months later, on 16 September 2016, a group of heavily armed terrorists targeted the rear administrative base of a unit in Uri, Kashmir. In the deadliest attack on security forces in almost two decades, suspected Pakistan-based terrorists, in a predawn ambush, lobbed seventeen grenades in three minutes, killing seventeen Indian Army personnel and injuring nearly 150 soldiers. Most of the soldiers who lost their lives were from 10 Dogra and 6 Bihar regiments. As 6 Bihar was replacing 10 Dogra, most of the troops were stationed in tents that were not fireproof and, as the men ran out to escape the fire, they were attacked by the terrorists. After a gun battle that lasted six hours, Indian soldiers killed four terrorists belonging to Jaish-e-Mohammed as per the identification found on them. Their equipment bore Pakistani markings.

The attack sent shockwaves across India. Condemning the incident as despicable and cowardly, Prime Minister Modi assured the nation that those behind the attack would not go unpunished.[69] Terming Pakistan a terrorist state, Rajnath Singh cancelled his scheduled visit to Russia and the United States to take stock of the situation. He pointed out that Pakistan's continued and direct support to terrorism and terrorist groups needed to be addressed in a befitting manner. Nearly every major interaction with Pakistan was put to an immediate halt. India cancelled its participation in the nineteenth SAARC summit that was to be held in Islamabad in November, following which Afghanistan, Bangladesh and Bhutan also withdrew from the summit.[70] One of the biggest media houses of India, Zee Entertainment Enterprise, discontinued its 'Zindagi' channel that showcased Pakistani shows. The Badminton Association of India boycotted the Pakistani International Series and the Board of Control for Cricket in India (BCCI) ruled out any possible revival of bilateral cricket ties with Pakistan.

Even though Islamabad continued to deny the role of jihadist groups based within Pakistan in the Uri attack, posters claiming that the LeT would hold the last rites for one of the four attackers killed by the Indian Army substantiated India's claim.[71] Rajnath Singh along with Manohar Parrikar, Ajit Doval and General Suhag met the prime minister to review the situation. Parrikar and General Suhag had visited Uri in the wake of the attack and the meeting also had briefings by officials of the ministries of home and defence, paramilitary forces and intelligence agencies. In the high-level meeting, Singh also reviewed the security situation across the entire western border.

The Uri assault was more than an infiltration bid. It was in many ways a direct attack on India and it needed a response more than simple verbal condemnation or tough posturing beyond the diplomatic front. Pakistan had also been soliciting support from global bodies such as the United Nations to investigate human rights violations by Indian armed forces and routinely accused India of sponsoring militancy in its

Balochistan province. Some commentators on international affairs had begun to talk about possible military retaliation from India but cautioned how it would not behove an emerging global power to do anything that would escalate the bilateral conflict.[72] Nawaz Sharif was expected to bring up the issue of India's human rights violation at the UN General Assembly (UNGA) that was to convene just a week after the attack on Uri.[73] Sharif's speech at the UNGA, where he brought up India's involvement in Balochistan and the development of the Chabahar Port in Iran, while highlighting how his own country had made great strides in tackling terrorism internally, not only attracted opposition from Baloch activists who held large-scale demonstrations outside the UN headquarters in New York but also India's minister for external affairs, Sushma Swaraj. In her address, Swaraj labelled terrorism as Pakistan's calling card, asking Sharif to abandon the dream that terrorism would enable Pakistan obtain what it 'coveted', Kashmir. She also rejected Sharif's contention that India was setting conditions for resuming peace talks.[74] She highlighted how India had time and again in the previous two years reached out for friendly relations, in a manner that was without precedent. Reiterating India's desire to cultivate normal relations with Pakistan, she listed Modi's surprise visit to Lahore in December.

A few days after the UNGA, on 29 September 2016, eleven days after the Uri attack, the Indian Army told the world that it had successfully carried out surgical strikes in Pakistan-occupied Kashmir (PoK). In an address to the media, the then director general of military operations (DGMO) Lt Gen. Ranbir Singh revealed that the Indian Army had carried out pre-emptive strikes against militant outfits in the light of intelligence reports of more attacks like the one in Uri being planned across the state of Jammu and Kashmir. This response was the first of its kind, with the Indian Army conducting strikes across the border during peacetime—something they had not done in decades. They were crossing a threshold embedded in their minds and had to reorient their outlook in order to apply their skill and training to a different set of circumstances.[75]

According to numerous unofficial accounts, three to four teams of seventy to eighty soldiers from the 4 and 9 Parachute Regiment Special Forces were airdropped at the Line of Control. They crossed over under the cover of firing by the Indian artillery.[76] The commandos travelled nearly three kilometres on foot and destroyed terror camps in Bhimber, Hotspring, Kel and Lipa sectors in PoK and eliminated thirty-eight terrorists and two soldiers of the Pakistan Army.[77] The commandos returned safely without a single casualty. After the operation, the teams even informed Pakistan about the surgical strike. Denying any such strike, Pakistan dismissed it as regular cross-border firing.

After the DGMO's press briefing, Rajnath Singh called an all-party meet and briefed leaders of all major political parties about the surgical strike. The historic mission was so secretive that nobody in the military or the government, besides a carefully pruned chain of command stretching from the prime minister on one end and the special forces team commanders on the other, knew about it.[78] Setting aside all political differences, nearly every single Indian political party hailed the government's actions. Congress president Sonia Gandhi acknowledged that the surgical strikes had sent across a strong message. She offered her party's support to the government in the war against terror, underlining that the action conveyed India's resolve to prevent further infiltration and attacks on its security forces as well as is people.[79]

At the time of the surgical strike, the BJP was a part of the state government of Jammu and Kashmir along with the Jammu and Kashmir Peoples Democratic Party (PDP).

Barring the BJP's coalition partner and Jammu and Kashmir chief minister, Mehbooba Mufti, who was concerned that escalation of the situation along the border in the form of a confrontation could lead to a disaster of epic proportions, there were also some like Arvind Kejriwal, the founder-leader of the Aam Aadmi Party (AAP) and the chief minister of Delhi who, while lauding the prime minister, asked the government to release footage of the strikes ostensibly to counter Pakistan's smear campaign.[80] Pakistan flew in a group of forty journalists representing international media outlets, including CNN, BBC, Reuters, Associated Press, *Newsweek*, to areas around the LOC to independently investigate and debunk India's claims of the cross-border strike.[81] When asked by the Indian media if the government planned to release any footage of the surgical strike, Rajnath Singh simply said: 'Wait and watch.' Following the September 2016 surgical strike, there was a 45 per cent drop in cross-border infiltration. In June 2018, a video of the surgical strike was made public and, in September 2018, as the second anniversary of the surgical strike approached, a second video from a UAV (unmanned aerial vehicle) showing a terror launch pad being destroyed was released by the Modi government.[82]

Despite the massive press that the surgical strike generated, a significant repercussion went largely under-reported in the Indian media. A thirteen-member committee of the Aiwān-e-Bālā or Senate, the Pakistani equivalent of the Rajya Sabha, came up with 'policy guidelines' that suggested a new strategy to check India's growing stature in a diplomatic battle with Pakistan. The Senate made tactical recommendations to the Nawaf Sharif government to play up caste and religious fissures in India by talking about Dalits, unhappy Muslims and encourage those opposing Prime Minister Modi. Adopting the report of the committee, the Senate also recommended revival of backchannel talks with India and bilateral confidence-building measures as well as the ones related to the Kashmir issue. It recommended hiring international lobbyists and strategic communication firms besides engaging the Pakistani community living abroad to change the global narrative about Pakistan. The twenty-two-point policy guidelines unabashedly advised the Pakistan government to exploit 'India's own fault-lines in their alienated Muslims, Sikhs, Christians and Dalits' as also that 'the growing Maoist insurgency (should) be highlighted'.[83] The Sharif government was advised to reach out to those segments of Indian public opinion that were opposed to [PM] Modi's 'extremism and his anti-Pakistan policies including political parties, media, civil society organizations and human rights groups'.[84] The Senate's document in effect put in public domain what had always been the unsaid official policy of Pakistan and its bodies such as the ISI.

The year that had started with a terrorist attack on Pathankot and witnessed India retaliate like never before to cross-broader terrorism would eventually end up with a surgical strike of another kind, on black money—the bold and unexpected decision of the Modi government to demonetize all 500- and 1000-rupee bank notes. On 8 November 2016, in a live television address to the nation, Prime Minister Modi announced that currency notes of both denominations would no longer be valid and that the government would issue new 500- and 2000-rupee bank notes in exchange for the demonetized ones. The urgent action was undertaken to curtail the shadow economy, reduce the use of illicit and counterfeit cash to fund illegal activity and terrorism. The purpose would have been defeated if the plans were leaked and besides Modi, only a handful of people knew about the demonetization move. The plan was initiated nearly six to ten months before it was announced but such was the secrecy that even the Union cabinet had no clue. In fact, it was believed that most of the cabinet, including Finance Minister Arun

Jaitley, was briefed just minutes before the prime minister's television appearance.[85] Most political parties that opposed the BJP such as the Trinamool Congress (TMC), the AAP and the CPI (M) criticized the move but Bihar's Nitish Kumar and Andhra Pradesh's N. Chandrababu Naidu supported Modi's decision.[86] Former chief election commissioner of India S.Y. Quraishi opined that demonetization could lead to long-term electoral reforms and the Congress, while welcoming the move as an instrument to fight corruption and black money, raised serious apprehensions over the fallout.

The decision momentarily slowed India's growth rate and industrial production but there was also an increase in the number of income tax returns filed, from 43.3 million to 52.9 million in the financial year 2016–17. There was a decrease in Maoist activities too. According to security agencies, Naxalites envisage collecting thrice their annual requirement (one year's requirement, plus one year's reserve and another year's requirement). Demonetization invalidated a lot of the stored currency of high denominations, so the activities of the ultras could be controlled. Terror activities in Jammu and Kashmir also reportedly came down.[87]

With state legislative elections scheduled in seven states in 2017, the move was considered suicidal by most experts. It took the economy a couple of quarters to get back on track and the period of October to December 2017 saw the GDP touch a growth rate of 7.2 per cent. Irrespective of the initial reactions and the effects, the average citizen not only seemed to welcome Modi government's move but also gave it a resounding approval.[88] The BJP and its allies formed the government in six out of seven state legislative assemblies, including Rajnath Singh's home state, Uttar Pradesh.

13

The Sky As a Shelter

When Rajnath Singh took over as the home minister of India, the general approach of the ministry was to try and cope rather than get on top of things. The 'will cope' attitude had invariably become the standard way of handling things largely because of the lag between intention and action. Under Singh, the MHA shifted gears to 'resolve' things as opposed to 'managing' them. This has been the approach of the Modi government across various ministries. Since 2014, the government has initiated new measures and schemes, tweaked the already existing ones and streamlined delivery mechanisms.

The change in the overall approach towards internal and external security concerns of India, initiated by the government, were visible in a number of cases through 2017–18. As a policy, the government has given security forces a free hand to engage with the enemy, be it within the geographical border or beyond, as long as protocol is followed. Singh told the forces in Kashmir to not be the first to engage, but if it came to action to not count their bullets while retaliating. Compared to the corresponding period of the previous year, there was a 45 per cent decrease in cross-border infiltration from Pakistan over a six-month period.[1] The message had gone across that response was going to be swift and unforgiving and that India would no longer be pushed around.

The MHA constantly reviewed the ground situation to ensure that any tactic to weed out insurgency or threat to national security was not cast in stone. An ever-evolving approach made changing tactics and adapting to progressing scenarios a way of life for security forces. Attempts were still under way to thwart the progress the paramilitary forces were making. In April 2017, in the deadliest Naxalite–Maoist attack in seven years, 300 insurgents ambushed a ninety-nine-member strong CRPF battalion that left twenty-six jawans dead. This was the largest ambush since the 2010 Dantewada attack. The battalion, entrusted with the task of providing security to a road construction project, was patrolling an interior road.[2] Three or four sections of the battalion, which had nearly 1000 personnel, were separated from each other by about 600 to 700 metres. The Naxals took away the radio sets of the CRPF so they would not be able to call for help and a second team walked right into the ambush as they had not heard from their colleagues at the scheduled time.[3]

As he paid homage to the martyrs in Chhattisgarh, Singh said that the cold-blooded killing of the CRPF personnel would not deter either development work or anti-insurgency operations. Taking stock of the situation, Singh briefed the prime minister upon his return to Delhi and later called a meeting to initiate an overhaul of the operations in Bastar. The attack called for a revision of the standard operating procedure. In addition to a redeployment of forces, special operations under the command of COBRA (Commando Battalion for Resolute Action), the CRPF's elite jungle warfare unit, were going to be a part of the operations. Singh asked the forces to go on an 'all-out offensive' towards which end the government made strategic changes.[4] The CRPF's central zone was shifted to the capital of Chhattisgarh from Kolkata. In addition to nearly 40,000 boots on the ground, there were also thirty-six flying assets of different categories operating from Bhilai, which was nearly 300 kilometres from Sukma and Bastar. Travelling that big a distance before they could be deployed to conduct any operation defeated their purpose.[5] As such, the technical command centre of the unmanned aerial vehicles was shifted to Bastar, the Naxal hotbed in the state, to provide the security forces enhanced aerial surveillance to conduct anti-Maoist operations. The MHA also sanctioned the expansion of the base to hold at least 300 UAVs to provide technical intelligence and information to the troops.

In a review meeting with the district magistrates and superintendents of police of the thirty-five districts that bore the brunt of left-wing extremism, Rajnath Singh outlined the government's strategy, 'SAMADHAN', to tackle the issue—a mix of smart leadership, aggressive strategy, motivation and training, actionable intelligence, dashboard-based key result areas and key performance indicators, harnessing technology, action plan for each theatre and no access to financing. Singh also pushed for the fulfilment of the development projects under the additional central assistance (ACA), which furthered the previous integrated action plan (IAP) with a focus on expediting the construction of roads under the Road Requirement Plan (RRP-I).[6] Between 2014 and 2017, roads covering a distance of nearly 1504 kilometres were constructed in the most difficult areas, efforts were made to enhance skill development with the sanction of nine ITIs and fourteen skill development centres. There was also a concentrated effort to boost education infrastructure in Bijapur and Sukma by starting two Kendriya Vidyalayas along with three Jawahar Navodaya Vidyalayas (JNV), a school for gifted students.[7] The government also approved a Rs 200-crore upgradation of the Jagdalpur Medical College as a centre of excellence.

To increase local representation in CRPF's combat layout in the Bastar area, the MHA formed a 'Bastariya Battalion'—consisting of 534 tribal youth, including 189 women, from the most 'highly Naxal-infested' districts of Chhattisgarh: Bijapur, Dantewada, Narayanpur and Sukma—in April 2017. Arising from the CRPF's civic action programme that was designed to win hearts, the Bastariya Battalion recruits came from deep within the jungles of Bastar and were trained for a year in drills, physical and unarmed combat training, the handling of weapons and also in survival techniques in the jungle, which included living off the land, casualty evacuation and jungle warfare exercises and tactics.

On 21 May 2018, Singh, along with Chhattisgarh chief minister Raman Singh, was present at the passing-out parade of Battalion 241 of the CRPF, the first-ever Bastariya Battalion, in Ambikapur. Rajnath Singh told the media that the decision to raise a local battalion was a well-thought-out one. The recruits were trained knowing that there could be a conflict in their minds as the Maoists they had to fight could be from their own villages, and even people they grew up with. As a result, a considerable amount of time was spent in telling them that there was no 'enemy' but that people had to be brought back to the right path.[8]

Besides the development push and strengthening of operations, there was another factor that led to a decrease in Naxalite–Maoist attacks towards the end of 2017—ageing leadership and the lack of an effective second-rung. The average age of the leadership in the central committee, the apex decision-making body of the outlawed Communist Party of India (Maoist), was in the mid-fifties.[9] In the last week of December 2017, fifty-five-year-old Ginugu Narsimha Reddy, known as 'Jampanna', a much-celebrated member of the central committee, surrendered along with his wife,

Hinge Anitha, thirty-seven, a district committee member of
the CPI (Maoist)'s Kalahandi–Kandhamal–Boudh–Nayagarh
divisional committee. After spending thirty-three years as a
Maoist, Reddy, who carried a reward of Rs 25 lakh, chose to
give up the extremist ideology after differences with the party.[10]
The year 2016 reflected a decline of 53 per cent in the number
of violent incidents and a nearly 72 per cent decrease in deaths
caused by left-wing extremism when compared to the previous
year. The trend continued and in 2017 there was a further
decline by 25.6 per cent. Over a four-year period, from 2014 to
2018, fifty-eight of the seventy-six districts reported a drop in
violence. Of the fifty-eight districts, thirty accounted for nearly
90 per cent of cases of left-wing extremist violence.

All this while the MHA was in consultation with the states,
continuously reviewing the affected districts to keep resources
in sync with the changes on ground. In 2018, the MHA
added eight districts to the security-related expenditure (SRE)
scheme, but the biggest indicator of the transformation was the
exclusion of forty-four districts from the list.[11] During the 2018
'Vijay Diwas' celebrations that mark India's military victory over
Pakistan on 16 December 1971 during the war for the liberation
of Bangladesh, Singh informed members of the media that the
number of districts affected by left-wing extremism had gone
down from ninety to just twelve.[12] Although Singh was satisfied
with what the security agencies had achieved, not being able to
wipe out the Naxal–Maoist menace completely remained one
of his unfulfilled dreams.

The Modi government's decision to come down heavily
on the routes that fuelled the financial component of terror
organizations as well as the ones suspected of funnelling money
for such outfits played a major role in checking Naxalite–Maoist
insurgencies and also terror activities in Kashmir. There had
been concerted efforts from various governments in India to

regulate the acceptance and utilization of foreign contribution or foreign hospitality. In 2010, the UPA government had updated the Foreign Contribution Regulation Act (FCRA) towards this end. Under the Act's terms, civil society groups could receive funds from abroad—whether from governments or private foundations and individuals—only if they were granted the right by the Indian government, and such permission could be denied if the activities were found to be against national interest.

In 2008, a report submitted to the Maharashtra state home department had listed concrete evidence of nearly fifty-six NGOs that were raising funds and conducting recruitment for Naxalites. In a report published in *Daily News & Analysis* in March 2008, a senior officer from the state intelligence department who had sent the report shared how NGOs based out of Mumbai, Pune and Nagpur, working under the umbrella of the Tactical United Front (TUF) and the All India People's Resistance Forum (AIPRF)—a conglomerate of groups sympathizing with the Naxal cause—were channelling funds through various conduits. They were also instrumental in brainwashing new recruits, primarily locals and tribals from Gadchiroli, Chandrapur, Bhandara and Yavatmal districts.[13] By 2013, the UPA government had identified 128 such organizations working under various pretexts for Naxals in sixteen Indian states, including even relatively unaffected areas, which highlighted the spread of left-wing insurgency.[14] According to an internal report prepared by the Intelligence Bureau, these bodies were active even in states such as Uttarakhand and Uttar Pradesh that have seen little or no Naxal-related violence. In 2013, the NIA unearthed ten cases related to funding of terrorist groups. Investigations revealed how almost Rs 600 crore had been pumped in for terror operations through donations and relief funds collected over a period of two years. The NIA followed the money trail to discover how the Jammu and Kashmir Affectees Relief Fund Trust (JKART), an organization founded in the early 1990s to provide health care, food and shelter to Kashmiri families displaced by the conflict, single-handedly diverted nearly Rs 95 crore to Pakistan-based militant groups, chiefly the Hizbul Mujahideen.[15]

Unlike the previous dispensation, the Modi government tackled the issue of foreign funding of NGOs for suspected anti-national activities head-on. In September 2015, much to the chagrin of international bodies that termed the government's crackdown aggressive, the MHA cancelled the registration of Greenpeace India. Five months before the cancellation, the MHA suspended the organization's licence, giving it a 180-day notice to reply to charges of attempting to 'delay and place illegal obstructions to India's energy plans', 'campaigning, protesting and lobbying against government of India's policies', and also playing an anti-nuclear 'full page colour advertisement'. The notice also cited 'talks' with the Aam Aadmi Party.[16] Although there was much chest-beating about the manner in which the MHA had cracked down on NGOs, it wasn't long before the question of why some NGOs would be reluctant to declare details about funds received from overseas sources and how they were utilized in India came up.

In its investigation, the MHA found over 1000 NGOs that were using foreign funds in clear violation of various provisions of FCRA, 2010. In May 2017, the MHA asked NGOs to file their missing annual returns pertaining to financial years 2010–11 to 2014–15. Organizations and NGOs that received foreign funding but had failed to file annual returns included educational institutions as well. Once the stipulated one month was over, it served a show-cause notice to 5922 NGOs to explain why their FCRA registration may not be cancelled and asked over 2000 NGOs to validate their FCRA-designated bank accounts.[17] Through the year the MHA gave several opportunities to defaulting NGOs, but a large number of these organizations did not adhere to the stipulated rules and, by the end of 2017, the MHA cancelled the licences of 4842 such organizations and NGOs. In April 2018, the MHA informed the Parliament that the government had cancelled licences of over 14,000 NGOs/associations over a four-year period from 2014 to 2018.[18]

Nearly every major people's movement showed links to certain elements taking advantage of disaffection through various social media platforms to fuel violent agitation. In some cases, the Twitter handles pushing the agenda originated from outside the country. With 20,000 active FCRA-registered organizations receiving foreign currencies worth Rs 18,065 crore to execute various social, cultural, economic, educational and religious activities in a single financial year, 2016–17, the security implications were scary. The clampdown had international ramifications as well. Following an audit that had been under way since 2011, the Government of Canada revoked the 'charity' status of two NGOs—Islamic Services of Canada and Canadian Islamic Trust Foundation—for possibly funding Pakistani militants.[19] The money collected in Canada was being remitted to the Relief Organization of Kashmiri Muslims (ROKM) that the Canada Revenue Agency discovered was the charitable arm of Jamaat-e-Islami. By mid-2018, the MHA put in place an 'Online Analytical Tool' to monitor flow and utilization of authorized foreign contributions received by various organizations. The portal integrated the bank accounts of the FCRA-registered entities through the public financial management system and provided real-time update of transactions, allowing government departments to conduct big data mining of foreign funds, their actual use in the country and allowed evidence-based decisions to enforce FCRA compliance.[20]

Even as the government sought to check the funding mechanism that fuelled insurgency in Kashmir, it continued to engage across the political spectrum both at the state as well as national level. Since taking over as home minister, Rajnath Singh had visited Kashmir on multiple occasions to conduct on-the-spot assessment of the situation and interact with officers of security agencies and a cross-section of society. The BJP was in alliance with the PDP in Jammu and Kashmir since 2016, after a fractured mandate saw both parties join hands to form a coalition government. To find a possible solution to the prolonged unrest following the death of Burhan Wani, Singh led an all-party delegation on a two-day visit to the state in September 2016. Besides the minister of state in the PMO, Jitendra Singh, and then finance minister, Arun Jaitley, Singh was accompanied by leaders of the opposition in the Rajya Sabha and the Lok Sabha, Ghulam Nabi Azad and Mallikarjun Kharge respectively, senior Congress leader Ambika Soni, Ram Vilas Paswan of the Lok Janshakti Party, Sharad Yadav of JD (U), CPI's Sitaram Yechury and D. Raja, the NCP's Tariq Anwar and Saugata Roy, the Shiv Sena's Sanjay Raut and Anandrao Adsul, the TDP's Thota Narasimham, the Shiromani Akali Dal's Prem Singh Chandumajra, the Biju Janata Dal's Dilip Tirkey, Asaduddin Owaisi of the All India Majlis-e-Ittehad-ul Muslimeen (AIMIM), the All India United Democratic Front's Badaruddin Ajmal and the Muslim League's E. Ahamed, besides representatives of the Telangana Rashtra Samithi, Revolutionary Socialist Party, AIADMK, DMK, YSR-Congress, RJD, AAP and the Rashtriya Lok Dal.[21]

Apart from meeting the governor and the chief minister of the state, the MPs held meetings with representatives of all political parties and other delegations. To counter incidents of stone pelting in the state, security forces had been using pellet guns which were considered non-lethal. But following reports of some incidents, the MHA decided to constitute a seven-member expert committee to explore other alternatives. The committee, headed by the joint secretary in the home ministry, T.V.S.N. Prasad, submitted its report in August 2016 and recommended the use of Pelargonic Acid Vanillyl Amide (PAVA), an organic compound in chilli pepper as an alternative to pellet guns. In September 2016, Singh approved the use of the bio-safe PAVA shells that would cause severe irritation and paralyse the victim for a short duration but with a caveat that it would be used only in the 'rarest of the rare' cases.[22]

Despite all efforts, the situation in the Valley continued to remain tense from mid-2016 till early 2017 due to what was being called the 'Burhan aftermath'. Stone pelting, a prominent feature of protests from 2008 onwards, had attained a whole new dimension by 2016–17 when over 2690 stone-pelting incidents were reported across various districts, with Baramulla alone witnessing 492 incidents followed by Srinagar and Kupwara with 339 each. While journalists and other experienced observers felt there was a difference between the protests of the 1990s and those after 2010—the former had a strong anti-India undercurrent, the latter, despite featuring anti-India slogans like 'aazadi', was 'specifically directed at the security forces in the context of the brutal killings of innocent boys'[23]—local commentators were of the opinion that the street protests were spontaneous gatherings and warned that if such manifestation of outrage was suppressed by force it could merge with the larger separatist movement. An investigation conducted by *India Today* in March 2017 revealed these so-called 'spontaneous' protests as planned events organized by people based out of the Valley where each stone-pelter was paid anywhere between Rs 5000 and 7000 a month.[24] The masterminds used the Internet to organize stone-pelting across various locations and gave specific instructions to target JK police personnel, army jawans, MLAs and government vehicles.

In July 2016, the Army moved an entire brigade into south Kashmir as a part of 'Operation Calm Down' that commenced in September to put an end to the protests that had gone on for nearly three months. With over 4000 additional troops deployed under Operation Calm Down to clear militants, the MHA had issued direct instructions to use minimal force. There were reports of nearly 100 militants also crossing into south Kashmir since the unrest broke and the Army had fanned out in all the four districts of south Kashmir—Pulwama, Shopian, Anantnag and Kulgam. After a few instances of the Army facing stone-pelting, the MHA got the local police to rent out armoured jeeps to the Army to help in the combing operations. The CRPF and the state police also assisted the MHA in clearing the roadblocks the protesters had put up by felling trees, electric poles and placing huge boulders and burnt vehicles.

The government's attempt to check the inflow of foreign funding of NGOs also led to the NIA claiming that the hardline Syed Ali Shah Geelani faction of the All Parties Hurriyat Conference (APHC) was involved in running hawala networks to finance the Hizbul Mujahideen and other militant groups in Jammu and Kashmir.[25] A charge sheet filed by the NIA in January 2018 in the terror-funding case that named the Lashkar-e-Taiba chief Hafiz Mohammed Saeed and Hizbul Mujahideen chief Syed Salahuddin pointed to links between them and the top leadership of several Kashmiri separatist groups that are part of the All Party Hurriyat Conference.[26] The ISI had not only used Wani's encounter to ignite rebellion across the state by supplying money to the tune of nearly Rs 800 crore to Kashmiri separatist leaders, but also patronized stone-pelters by releasing a song titled 'Sangbaaz' or stone-pelters with lyrics that went, 'You can gouge out our eyes, but you cannot snatch our dream'.[27]

Between July 2017 and May 2018, the government of India undertook a massive mission to deliver what could probably be the final body blow to terrorism in Jammu and Kashmir. After months of planning and research, the MHA, along with the country's top security establishment, came up with a list of as many as 258 militants belonging to different terror groups like LeT, JeM, HM and Al-Badr to be flushed out as part of an operation to establish lasting peace in the Valley. The list included 130 local and 128 foreign terrorists who were identified after a secret district-wise survey that also earmarked prime locations of terrorist activities as well as hideouts. The operation included the Indian Army, CRPF, the BSF, the IB and Jammu and Kashmir Police and was initiated by the MHA with the singular aim of not stopping until there was complete peace. Although some media outlets shared a few details of the mission that had come to be referred as 'Operation All Out', the top-secret mission shifted gears after suspected LeT operatives attacked Amarnath pilgrims in July 2017, killing eight civilians and leaving eighteen grievously injured. In the midst of recurring stone-pelting incidents, the Central government decided to suspend operations in May 2018, which also coincided with Ramzan, but a later review made extending the ceasefire beyond Ramzan untenable. As of December 2018, 238 terrorists had been killed in 587 incidents that also saw eighty-six security personnel lay down their lives in the course of duty.

During a two-day visit to the state in June 2018, Rajnath Singh sanctioned Rs 14.30 crore for block-level sports in Jammu and Kashmir to enable the youth in the state to participate in the Union sports ministry's 'Khelo India' scheme along with the rest of the country. When Singh revisited the state a month later, he assessed the security situation and found it conducive enough to go ahead with the decision to conduct the first-ever local-body elections in over a decade and panchayat elections that were last held in 2011. Singh's decision was epoch-making as it would not only ensure the long-overdue restoration of democracy at a grass-roots level in the state, but also push the average Kashmiri to participate in making decisions that would impact them directly.

When it came to Kashmir, nearly every single expert mentioned 'Kashmiriyat', 'Insaniyat' and 'Jamhooriyat' or the social consciousness and cultural values of the Kashmiri people, humanitarianism and democracy. The government's decision to try Jamhooriyat with the same gusto as Kashmiriyat and Insaniyat gave an entire generation of Kashmiris the power to be masters of their own destiny for the first time. The elections were held in nine phases between October and December 2018 and paved the way for the duly constituted local bodies receiving central grants to the tune of nearly Rs 4335 crore from the Fourteenth Finance Commission. Despite the two main political parties of the state, the NC and the PDP, calling for a boycott of the elections on the grounds of the Central government's stand on Article 35A, which grants special privileges to residents of Jammu and Kashmir, the elections saw people turn up and elect representatives who would be directly responsible for the implementation of subjects under the 73rd Amendment of the Constitution of India, such as the primary health centres, primary schools, Anganwadi centres, etc. The polls gave the panchayats the power to generate their own funds, including building permission fee, taxes on entertainment, advertisement, hoardings, various kinds of businesses and profession. They also made the local representatives responsible for the implementation of national schemes and supplemented their coffers by both central and state government funds for

MGNERGA, PMAY, ICDS, Mid-Day Meal, etc., schemes. The local body elections increased the financial powers of a standard panchayat tenfold from Rs 10,000 to Rs 1 lakh, gave block councils Rs 250,000 instead of Rs 25,000 and also made the chief executive councillors the chairman of all tourism development authorities.

These were more than mere indicators of power trickling down. By making the grass-roots play a role in revenue generation, Rajnath Singh brought the concern for safety to the doorsteps of each and every home across towns and villages of Jammu and Kashmir and made the common folk initiators of the peace process.

If India confronted its internal security threats with an iron hand, it also demonstrated a tough stance while addressing external issues. The country adopted a mix of diplomacy, soft power and tough posturing to change its image across global platforms. In his maiden speech at the United Nation General Assembly in 2014, Modi chose to shun playing to the gallery. Instead of the traditional approach of simply reiterating India's commitment to peace and the United Nations' endeavours across the globe or calling for reforms in the UN's Security Council, thus underlining India's claim for a permanent seat, Modi used the platform to set out the agenda of India that he envisioned. The first tool he used to make India a global trailblazer was to call for an International Day of Yoga. Modi's offer to let yoga lead a shift in the world's consciousness was testimony to India's out-of-the box thinking in diplomacy and foreign policy. Also, for the first time in the history of the United Nations, 177 member states decided to co-sponsor a resolution, thus ensuring it was adopted without a vote.

Keeping the spread of yoga in mind and the increased interest in Indian medicinal systems, the MHA included yoga-based programmes in the list of permissible activities under the tourist visa. Besides soft power such as yoga and culture, the

Modi government—through the visits of the prime minister himself and senior cabinet ministers such as Rajnath Singh and Sushma Swaraj—laid the foundation of new working relationships with most countries of the Middle East that were previously driven either by economic compulsion or a general resentment towards Pakistan.

In August 2015, Modi became the first Indian prime minister to visit the United Arab Emirates (UAE) in over three decades after Indira Gandhi in 1981. In the course of the historic visit, the UAE assured increasing trade between the two nations by 60 per cent, announced an initial allocation of US$ 2 billion for investments in infrastructure projects in India along with a promise to invest US$ 75 billion in India's plans for rapid expansion, while allocating 55,000 sq. m. of land for the construction of the first traditional Hindu stone temple in the Middle East.[28] During his visit to Bahrain in October 2016, Rajnath Singh met King Hamad bin Isa Al Khalifa. In the course of his interactions with the interior minister, Lt-General Shaikh Rashid bin Abdullah Al Khalifa, as the two countries reaffirmed their strong stance against all forms of terrorism, Singh repeated what he had said during his visit to Pakistan: a terrorist in one country cannot be glorified as freedom fighters by another.

Singh's visit assumed greater importance as the Organisation of Islamic Cooperation (OIC), of which both Pakistan and Bahrain were members, had backed Pakistan on the Kashmir issue and had also asked India to cease 'atrocities' in the Valley.[29] Singh was expected to not only address this prickly issue but also nurture an environment that would garner support for India's stand vis-à-vis Kashmir by pointing to Pakistan's role in waging a proxy war against India through cross-border terrorism. In his meeting with both King Hamad and the interior minister, Singh conveyed Pakistan's refusal to give up terrorism as an instrument of state policy and, as a result, India's reluctance to take at face value any assurances that Pakistan provided in this regard. Singh signed a number of MoUs whereby both India and Bahrain would combat international terrorism, transnational organized crime and human trafficking as well as trafficking in illicit drugs and narcotics, and also fight money laundering.

In Saudi Arabia, PM Modi renewed the 2006 information-sharing agreement between the two countries signed by King Abdullah and Manmohan Singh, and signed agreements pertaining to cooperation in exchange of intelligence related to money laundering, crimes and terrorism financing. Both countries further agreed to take action against illegal transfer of money.[30] During his visit, Modi and Crown Prince Mohammed bin Salman, who was also the defence minister, decided to intensify bilateral defence cooperation through visits by military personnel and experts, joint military exercises and visits of ships and aircraft and supply of arms and ammunition and their joint development.

Between 2014 and 2018, India signed a series of agreements with the United States of America, Switzerland, United Arab Emirates, the Russian Federation, the United Kingdom, Australia and Thailand, among others, on exchange of terrorist-screening information, return of illegal migrants, intelligence sharing, cybercrimes, coordination of home land security, checking extremism and radicalization, besides steps to check illegal financial transaction. India also entered into an understanding on capacity building to fight terrorism and police training development activities with Maldives and Afghanistan, besides regular interactions with other Asian countries, including SAARC partners and Japan cemented India's new approach.

India's commitment to upholding democratic values was emphasized every time the government interacted on an international platform. During a symposium in Tokyo on Shared Values and Democracy in Asia, the MHA, represented by Kiren Rijiju, underlined India's devotion to working together with the world to preserve and promote non-conflicting traditions.[31]

The defining moment of how the 'new' India responded came in the middle of the Modi government's term in office during the two-month-long border stand-off between the Indian armed forces and the People's Liberation Army of China over the construction of a road in Doklam by the Chinese. On 16 June 2017, Chinese troops started extending a road southward of Doklam, a territory that both China and Bhutan claim. India stood by its ally Bhutan and, on 18 June 2017, around 270 Indian troops stopped the Chinese from constructing the road. One of the worst border disputes between India and China in decades, the stand-off attracted international attention. The dispute over whether a small piece of land, only about 34 sq. miles, belonged to China or Bhutan was seen as pivotal in the growing competition between China and India over the future of Asia. Throughout the confrontation, India refused to blink or give in to the demands of the Chinese, even as the latter termed India's action a pretext to interfere in and impede the boundary talks between China and Bhutan, accused India of standing in the way of peace and also indicated that it had notified India in advance about its plans to construct a road.[32]

As the Indian army was squaring off against the Chinese troops, Rahul Gandhi, who was then vice-president of the Congress, met the Chinese ambassador and said that it was his job to be informed. Although initially the Congress party refused to confirm or deny the meeting, later Rahul Gandhi tweeted, 'And for the record, I am not the guy sitting on the swing while a thousand Chinese troops had physically entered India,' a reference to the photo-op between Narendra Modi with Chinese President Xi Jinping during the Chinese premier's visit to India in 2014.[33]

After two months, the crisis that threatened to erupt into an armed conflict between the two nations finally blew over when, on 28 August 2017, both China and India pulled back troops.[34] From India's point of view, the Chinese stopping construction and withdrawing to its June 2017 position was what it had set out to achieve, but from the Chinese perspective it was India that withdrew from what it claimed to be their territory. There were two 'victories' for India in the entire episode. One, both China and India had maintained diplomatic communication throughout, which showed that diplomacy could avert military confrontation. Two, and more importantly, the manner in which India dealt with the deadlock by standing firm in the face of China's relentless provocation showed the world that Beijing's expansionist ambition is not unstoppable.[35]

India's restraint in the Doklam stand-off enhanced its profile amongst nations emerging as new powers in the region. With Doklam, India also strengthened partnerships with South and Southeast Asian nations, especially those who have territorial and maritime disputes with China. On 9 June, a few days before the Doklam crisis erupted, India was invited to become a full-time member of the Shanghai Cooperation Organisation (SCO), which was being seen as the Asian answer to NATO (North Atlantic Treaty Organization). India becoming a permanent member of the SCO with China and Russia, besides Kazakhstan, Kyrgyzstan, Tajikistan and Uzbekistan, gave the SCO a pan-Asian identity. Also with two of the world's most populous nations as members, the SCO would effectively be speaking on behalf of half of humanity.

On 24–25 August 2017, before the de-escalation of troops in Doklam, Rajnath Singh led the Indian delegation to the SCO summit in Ata, Kyrgyz Republic.[36] In his opening statement,

Singh expressed his gratitude to all member-states of the SCO for their support for India's membership and moved a proposal to organize a joint urban earthquake search and rescue exercise to improve collective preparedness. The visit was of immense bilateral significance and showed India's growing heft as a power worth engaging with. Singh's meeting with his Chinese counterpart at the SCO summit was also a precursor to the Modi–Xi Jinping bilateral meet during the BRICS (Brazil, Russia, India, China and South Africa) summit in Beijing from 3 to 5 September.[37]

The basic difference in the approach of the Modi-led NDA-II government and UPA-I and UPA-II under Manmohan Singh was the manner in which India enhanced its clout as a major player in nearly every sphere. Both internally as well as while negotiating with the outside world, the mantra was simple—this 'new' India was not going to be second to anyone. This new approach was most visible in the way India began to deal with its oil imports. Through 'oil diplomacy' efforts focused on Russia, Latin America and Africa between 2014 and 2018, India renegotiated supply contracts with countries that it bought oil from, increased its investments in buying oil fields in Russia where, taken together with older investments in Sakhalin, Indian investment in strategic oil and gas sectors touched nearly US $10 billion, and engaged with both the United States and Russia as part of its agenda to diversify away from acute dependence on the OPEC.[38] India changed the rules of the game when it began to import crude oil from the United States and the move sent a message to the OPEC that the world's third-largest consumer had other options.

India managed to do the near impossible by getting other Asian giants such as China, Japan and South Korea to come onboard to push OPEC to treat Asian buyers as primary markets. With Dharmendra Pradhan, the petroleum minister, raising the issue of OPEC charging Asian nations a premium for imported crude when compared with European and US importers, talks about China and India forming an oil buyers' club were seen as an indication of the rise of a new cartel that could force OPEC to think of setting new and fair prices for Asian consumers.[39] The realization that India and China alone accounted for 17 per cent of the world's oil consumption and India's willingness to explore new markets like Venezuela which was ready to sell in Indian rupees to circumvent US sanctions, pushed OPEC to place India in a different league.[40]

In December 2018, despite US President Donald Trump urging[41] OPEC to keep oil prices low by not restricting its production, the Saudi energy minister Khalid Al-Falih publicly said that OPEC would consider Prime Minister Modi's views before taking any decision on global crude oil prices.[42] Moving beyond physical connectivity, through energy diplomacy India quietly created grids in its neighbourhood that matched China's ambitious One Belt One Road (OBOR) initiative in which India was the only South Asian country not to be involved. Singh visited Mongolia in June 2018 and, along with the Mongolian prime minister, Ukhnaagiin Khürelsükh, attended the ground-breaking ceremony of the construction of the first-ever oil refinery in the country that was funded by India.[43] The refinery would end Mongolia's dependence on Russian fuel and the refinery based in the southern Dornogovi province would be capable of processing 1.5 million tonnes of crude oil per year, which amounts to 30,000 barrels per day.

India broke geopolitical barriers through enhanced cooperation with Nepal, Bhutan, Bangladesh, Sri Lanka, Mauritius, Indonesia and Myanmar by pushing old projects that had been languishing for years and initiating new ones as well in hydroelectric power generation and distribution, supplying diesel, supplying gas to power plants, upgrading refineries, building floating storage and regasification units (FSRU) for countries such as Indonesia to help it supply energy to thousands of its islands and sharing technical know-how in the use of LEDs and renewable energy.[44]

By the end of 2018, there were visible signs of the MHA managing to get an upper hand in dealing with issues that only a few years ago seemed an uphill task. Rajnath Singh's efforts to streamline the functioning of the MHA showed great results. Better inter-agency coordination between the army, paramilitary forces, the states' police, NIA and IB resulted in success in nearly every single mission undertaken. This coordination was responsible for the favourable outcomes security agencies enjoyed in Jammu and Kashmir, areas infested with left-wing extremism, insurgency in the north-east as well as the missions involving the killing of Lashkar-e-Taiba's top commander Abu Dujana, the arrest of Rubel Ahmed alias Munir ul Islam and Musharraf Hussain alias Musa of the Jamaat-ul-Mujahideen who had escaped from Bangladesh to Greater Noida, and those of individuals in Hyderabad with links to the Islamic State (IS).

Following months of investigation into the violence that erupted during the celebratory gathering of Dalit and Bahujan groups to mark the 200th year of the Bhima–Koregaon battle, in January 2018, the Pune police arrested activists Surendra P. Gadling, Sudhir P. Dhawale, Rona Jacob Wilson, Shoma Sen and Mahesh S. Raut under the Unlawful Activities Prevention Act.[45] The police claimed that evidence gathered during searches at different locations that led to these arrests indicated links between the five people and the banned outfit CPI (Maoist). Further investigations in August 2018 saw the arrests of more activists, including Maoist ideologue Varavara Rao, Arun Ferreira, lawyer Sudha Bharadwaj and Gautam Navlakha for their alleged links with Maoists.

The spread of the Naxalite–Maoist ideology in urban centres through sympathizers and front men acquired a frightening dimension following alleged threats against the prime minister in a laptop belonging to Rona Wilson the public relations secretary of the Committee for Release of Political Prisoners (CRPP). In the material recovered, the police claimed that Maoists proposed concrete steps to end the Modi era and plotted to kill the prime minister 'along the lines of another Rajiv Gandhi-type incident'.[46] Rajnath Singh chaired an inter-agency meeting to review the PM's security arrangements that was attended by senior officials of the Ministry of Home Affairs as well as NSA Ajit Doval, Home Secretary Rajiv Gauba and IB chief Rajiv Jain. He also directed all agencies to beef up the PM's security in the wake of the assassination threat.

The police crackdown on 'urban Naxalism' triggered massive outrage with politicians, activists and authors terming it as an attack on democratic rights. Some even likened the detention and raids to the declaration of Emergency.[47] A petition moved before the Supreme Court by historian Romila Thapar, economists Prabhat Patnaik and Devaki Jain, sociology professor Satish Deshpande and human rights lawyer Maja Daruwala challenged the arrests of Varavara Rao, Vernon Gonsalves, Arun Ferreira, Sudha Bharadwaj and Gautam Navlakha. Represented by a bunch of senior lawyers, including Abhishek Manu Singhvi, Dushyant Dave, Prashant Bhushan, Indira Jaising and Vrinda Grover, the petitioners claimed that the government was 'quelling dissent'. The three-judge SC bench headed by the then Chief Justice of India Dipak Misra directed the Pune police to place them under house arrest as they were 'professors and lawyers'.[48] The petitioners asked the SC for an independent probe into the arrests but the government, represented by Additional Solicitor General Tushar Mehta, argued that the arrests were made after an extensive investigation. In subsequent hearings, the SC in a 2:1 verdict not only refused the plea seeking the immediate release of the activists but also refused to interfere.

Justice D.Y. Chandrachud dissented with the majority view and noted that the arrest of the five accused was an attempt by the state to muzzle dissent and that, short of incitement to violence and subversion of elected government, dissent must be allowed in a democracy. The majority verdict, on the other hand, by CJI Misra and Justice A.M. Khanwilkar said the arrests were not merely because of differences in political views or dissent but that there was prima facie material to show their link with banned Maoists.[49]

India's internal security improved vastly under Rajnath Singh with no major terror attacks since June 2014. While earlier the news of a terror attack was commonplace, since Singh assumed charge, terror plans being foiled became a part and parcel of everyday news. One such big breakthrough came about in December 2018 when, after months of investigations, the NIA busted an ISIS-inspired module called Harkat-ul-Harb-e-Islam and arrested ten persons, foiling their attempts to carry out a series of blasts in and around the national capital.

This happened around the same time that the Opposition raked up the issue of the MHA allowing select security and intelligence agencies to intercept, monitor and decrypt any information generated, transmitted, received or stored in any computer resource. The MHA directive invited the collective ire of the Opposition that termed it an attempt to convert India into a surveillance state. The MHA was, in fact, only following an order in place since 2009 pertaining to surveillance.[50] Rule 4 of the Information Technology (Procedure and Safeguards for Interception, Monitoring and Decryption of Information) Rules, 2009, read with the Information Technology Act, 2000, gave the MHA the necessary authority.

The raids across seventeen places—six at Jaffrabad in
Seelampur of East Delhi and the rest in Lucknow, Amroha,
Hapur and Meerut districts of UP—also gave the average
Indian an idea of how the security agencies were on top of
their game. During the raid, 25 kg of explosives, a country-
made rocket launcher, twelve pistols, 112 clocks to work as
timers, 150 rounds of live ammunition, mobile-phone circuits,
batteries, fifty-one pipes, remote-control car-triggering switch,
wireless digital doorbell for remote switch, steel containers,
electric wires, ninety-one mobile phones, 134 SIM cards, three
laptops, knives, swords, ISIS-related literature and cash of
about Rs 7.5 lakh were recovered.[51]

A major contributor to the success security forces enjoyed
during this period was the effort to modernize the forces both in
terms of equipment as well as logistics and boosting their general
morale. At the twenty-second meeting of eastern and western
zonal councils in June 2016, that saw the participation of states
and Union Territories, in addition to discussing issues such as
measures to curb communal tensions, drug trafficking, those
related to fisheries, coastal security, issuance of biometric identity
cards and others, Singh broached the topic of modernization of
state police forces. Taking suggestions from various quarters, the
Union cabinet approved an umbrella scheme of 'Modernization
of Police Forces (MPF)' for the years 2017–18 to 2019–20 and
earmarked Rs 25,060 crore for the three-year period. Making
special provisions for internal security, law and order, security
for women, availability of modern weapons, mobility of police
forces, logistics support, hiring of helicopters, upgradation of
police wireless, operationalizing a national satellite network,
implementing the Crime and Criminal Tracking Network
and System (CCTNS) project, E-prison project and more, the
central government put up Rs 18,636 crore of the total financial
outlay while the rest, Rs 6424 crore, would be the states' share.

Nearly Rs 2000 crore of the modernization plan was dedicated
to the implementation of the CCTNS project under which the
MHA planned to integrate the various organs of the criminal
justice system such as the police, courts, prisons, prosecution,
forensic laboratories, fingerprints and juvenile homes under one
comprehensive database, which would provide investigators the
complete record history of any criminal anywhere across the
country.

On 21 August 2017, Rajnath Singh launched the Digital
Police Portal under the CCTNS project that enabled citizens
to register FIRs online and also seek antecedent verification
of prospective employees and tenants. In order to increase the
representation of women in police, Singh urged state governments
to reserve 33 per cent posts in police forces for women. Since
the then Tamil Nadu chief minister J. Jayalalithaa's decision to
start an All Women Police Station (AWPS) in 1992, India had
seen a steady increase in the number of AWPS that encouraged
more women to report crimes. Under Singh, several such police
stations were set up in Kohima and Dimapur and the state
government of Nagaland also raised a Mahila Battalion. The
MHA approved raising two women battalions for Jammu and
Kashmir Police while the CRPF deployed women commandos
in COBRA force for anti-Naxal operations.[52]

The MHA took cognisance of grievance redressal amongst
the Central Armed Police Forces (CAPF) and launched
a mobile application called 'BSF My App' that provided
a common system for all CAPF personnel to submit their
grievances. It also featured an in-built provision through which
a jawan could connect with the MHA and Singh personally,
who assured the jawans that the home minister of India was
just a click away.[53] To inspire the forces, the MHA enhanced
the honorarium of Special Police Officers (SPOs) of Jammu
and Kashmir to Rs 6000 per month from Rs 3000 per month

and made arrangements to increase the compensation to CAPF martyrs. Singh's top priority was to ensure that the families of those who laid down their lives in the line of duty get a compensation of at least Rs 1 crore. The family of a slain soldier of the Central Armed Police Forces that included the CRPF, the BSF, the ITBP, the CISF, the SSB, the NSG and Assam Rifles got about Rs 50–60 lakh. In addition to doing whatever the MHA could do officially, Singh connected with the average citizen to help fill the gap. The MHA launched a new website 'Bharat Ke Veer' where any Indian could donate up to Rs 15 lakh to any CAPF personnel killed in the line of duty.[54]

In its efforts towards strengthening the borders, India deployed Israeli 'SPYDER' air defence system for the Pakistan border. The state-of-the-art SPYDER (Surface-to-air PYthon and DERby missiles) replaced the Soviet-era Osa-AKM and 9K35 Strela-10 at six airbases and other critical locations along the western border. With a capability of neutralizing hostile targets up to 15 km away and at heights between 20 and 9000 metres, it would help in tackling any aircraft, cruise missile, surveillance plane or drone that tried to violate Indian airspace. The induction of SPYDER was delayed by three years after it was finalized in 2008 due to the non-availability of the Czech-made Tatra trucks, the acquisition process for which had got mired in a controversy over bribery allegations.[55]

Rajnath Singh also put in place a mix of measures such as fencing, increased border posts, making ten-metre-high walls stretching across 190 km and hi-tech surveillance systems to secure India's borders on both the western and eastern fronts. Singh inaugurated two pilot projects of smart fencing along the India–Pakistan border in Jammu under the Comprehensive Integrated Border Management System (CIBMS) programme that he had seen at work in Israel during his 2014 visit.[56]

The MHA had been considering the use of high-tech solutions for border security since 2012. In 2014, the BSF had submitted a detailed report on the CIBMS to the MHA. There was a meeting between the MHA and the BSF in March 2014 but no decision was taken to implement the system until January 2016. The Pathankot attack in early 2016 saw the MHA step on the accelerator to implement the CIMBS.[57] A first of its kind in India, the CIMBS covered a 5.5 km stretch along the international border and is designed to guard stretches where physical surveillance is not possible either due to inhospitable terrain or riverine borders. It created an invisible electronic barrier on land, water and even in air and underground that helped the BSF to detect and foil infiltration and smuggling bids.

The MHA also decided to launch a similar 60-km-long pilot project in Assam where internal security had already shown signs of improvement since Singh took office. The year 2017 recorded the lowest insurgency incidents and causalities amongst both civilians and security forces in nearly two decades. The region has seen a 63 per cent reduction in insurgency since 2014 and the lifting of the Armed Forces (Special Powers) Act (AFSPA) from all areas of Meghalaya on 31 March 2018 illustrated the vastly improving security scenario. The AFSPA was also abrogated in eight out of sixteen areas in Arunachal Pradesh. The Centre also extended the ceasefire with the National Socialist Council of Nagaland and the National Socialist Council of Nagaland/Reformation.

In a marked departure from before, the MHA interacted with the eight member states of the North Eastern Council for the effective implementation of the central government's financial packages such as the Rs 3000-crore special scheme to incentivize micro, small and medium enterprises sector in the region and an additional Rs 4500-crore package in 2018 to help focus on specific areas and better delivery of government-sponsored schemes.

The MHA also undertook the rollout of the draft National Register of Citizens (NRC) in Assam to update the register in compliance with the demands of the Assam Accord of 1985. Since Independence till 1971 Assam witnessed large-scale migration from East Pakistan. The migration continued even after the 1971 war for the liberation of Bangladesh. As per the Assam Accord, the NRC needed to be updated to identify and deport illegal migrants in the state. The cut-off date for inclusion in the NCR was 25 March 1971 when the war for the liberation of Bangladesh commenced. Indian citizens, including their children and descendants, who moved to Assam after 24 March 1971, would be eligible for inclusion in the updated NRC only after satisfactory proof of residence in any part of the country (outside Assam) as on 24 March 1971 was provided. Addressing the fears among various groups in the run-up to the draft NRC publication in Assam, Rajnath Singh assured every individual of justice and humane treatment. The process of updating the NRC was generally peaceful though the SC slammed the MHA in early 2019 for delays as the government sought permission to suspend all activities in view of the impending 2019 general elections.[58]

The NDA lost its ally in Assam, the Asom Gana Parishad, when the government presented the Citizenship (Amendment) Bill 2016 that aimed to provide citizenship to those displaced due to religious persecution for being from minority groups in Bangladesh, Pakistan and Afghanistan after due scrutiny and recommendations of district and state authorities. The government's decision to provide for persecuted Hindu, Sikh, Buddhist, Jain, Parsi and Christian communities from the neighbouring countries did not go down well. Protestors in Assam maintained that all immigrants who entered the country after 1971 should be deported irrespective of their religion. While presenting the Bill in Parliament, Singh said that these people for whom India was amending its law had no place to go to except India. He also assured that the Bill would not be limited to Assam.[59] The Bill was originally introduced in 2016 and tabled in early 2019 after including the recommendations of the Joint Parliamentary Committee.

The MHA also gave financial assistance to 5764 West Pakistan refugees settled in Jammu and Kashmir and facilitated the repatriation of Rohingya refugees from Bangladesh to Myanmar's Rakhine state. Singh's meeting with the prime minister of Bangladesh, Sheikh Hasina during his visit to Dhaka in 2018 went beyond the trappings of a routine event. During the meeting, Singh shared New Delhi's efforts to help. India constructed prefabricated houses in Rakhine for Rohingya returnees and also continued to provide relief materials to help Bangladesh deal with the needs of the refugees in relief camps.[60]

As a part of its neighbourhood-first policy, India also gifted the South Asia Satellite for the SAARC region that provided crucial information on tele-medicine, tele-education, banking and television broadcasting opportunities. The geostationary satellite was developed by the Indian Space Research Organization (ISRO) after PM Modi asked the scientists to work on a satellite that would provide a full range of applications and services to all of India's neighbours. While Pakistan did not join the project, Afghanistan, Bangladesh, Bhutan, the Maldives, Nepal and Sri Lanka make use of the multidimensional facilities provided by the satellite that is also equipped with remote sensing state-of-the-art technology which enables collection of real-time weather data and helps in observations of the geology of South Asian nations.

The Ministry of Home Affairs also pushed for an amendment of the five-decade-old Enemy Property (Amendment and

Validation) Act that ensured that the heirs of those who had migrated to Pakistan and China during Partition and afterwards will have no claim over the properties left behind in India. Rajnath Singh's push to change the forty-nine-year-old Act resulted in a windfall of Rs 100,000 crore for the government through the sale of nearly 9400 such properties.

In December 2018, ISRO launched the GSAT-7A, a satellite exclusive for the MHA to help further strengthen frontiers with Pakistan and Bangladesh. The GSAT-7A would enable real-time control and communication for the helicopters and UAV's operations, helping the Indian Air Force and the Indian Army to protect citizens. With this, Rajnath Singh made the sky a shelter for 1.25 billion Indians.

In early 2019, a Mood of the Nation poll conducted among 13,000 participants voted Rajnath Singh as the best-performing minister in the Narendra Modi government, which summed up both Singh and the MHA's impact on the lives of Indians. During the initial period of his tenure as home minister, Singh, always a man of few words, was often derided for his taciturn approach. Singh's use of the Hindi word 'ninda' or censure was ridiculed as the only response he had to acts of terror. However, it is under him that the security forces have made India much safer for the average man than ever before.

Epilogue

In March 2018, the Bharatiya Janata Party got an overwhelming majority in the Uttar Pradesh Assembly elections. It won 312 out the 403 legislative seats, even though it did not project a chief ministerial candidate before the election. Three days before the chief minister was announced, a reporter caught up with Rajnath Singh as he was entering the Parliament. The reporter asked him for a comment on the rumours that he was, in fact, a front runner for the post. Given his nature, one would have expected Singh to acknowledge the question and reply with either a 'no comment' or a smile. But this one time, Singh sternly said, '*Kya faltu baat hain? Sab anavashyak baatein hain.*' (What nonsense! It's all unnecessary talk.)

The general perception about people in public life applies to Singh as well. People believe they know Rajnath Singh because they have seen him in person or heard him speak. Singh chooses to speak less and, as a result, even those who might have interacted with him for several years cannot help but wonder if there is indeed more than what meets the eye. Till the age of thirty, Singh often found himself too eager to set things right. The exuberance he exuded made him a natural leader. As the years passed, there was a change in his persona. He was no longer rushed. He continued to do the right thing but his approach underwent a transformation. He became calmer. To the outside world, Singh's calmness, at times, began to be interpreted as reticence.

While his frugality with words has not cast a shadow on his ability to connect with the masses, it has created a perception of him being an astute politician. Singh is not unaware of the image that he has come to be identified with, but does find it difficult to come to terms with the manner in which it came to be associated with him. On his own, he accepts that he did little over the years to alter such a perception. Perhaps he believed such misconceptions would get dispelled over time.

Even when it comes to his family, Singh's mind can be misread. Never has this been more in evidence than in the case of his son Pankaj's foray into active politics. Singh might not have wanted his children, two sons and a daughter, to follow in his footsteps but he never imposed any restrictions on them either when it came to them choosing what they wanted to do. In 2007, Kalyan Singh proposed Pankaj Singh's candidature from the Chiraigaon seat in Varanasi but Rajnath Singh opposed it for the simple reason that he was then the national president of the party. Both Atal Bihari Vajpayee and Lal Krishna Advani were in-charge of the election committee and they disagreed with Rajnath Singh. In fact, Vajpayee famously told everyone present that the committee had noted the president's dissent and proceeded with business as usual. As the meeting wound up, Singh once again said that Pankaj's name should be struck out as he was his son and he did not want people to question both him and his son's intentions. But Vajpayee would have none of it and instructed senior leader Ananth Kumar to announce Pankaj as the candidate.

The news reached the Singh household and by the time Rajnath Singh returned there was celebration in the air. Pankaj touched his father's feet and sought his blessings but all he got was a pat on the back before Singh retired to his room. A few minutes later, Savitri entered the room to chastise her husband from being so dour on such a day. Singh had relied heavily on Savitri ever since they were married to help maintain balance in his life. When she told him to bless his son, he called for Pankaj. Seeing his father dejected, Pankaj enquired if he was unhappy with what had happened. Singh expressed his misgivings. He told Pankaj that unfair as it may seem to him, as the national president he could not give a ticket to his son. Singh asked Pankaj to go to Vajpayee's house and apologize that he would not be able to fight the elections as his father was not happy. When Pankaj met Vajpayee to tell him precisely this, the senior leader admonished the young man's 'Papa' and told him to buckle up, until Pankaj finally managed to prevail.

Later, when Nitin Gadkari was the party president and proposed Pankaj's name as a general secretary in Uttar Pradesh, Singh once again put his foot down. Despite beginning at the grass roots and being actively involved in the state's politics since 2002, it was only during the 2017 Uttar Pradesh Assembly elections that Pankaj Singh's career commenced after BJP national president Amit Shah gave him the ticket from Noida.

Rajnath Singh's acumen and clarity on issues both personal and political are well known. His stance on matters often makes news as they are rarely half-hearted and mostly unwavering. Yet that doesn't mean he imposes his thoughts on anyone. Even as he told Pankaj to withdraw his name despite Vajpayee insisting, Singh was clear in his mind that he could not push his son beyond a point. He insisted that it was not incorrect for any leader's son or daughter to fight elections, but they should not shy away from working like the others for the party if that was their calling. Similarly, Singh's comment on how English had caused a great loss to the country by eroding Indian culture and language had 'elite intellectuals' see red. But Singh has never implied or forced any 'non-English' rule and if an opinion is read as a diktat, who is at fault?

Much was also made of Singh's 2013 statement as the BJP president that homosexuality was an unnatural act and could not be supported. At the same time, the BJP-led government in which Singh has been a high-ranking cabinet minister decided to not contest the batch of petitions seeking to decriminalize homosexuality in the Supreme Court and left it to the wisdom of the Court to decide on the constitutional validity of Section 377 of the Indian Penal Code, which criminalizes same-sex acts. Ironically enough, when the history of the LGBT (lesbian, gay, bisexual and transgender) rights movement in India will be written, it will feature the BJP in power at the Centre when the apex court of the country decriminalized consensual gay sex.

In October 2018, nearly 30,000 farmers reached the border of the National Capital Region to protest in New Delhi. The police halted them at the Delhi border and the angry farmers tried to break the barriers, raised slogans and forced the police to use batons, tear gas shells and water cannons to disperse them. Several protesters and policemen were injured in the clash and the situation had reached a flashpoint when the government announced that Rajnath Singh would meet with the farmers. Singh's presence allayed the fears of the farmers and many of them returned with both assurance and hope that their demands would be met.

Later in the same month, in the wake of the #MeToo movement in India, as several women publicly named people who had sexually harassed them, the government constituted a group of ministers to strengthen the framework to deal with and prevent sexual harassment at the workplace. Reiterating the government's commitment to ensuring the safety and dignity of working women, Singh headed the group that included Surface Transport Minister Nitin Gadkari, Defence Minister Nirmala

Sitharaman and Women and Child Development Minister Maneka Gandhi.

Singh's journey has seen him through many ups and downs. His life is a success in many aspects but what stands out is his intent to do what he thinks is right. As far as he is concerned, greatness is within the grasp of anyone who aspires to it. His own resolve to overcome challenges, to inspire others, remains as important as ever. In this, Rajnath Singh continues to be committed to the ideals of social justice, political equality and civil liberty.

Notes

Chapter 1: The Son of a Farmer

1. 'The Indian Elections–1946'. *The World Today*, Vol. 2, No. 4, pp. 167–75. JSTOR, www.jstor.org/stable/40391905
2. Dinesh Chandra Sinha and Ashok Dasgupta. *1946: The Great Calcutta Killings and Noakhali Genocide: A Historical Study*, Tuhina Prakashani, 2011, p. 45.
3. Balraj Madhok. *Portrait of a Martyr: A Biography of Dr Shyama Prasad Mookerji*, Jaico Publishing House, 1969, p. 69.
4. Craig Baxter. *The Jana Sangh: A Biography of an Indian Political Party*, Oxford University Press, 1971, p. 26.
5. Walter K Andersen. 'The Rashtriya Swayamsevak Sangh–III: Participation in Politics'. *Economic and Political Weekly*, March 1972, www.epw.in/journal/1972/13/special-articles-special-articles/rashtriya-swayamsevak-sangh.html
6. Madhav Sadashiv Golwalkar. *Justice on Trial: A Collection of the Historic Letters between Sri Guruji and the Government (1948–49)*, Prakashan Vibhag, 1969.
7. Walter K. Andersen and Shridhar D. Damle. *The Brotherhood in Saffron: The Rashtriya Swayamsevak Sangh and Hindu Revivalism*, Westview Press, 1987, p. 54.
8. Rakesh Ankit. 'How the Ban on the RSS Was Lifted'. *Economic and Political Weekly*, 21 April 2012, www.epw.in/journal/2012/16/special-articles/how-ban-rss-was-lifted.html
9. Balraj Madhok. *Portrait of a Martyr: A Biography of Dr Shyama Prasad Mookerji*, Jaico Publishing House, 1969, p. 96.

10. Anthony Elenjimittam. *Philosophy and Action of the R.S.S for the Hind Swaraj*, Laxmi Publications, 1951, p. 149.

11. Walter K. Andersen, and Shridhar D. Damle. *The Brotherhood in Saffron: The Rashtriya Swayamsevak Sangh and Hindu Revivalism*, Westview Press, 1987, p. 55.

12. 'Tandon Resigns; Nehru New President'. *The Hindu*, 10 September 1951, www.thehindu.com/thehindu/2001/09/10/stories/10101045.htm

13. Balraj Madhok. *Portrait of a Martyr: A Biography of Dr Shyama Prasad Mookerji*, Jaico Publishing House, 1969, p. 100.

14. Walter K. Andersen and Shridhar D. Damle. *The Brotherhood in Saffron: The Rashtriya Swayamsevak Sangh and Hindu Revivalism*, Westview Press, 1987, p. 128.

15. Election Commission of India. 'First General Elections in India, Vol. I (1951–1952)', 26 September 2018, eci.gov.in/files/file/7448-first-general-elections-in-india-vol-i-1951-1952/

16. Craig Baxter. *The Jana Sangh: A Biography of an Indian Political Party*, Oxford University Press, 1971, pp. 108–109.

17. Jammu & Kashmir Legislative Assembly, 'Constitution of Jammu & Kashmir', jklegislativeassembly.nic.in/Costitution_of_J&K.pdf

18. Balraj Madhok. *Portrait of a Martyr: Biography of Dr Shyama Prasad Mookerji*, Jaico Publishing House, 1969, p. 157.

19. 'From the 1953 Agreement'. *Front*, July 2000, frontline.thehindu.com/static/html/fl1714/17140060.htm

20. Ibid.

21. Balraj Madhok. *Portrait of a Martyr: Biography of Dr Shyama Prasad Mookerji*, Jaico Publishing House, 1969, p. 216.

22. Tathagata Roy. *Syama Prasad Mookerjee: Life and Times,* Viking, 2018.

23. Balraj Madhok. *Portrait of a Martyr: A Biography of Dr Shyama Prasad Mookerji.* Jaico Publishing House, 1969, p. 233.

24. Prabhash Dutta. 'Why Syama Prasad Mookerjee Remains a Deity for BJP and Pariah for Congress'. *India Today*, 6 July 2018, www.indiatoday.in/india/story/why-syama-prasad-mookerjee-remains-a-deity-for-bjp-and-pariah-for-congress-1278867-2018-07-06

25. Claude Arpi. 'The Blunder of the Pandit'. Rediff.com, 16 June 2004, www.rediff.com/news/2004/jun/16spec3.htm

Chapter 2: The Student and the Teacher

1. Walter K. Andersen and Shridhar D. Damle. *The Brotherhood in Saffron: The Rashtriya Swayamsevak Sangh and Hindu Revivalism*, Westview Press, 1987, p. 84.

2. Narisetti Innaiah. *The Birth and Death of Political Parties in India*, Booklinks Corp., 1982, p. 48.
3. Walter K. Andersen and Shridhar D. Damle. *The Brotherhood in Saffron: The Rashtriya Swayamsevak Sangh and Hindu Revivalism*, Westview Press, 1987, p. 165.
4. Ibid., 172.
5. 'Balraj Madhok (1920–2016) Gave Us Definition Of Indianisation.' *Swarajya*, 5 May 2016, www.swarajyamag.com/columns/balraj-madhok-1920-2016-gave-us-definition-of-indianisation
6. Ananya Awasthi. 'Explained: What Integral Humanism Is and Why India Needs It.' *Swarajya*, 25 September 2017, swarajyamag.com/blogs/explained-what-integral-humanism-is-and-why-india-needs-it
7. Walter K. Andersen and Shridhar D. Damle. *The Brotherhood in Saffron: The Rashtriya Swayamsevak Sangh and Hindu Revivalism*, Westview Press, 1987, p. 174.
8. Ibid., p. 175.
9. Ibid., p. 119
10. Vinay Sahasrabuddhe. 'Criticise ABVP If You like, Don't Dismiss Their Good Work.' *DailyO*, 25 February 2016, www.dailyo.in/politics/abvp-bjp-rss-sangh-parivar-jnu-dalits-narendra-modi-hindutva-rightwing/story/1/9224.html
11. Vasant Kaiwar and Sucheta Mazumdar, editors. *Antinomies of Modernity: Essays on Race, Orient, Nation*, Duke University Press, 2003.
12. Bipin Chandra, et al. *India after Independence: 1947–2000*, Penguin, 1999.
13. Sanjoy Hazarika. 'Raj Narain, 69, Indian Socialist: Helped Defeat Two Governments.' *New York Times*, 1 January 1987, www.nytimes.com/1987/01/01/obituaries/raj-narain-69-indian-socialist-helped-defeat-two-governments.html
14. P.N. Dhar. *Indira Gandhi, the 'Emergency', and Indian Democracy*, Oxford University Press, 2001
15. Priyanka Dubey. 'Student Days: The Age of ABVP'. *Caravan*, October 2017, caravanmagazine.in/reportage/age-of-abvp
16. Kaushal, Pradeep. 'A Jana Sangh Founder Who Brooked No Diktat'. *Indian Express*, 2 May 2016, indianexpress.com/article/india/india-news-india/former-jana-sangh-president-balraj-madhok-passes-away-pm-modi-offers-condolences-2780902/
17. R.K. Sinha. 'In Memory of Balraj Madhok'. *Pioneer*, 11 May 2016, www.dailypioneer.com/2016/columnists/in-memory-of-balraj-madhok.html
18. Katharine Frank. *Indira: The Life of Indira Nehru Gandhi*, HarperCollins, 2001.

19. Rakesh Ankit. 'Janata Party (1974–77): Creation of an All-India Opposition'. *History and Sociology of South Asia*, Vol. 11, No. 1, January 2017, pp. 39–54.

20. Khushwant Singh. 'A New Wave from the Old India'. *New York Times*, 30 March 1975, www.nytimes.com/1975/03/30/archives/a-new-wave-from-the-old-india-out-of-the-past-comes-jp-narayan-a.html

21. K.N. Govindacharya. 'The Emergency Started Long before 25 June 1975'. *Livemint*, 22 June 2015, www.livemint.com/Politics/dtQymwkmkAEaOOrDUJ6ASI/The-Emergency-started-long-before-25-June-1975.html

22. 'Mrs Gandhi Vows to Stay in Office in spite of Ruling'. *New York Times*, 13 June 1975, www.nytimes.com/1975/06/13/archives/mrs-gandhi-vows-to-stay-in-office-inspite-of-ruling-indian-prime.html

23. Eric Pace. 'Removal of Mrs Gandhi Put Off by Supreme Court'. *New York Times*, 25 June 1975, www.nytimes.com/1975/06/25/archives/removal-of-mrs-gandhi-put-off-by-supreme-court-court-permits-mrs.html

24. V. Kumara Swamy, et al. 'The Night of the Long Knives'. *Telegraph*, 28 June 2015, www.telegraphindia.com/7-days/the-night-nbsp-of-the-nbsp-long-nbsp-knives/cid/1313962

Chapter 3: The Emergency and Its Aftermath

1. Rohit Kumar. 'The Judge Who Stood Up To Indira Gandhi and Whose Judgment Shook India'. *Swarajya*, 20 March 2016, swarajyamag.com/politics/the-judge-who-stood-up-to-indira-gandhi-and-whose-judgment-shook-india

2. Manu Joseph. 'How Indians Protest'. *Times of India*, 19 May 2007, timesofindia.indiatimes.com/How-Indians-Protest/articleshow/2061978.cms

3. Arun Jaitley. 'A Tale of Three Emergencies: Real Reason Always Different.' *Indian Express*, 5 November 2007, archive.indianexpress.com/news/a-tale-of-three-emergencies-real-reason-always-different/235992/0

4. 'Cong Book Blames Sanjay for Emergency Excesses'. *India Today*, 29 December 2010, www.indiatoday.in/india/north/story/congress-sanjay-gandhi-emergency-87911-2010-12-29; C. Brian Smith. 'In 1976, More Than 6 Million Men in India Were Coerced into Sterilization'. *MEL Magazine*, May 2018, melmagazine.com/en-us/story/in-1976-more-than-6-million-men-in-india-were-coerced-into-sterilization

5. Nayantara Sahgal. *Indira Gandhi: Tryst with Power*, Penguin Random House India, 2012.

6. *Associated Press*. 'Mrs Gandhi Easing Crisis Rule, Decides on March Election.' *New York Times*, 19 January 1977, www.nytimes.com/1977/01/19/archives/mrs-gandhi-easing-crisis-rule-decides-on-march-election-key.html

7. John Dayal. 'What Drove Sanjay Gandhi and His Coterie during the Emergency?' Scroll.in, 26 June 2015, scroll.in/article/735576/what-drove-sanjay-gandhi-and-his-coterie-during-the-emergency

8. Pretika Khanna. 'The 44th Amendment Ensured Democracy's Survival in India: Shanti Bhushan'. *Livemint*, 22 June 2015.

9. Durvasa. 'Janata Party: Still Teething–How Long?' *India Today*, 31 August 1977.

10. Walter K. Andersen and Shridhar D. Damle. *The Brotherhood in Saffron: The Rashtriya Swayamsevak Sangh and Hindu Revivalism*, Westview Press, 1987, p. 215.

11. Ibid., p. 216.

12. Shanti Bhushan. *Courting Destiny: A Memoir*, Penguin India, 2008.

13. Walter K. Andersen and Shridhar D. Damle. *The Brotherhood in Saffron: The Rashtriya Swayamsevak Sangh and Hindu Revivalism*, Westview Press, 1987, p. 219.

14. Anirban Ganguly. 'How the Lotus Bloomed: A Look Back in Time'. *Pioneer*, 6 April 2018, www.dailypioneer.com/2018/columnists/how-the-lotus-bloomed-a-look-back-in-time.html

15. Sunil Sethi and Prabhu Chawla. '1980 Lok Sabha Elections See Virtual Eclipse of Jana Sangh in Parliament'. *India Today*, 31 January 1980, www.indiatoday.in/magazine/cover-story/story/19800131-1980-lok-sabha-elections-see-virtual-eclipse-of-jan-sangh-in-parliament-821699-2014-12-19

Chapter 4: Sun-ward Climb

1. Walter K. Andersen and Shridhar D. Damle. *The Brotherhood in Saffron: The Rashtriya Swayamsevak Sangh and Hindu Revivalism*, Westview Press, 1987, p. 226.

2. Walter K. Andersen and Shridhar D. Damle. *The Brotherhood in Saffron: The Rashtriya Swayamsevak Sangh and Hindu Revivalism*, Westview Press, 1987, p. 227.

3. Anirban Ganguly. 'How the Lotus Bloomed: A Look Back in Time'. *Pioneer*, 6 April 2018, www.dailypioneer.com/2018/columnists/how-the-lotus-bloomed-a-look-back-in-time.html

4. Makiko Kimura. *The Nellie Massacre of 1983: Agency of Rioters*, Sage Publications India Pvt. Ltd., 2013, pp. 100–01.
5. Kuldip Nayar. *Beyond the Lines: An Autobiography*, Lotus, 2012.
6. '34 Years On, A Brief History about Operation Bluestar, And Why It Was Carried Out'. NDTV.com, 6 June 2018, www.ndtv.com/india-news/operation-bluestar-34th-anniversary-a-brief-history-about-operation-bluestar-and-why-it-was-carried--1863385
7. Ajmer Singh. 'Atal Bihari Vajpayee Had Warned Indira Gandhi against Operation Bluestar'. *Economic Times*, 7 February 2014, economictimes.indiatimes.com/news/politics-and-nation/atal-bihari-vajpayee-had-warned-indira-gandhi-against-operation-bluestar/articleshow/29972542.cms
8. Stanley A. Kochanek and Robert L. Hardgrave. *India: Government and Politics in a Developing Nation*, 7th ed., Wadsworth Publishing Co Inc., 2006.
9. Manoj Mitta and H.S. Phoolka. *When a Tree Shook Delhi*, Lotus, 2008.
10. Manini Chatterjee. 'The Debacle and After'. *Seminar*, July 2004, www.india-seminar.com/2004/539/539%20manini%20chatterjee.htm
11. Sumit Mitra. 'VHP-Organised Ekaimata Yagna to Roll across India with 92 Religious Caravans'. *India Today*, 30 November 1983, www.indiatoday.in/magazine/special-report/story/19831130-vhp-organised-ekaimata-yagna-to-roll-across-india-with-92-religious-caravans-771249-2013-07-12
12. Asma Khan Lone. 'Reading the Vote in the Valley'. *The Hindu*, 5 November 2016, www.thehindu.com/opinion/lead/Reading-the-vote-in-the-Valley/article14171409.ece
13. William K. Stevens. 'Mrs Gandhi's Party Fails in Kasmir Voting'. *New York Times*, 12 June 1983, www.nytimes.com/1983/06/12/world/mrs-gandhi-s-party-fails-in-kashmir-voting.html
14. Election Commission, 1983.
15. Robert L. Hardgrave, Jr. 'India on the Eve of Elections: Congress and the Opposition'. *Pacific Affairs*, Vol. 57, No. 3, 1984, pp. 404–428.
16. Coomi Kapoor. 'Delhi Civic Polls: Congress (I) Fights Back, Wins an Impressive Victory'. *India Today*, 28 February 1983, www.indiatoday.in/magazine/indiascope/story/19830228-delhi-civic-polls-congressi-fights-back-wins-an-impressive-victory-771275-2013-08-23
17. Suman Dubey and Prabhu Chawla. 'Opposition Unity: Once More with Hope'. *India Today*, 31 October 2014, www.indiatoday.in/magazine/indiascope/story/19831031-opposition-unity-once-more-with-hope-771139-2013-07-17

18. James Manor. 'Party Decay and Political Crisis in India'. *Washington Quarterly*, Vol. 4, Issue 3, 1981, www.tandfonline.com/doi/abs/10.1080/01636608109451789

19. Brewer S. Stone 'Institutional Decay and the Traditionalization of Politics: The Uttar Pradesh Congress Party'. *Asian Survey*, University of California Press Journals, October 1988, as.ucpress.edu/content/28/10/1018

20. Anand Sagar and Prabhu Chawla. 'Uttar Pradesh: Advantage Brahmin'. *India Today*, 15 August 1982, www.indiatoday.in/magazine/indiascope/story/19820815-uttar-pradesh-advantage-brahmin-772062-2013-10-07

21. B.D. Graham, 'The Succession of Factionalism Systems in Uttar Pradesh Congress Party, 1937–66'. *Local-Level Politics: Social and Cultural Perspectives*, edited by Mark J. Swartz, Chicago: Aldine Publishing Company, 1968.

22. Brewer S. Stone, 'Institutional Decay and the Traditionalization of Politics: The Uttar Pradesh Congress Party'. *Asian Survey*, University of California Press Journals, October 1988, as.ucpress.edu/content/28/10/1018.

23. Deepak Lavania. 'When Atal Bihari Vajpayee Was Swamped with Flowers'. *Times of India*, 17 August 2018, timesofindia.indiatimes.com/city/agra/when-atal-was-swamped-with-flowers/articleshow/65444310.cms

24. 'BJP Makes First Overture at Its State Convention in Nagpur'. *India Today*, 30 November 1988, www.indiatoday.in/magazine/indiascope/story/19881130-bjp-makes-first-overture-at-its-state-convention-in-nagpur-798127-1988-11-30; Venkat Ananth. 'The Anatomy of an Alliance: The BJP-Shiv Sena Story'. *Livemint*, 22 September 2014, www.livemint.com/Politics/VbrxNc2FSZuGroknO7I97M/The-anatomy-of-an-alliance-The-BJPShiv-Sena-story.html

25. 'What the Bofors Scandal Is All About'. News18, 26 April 2012, www.news18.com/news/india/what-the-bofors-scandal-is-all-about-468591.html

26. Inderjit Badhwar. 'Euphoria of Rajiv Gandhi's Early Days in Office Vapourises into Despair and Disappointment'. *India Today*, 15 August 1987, www.indiatoday.in/magazine/cover-story/story/19870815-euphoria-of-rajiv-gandhis-early-days-in-office-vapourises-into-despair-and-disappointment-799841-1987-08-15

27. Sumantra Bose. *Kashmir: Roots of Conflict, Paths to Peace*, Harvard University Press, 2005

28. Praveen Donthi. 'How Mufti Mohammad Sayeed Shaped the 1987 Elections in Kashmir'. *Caravan*, 23 March 2016, caravanmagazine.in/vantage/mufti-mohammad-sayeed-shaped-1987-kashmir-elections
29. Koenraad Elst. *Ayodhya: The Case Against the Temple*, Voice of India, 2002.
30. Salman Rushdie. 'India Bans a Book For Its Own Good'. *New York Times*, 19 October 1988, www.nytimes.com/1988/10/19/opinion/india-bans-a-book-for-its-own-good.html
31. Smita Gupta. 'The Rise and Fall of Hindutva, 1989–2004'. *Political Process in Uttar Pradesh: Identity, Economic Reforms, and Governance*, edited by Sudha Pai, Pearson Longman, 2007, pp. 112–13.
32. Walter K. Andersen and Shridhar D. Damle. *The RSS: A View to the Inside*, Penguin Random House, 2018.
33. Barbara Crossette. 'Indian Opposition Chooses a Premier'. *New York Times*, 2 December 1989.
34. Harinder Baweja, et al. 'Mandal Report Touches a Peculiar Chord among Youth'. *India Today*, 31 October 1990, www.indiatoday.in/magazine/special-report/story/19901031-mandal-report-touches-a-peculiar-chord-among-youth-813187-1990-10-31
35. Ramchandra Guha. *India After Gandhi* (10th Anniversary Edition), Picador India, 2017, pp. 602–04.
36. 'The Drama of the Arrest'. *Frontline*, 6 February 2015, frontline.thehindu.com/the-nation/the-drama-of-the-arrest/article6808098.ece
37. 'Mulayam Singh Yadav Justifies Police Firing on Kar Sevaks in 1990'. *Times of India*, 22 November 2017, timesofindia.indiatimes.com/india/mulayam-singh-yadav-justifies-police-firing-on-kar-sevaks-in-1990/articleshow/61754186.cms

Chapter 5; Standing, Falling, Standing Again

1. Rasheed Kidwai. 'Ayodhya, a Reluctant Congress Story'. *Telegraph*, 4 October 2010, www.telegraphindia.com/india/ayodhya-a-reluctant-congress-story/cid/472844
2. Election Commission of India. 'Uttar Pradesh 1991'. 14 August 2018, eci.gov.in/files/file/3257-uttar-pradesh-1991/
3. Bharatiya Janata Party, Election Manifesto 1991, Bharatiya Janata Party, New Delhi, 1991, http://lib.bjplibrary.org/jspui/handle/123456789/239
4. Shyamlal Yadav. 'Uttar Pradesh: A Political History'. *Indian Express*, 11 March 2017, indianexpress.com/article/explained/uttar-pradesh-assembly-elections-2017-bjp-samajwadi-party-akhilesh-yadav-narendra-modi-rahul-gandhi-mayawati-mulayam-singh-yadav-congress-4562628/

5. Harold A. Gould. *Education and Political Processes in Faizabad District in Uttar Pradesh*, Randolph and Randolph, 1972.
6. Geeta Gandhi Kingdon and Mohd Muzammil. 'A Political Economy of Education in India–I: The Case of UP'. *Economic and Political Weekly*, 11 August 2001, www.epw.in/journal/2001/32/special-articles/political-economy-education-india-i.html
7. Ibid.
8. Deepak Gidwani. 'Learning Expedience'. *India Today*, 31 July 1994, www.indiatoday.in/magazine/education/story/19940731-learning-expedience-755752-1994-07-31
9. James Glover. 'Everything Vedic in "Vedic Maths"'. *The Hindu*, 17 October 2014, www.thehindu.com/todays-paper/tp-in-school/everything-vedic-in-vedic-maths/article6508218.ece
10. N.J. Nanporia. 'The Rites Of Passage'. *Outlook*, 17 August 1997.
11. Geeta Gandhi Kingdon and Mohd Muzammil. 'A Political Economy of Education in India–I: The Case of UP'. *Economic and Political Weekly*, 11 August 2001.
12. 'BJP Gaining Ground in UP'. *Times of India*, 8 January 1991.
13. Dilip Awasthi. 'Ayodhya Issue: CM Kalyan Singh's Fortunes Flounder as Hindu Hardliners Mount Pressure'. *India Today*, 15 September 1991.
14. 'Land Was Acquired to Facilitate Construction of Temple: Kalyan Singh'. *Zee News,* 27 January 2005, zeenews.india.com/news/nation/land-was-acquired-to-facilitate-construction-of-temple-kalyan-singh_198484.html
15. *Frontline*, 8 May 1992.
16. Yubaraj Ghimire and Dilip Awasthi. 'Kalyan Singh Struggles to Subdue Revolt Among Members Seeking His Removal'. *India Today*, 31 August 1992, www.indiatoday.in/magazine/special-report/story/19920831-kalyan-singh-struggles-to-subdue-revolt-among-members-seeking-his-removal-766755-2013-01-02
17. 'Babri Case: Kalyan Won't Be Tried While He's Governor'. *Times of India*, 19 April 2017, timesofindia.indiatimes.com/india/babri-case-kalyan-wont-be-tried-while-hes-governor/articleshow/58270461.cms
18. Chandra, Atul. '1991–2017: The Epic Saga of Elections in Uttar Pradesh'. *Swarajya*, 4 February 2017, swarajyamag.com/politics/1991-2017-the-epic-saga-of-elections-in-uttar-pradesh
19. Dhananjay Mahapatra. 'Rao, Who Defended in SC Dismissal of 3 BJP Govts, Dies'. *Times of India*, 14 September 2017, timesofindia.indiatimes.com/india/rao-who-defended-in-sc-dismissal-of-3-bjp-govts-dies/articleshow/60505519.cms
20. 'Janadesh Yatra'. *BJP*, www.bjp.org/en/leadership/shri-lk-advani/yatras/janadesh-yatra.

21. Election Commission of India. 'Uttar Pradesh 1993'. *Election Commission of India*, eci.gov.in/files/file/3258-uttar-pradesh-1993/
22. 'We Can Form the Government'. Kanshi Ram interview in *Sunday*, 16-22 May 1993.
23. Deepak Gidwani. 'Learning Expedience'. *India Today*, 31 July 1994, www.indiatoday.in/magazine/education/story/19940731-learning-expedience-755752-1994-07-31
24. Lalmani Verma. '1995: When BJP Leader "Rescued" Mayawati from SP Workers'. *Indian Express*, 15 March 2018, indianexpress.com/article/india/1995-when-bjp-leader-rescued-mayawati-from-sp-workers-5098374/
25. N.K. Singh. 'Elections 1996: BJP Launches High-Voltage Blitz with Atal Bihari Vajpayee as Central Theme'. *India Today*, 15 May 1996, www.indiatoday.in/magazine/cover-story/story/19960515-elections-1996-bjp-launches-high-voltage-blitz-with-atal-behari-vajpayee-as-central-theme-833193-1996-05-15
26. Thomas Blom Hansen and Christophe Jaffrelot. *The BJP and the Compulsions of Politics in India*, Oxford University Press, 2001.
27. V. Venkatesan. 'The Laxman Line'. *Frontline*, September 2000, frontline.thehindu.com/static/html/fl1719/17190040.htm
28. N.K. Singh. 'Elections 1996: BJP Launches High-Voltage Blitz with Atal Bihari Vajpayee as Central Theme'. *India Today*, 15 May 1996, www.indiatoday.in/magazine/cover-story/story/19960515-elections-1996-bjp-launches-high-voltage-blitz-with-atal-behari-vajpayee-as-central-theme-833193-1996-05-15
29. L.K. Advani. Speech at the National Executive, Hyderabad. 19 March 1994, lkadvani.in/bjp-speeches-5.php
30. M.J. Akbar. 'The Siege Within: Why Jyoti Basu Could Not Be PM'. *Times of India*, 10 January 2010, timesofindia.indiatimes.com/blogs/thesiegewithin/why-jyoti-basu-could-not/
31. 'Rajiv's Killer My Friend: Karunanidhi'. *Economic Times*, 20 April 2009, economictimes.indiatimes.com/news/politics-and-nation/rajivs-killer-my-friend-karunanidhi/articleshow/4422509.cms
32. 'BJP to Project Kalyan Singh as Father Figure'. *Telegraph* (Calcutta)
33. Sudha Pai. *State Politics: New Dimensions*, Shipra Publications, 2000, pp. 61–62.
34. Venkitesh Ramakrishnan. 'Shifting Alignments'. *Frontline*, 15 November 1996
35. A.S. Prashar. 'A Powder Keg about to Explode?' *The Tribune*, 25 July 1998, www.tribuneindia.com/1998/98jul25/saturday/head2.htm
36. Mohammad Amir. 'A Study of Electoral Participation of Bahujan Samaj Party in Uttar Pradesh since 1996'. *Shodhganga*, 2016, shodhganga.inflibnet.ac.in/handle/10603/186100

37. Farzand Ahmed. 'Uttar Pradesh Chief Minister Kalyan Singh Gets Tough with Errant Colleagues'. *India Today*, 2 November 1998, www.indiatoday.in/magazine/states/story/19981102-uttar-pradesh-chief-minister-kalyan-singh-gets-tough-with-errant-colleagues-830138-1998-11-02
38. Lubna Mustafa. 'Religion as a Factor: a Study of Parliamentary Elections in UP since 1984'. *Shodhganga*, 2007, shodhganga.inflibnet.ac.in/handle/10603/51963.
39. 'Sultan of somersaults'. *Indian Express*. 1 March 1998.
40. Sharad Pradhan. 'Ram Prakash Gupta to Replace Kalyan Singh'. Rediff.com, 9 November 1999, www.rediff.com/news/1999/nov/09up.htm
41. 'Kalyan Singh Expelled from BJP'. Rediff.com, November 1999, www.rediff.com/news/1999/dec/09kal.htm

Chapter 6: On the Road

1. George Iype. 'Vajpayee Drives across the Border into Pakistan and History'. Rediff.com, 20 February 1999, www.rediff.com/news/1999/feb/20bus1.htm
'BJP's Shatrughan Sinha Attends Marriage of Zia-Ul-Haq's Grandson in Pak'. *Indian Express*, 8 January 2013, archive.indianexpress.com/news/bjp-shatrughan-sinha-attends-marriage-of-ziaulhaqs-grandson-in-pak/1056369/
2. K.M. Thomas and K. Govindan Kutty. 'AIADMK Chief Jayalalitha's Pressure Tactics Paralyse BJP-Led Government'. *India Today*, 4 May 1998, www.indiatoday.in/magazine/cover-story/story/19980504-aiadmk-chief-jayalalithas-pressure-tactics-paralyses-bjp-led-government-826337-1999-11-30
3. *United News of India*. 'Swamy Urges Jayalalithaa to Withdraw Support to Vajpayee Government'. Rediff.com, 13 July 1998, www.rediff.com/news/1998/jun/13swamy.htm
4. 'Martyrs of Kargil War'. *Press Information Bureau of India*, 26 November 2012, pib.nic.in/newsite/erelcontent.aspx?relid=89410
Reddy, B. Muralidhar. 'Over 4,000 Soldiers Killed in Kargil: Sharif'. *The Hindu*, 17 August 2003, www.thehindu.com/thehindu/2003/08/17/stories/2003081702900800.htm
5. 'This Unquiet Land: Stories from India's Fault Lines'. *This Unquiet Land: Stories from India's Fault Lines*, by Barkha Dutt, Aleph Book Company, 2016, p. 214.
6. Elias Groll. 'The Story of How Nawaz Sharif Pulled Back from Nuclear War'. *Foreign Policy*, 14 May 2013, foreignpolicy.com/2013/05/14/the-story-of-how-nawaz-sharif-pulled-back-from-nuclear-war/

7. Ghani Ejaz, et al. 'Highway to Success in India: The Impact of the
    Golden Quadrilateral Project for the Location and Performance of
    Manufacturing'. *The World Bank*, 1 January 2013, documents.worldbank.
    org/curated/en/162351468267650898/Highway-to-success-in-India-
    the-impact-of-the-golden-quadrilateral-project-for-the-location-and-
    performance-of-manufacturing
8. *Press Information Bureau*, Government of India. 'Highway Development
    at an Unprecedented Scale', January 2004, pib.nic.in/newsite/
    erelcontent.aspx?relid=1025
9. 'PMGSY Roads Changing Lifestyle in Manipur'. *Assam Tribune*,
    29 October 2010, www.assamtribune.com/scripts/detailsnew.
    asp?id=oct2910/oth05
10. 'Golden Quadrilateral Highway Network'. *Road Traffic Technology*,
    20 March 2012, www.roadtraffic-technology.com/projects/golden-
    quadrilateral-highway-network
11. *Press Information Bureau*, Government of India. 'Highway Development
    at an Unprecedented Scale'. January 2004, pib.nic.in/newsite/
    erelcontent.aspx?relid=1025
12. Anil Sasi. 'NHAI Ordered To Award All Civil Contracts By June'.
    Business Standard, 15 August 2000, www.business-standard.com/
    article/specials/nhai-ordered-to-award-all-civil-contracts-by-
    june-100081501017_1.html
13. Ibid.
14. 'The Road to Profits'. *Outlook Money*, 16 December 2007, www.
    outlookindia.com/outlookmoney/archive/the-road-to-profits-87801
15. 15. Ajay Singh. 'Lunch With BS: Rajnath Singh'. *Business Standard*,
    1 November 2000, www.business-standard.com/article/opinion/lunch-
    with-bs-rajnath-singh-100110101015_1.html

Chapter 7: The Chief Ministerial Years

1. Subhash Mishra. 'Uttar Pradesh: After Series of Blunders, CM Ram
    Prakash Gupta May Be on His Way Out'. *India Today*, 14 February
    2000, www.indiatoday.in/magazine/states/story/20000214-uttar-
    pradesh-after-series-of-blunders-cm-ram-prakash-gupta-may-be-on-
    his-way-out-777064-2000-02-14.
2. Ibid.
3. Tara Shankar Sahay. 'Who Will Replace Rajnath Singh in UP?' Rediff.
    com, 23 November 1999, www.rediff.com/news/1999/nov/23tara.htm

4. 'UP's Own Anti-ISI War'. *Tribune*, 6 January 2000, www.tribuneindia. com/2000/20000106/edit.htm#2
5. 'Sonia Writes to President on U.P. Bill'. *The Hindu*, 4 April 2000, www. thehindu.com/2000/04/04/stories/02040003.htm
6. Ibid.
7. 'Want to Build a Mosque? Get Permission from Your DM!' *The Milli Gazette*, Vol. 1 No. 3, 1 February 2000, www.milligazette.com/ Archives/01-2-2000/Art2.htm; S.K. Ghosh. 'Pakistan's ISI: Network of Terror in India'. *Pakistan's ISI: Network of Terror in India*, APH Publishing Corporation, 2000, p. 61.
8. Pothik Ghosh. 'Indoctrination Lessons'. *Outlook*, 16 January 2000, www.outlookindia.com/magazine/story/indoctrination-lessons/208726
9. 'Muslims Protest against UP Bill'. *Tribune*, 22 April 2000, www. tribuneindia.com/2000/20000422/main1.htm
10. Saikat Datta and Sharat Pradhan. 'A Place and Its Negative'. *Outlook*, 5 October 2008, www.outlookindia.com/magazine/story/a-place-and-its-negative/238557
11. Varma, Purushottam. 'भारत का लादेन यूपी के इस जिले को बनाना चाहता था इंडियन मुजाहिदीन का गढ़, नेपाल से आता था यहाँ' India's Bin Laden Wanted to Make This District of UP into Indian Mujahideen Stronghold, Used to Enter from Nepal'. *Amar Ujala*, 24 January 2018, www.amarujala.com/ delhi-ncr/crime/indias-laden-abdul-subhan-qureshi-wanted-to-make-azamgarh-the-hub-of-indian-mujahideen?pageId=2
12. Tufail Ahmad. 'Travels of a Political Pilgrim: Madrassas Play Key Role in Inducing Orthodoxy among Azamgarh's Muslims'. *Firstpost*, 16 March 2017, www.firstpost.com/india/travels-of-a-political-pilgrim-madrassas-play-key-role-in-inducing-orthodoxy-among-azamgarhs-muslims-3337960.html
13. Radhika Ramaseshan and Anand Soondas. 'Crown of Thorns for Rajnath'. *Telegraph*, 25 October 2000, www.telegraphindia.com/india/crown-of-thorns-for-rajnath/cid/884887
14. A.K. Verma. 'UP: BJP's Caste Card'. *Economic & Political Weekly*, 1 December 2001.
15. Ibid.
16. Nailwal, R.P. 'Naresh Forced Rajnath to Sack Him'. *Times of India*, 10 August 2001, timesofindia.indiatimes.com/india/Naresh-forced-Rajnath-to-sack-him/articleshow/1135191537.cms
17. Subhash Mishra. 'UP Chief Minister Rajnath Singh Manages to Enhance Both His and BJP's Image'. *India Today*, 27 August 2001, www.indiatoday.in/magazine/states/story/20010827-up-chief-

minister-rajnath-singh-manages-to-enhance-both-his-and-bjp-image-774106-2001-08-27
18. Radhika Ramaseshan and Anand Soondas. 'Crown of Thorns for Rajnath'. *Telegraph*, 25 October 2000, www.telegraphindia.com/india/crown-of-thorns-for-rajnath/cid/884887
19. Masoodul Hasan. 'Amarmani Tripathi Is in the Dock Again'. *Hindustan Times*, 8 February 2007, www.hindustantimes.com/india/amarmani-tripathi-is-in-the-dock-again/story-Sa0lgUcx20k5NYmtZznUTJ.html
20. 'Out of Job UP Minister Ashok Yadav Projects Himself as Martyr to Backward Castes Cause'. *India Today*, 1 October 2001, www.indiatoday.in/magazine/indiascope/story/20011001-out-of-job-up-minister-ashok-yadav-projects-himself-as-martyr-to-backward-castes-cause-774336-2001-10-01
21. 'Modi Trying to Do What Rajnath Failed to Comply in UP'. *United News of India*, 10 September 2017, www.uniindia.com/modi-trying-to-do-what-rajnath-failed-to-comply-in-up/states/news/985516.html
22. Sutapa Lahiry. 'Bharatiya Janata Party in Uttar Pradesh: Ideology, Social Base and Strategies of Electoral Mobilisation'. *Shodhganga*, 2003, shodhganga.inflibnet.ac.in/handle/10603/19324
23. Ibid.
24. A.K. Verma. 'UP: BJP's Caste Card'. *Economic & Political Weekly*, 1 December 2001.
25. Tripathi, Purnima S. "Pre-Election Battle." *Frontline*, 27 October–09 November, 2001, frontline.thehindu.com/static/html/fl1822/18220310.htm
26. Purnima S. Tripathi. 'A Feud in Uttar Pradesh'. *Frontline*, 8 December 2001, frontline.thehindu.com/static/html/fl1825/18250370.htm
27. Ibid.
28. Praveen Swami. 'A Decade after 9/11, Indian Jihad Still Thrives'. *The Hindu*, 12 September 2011, www.thehindu.com/opinion/lead/a-decade-after-911-indian-jihad-still-thrives/article2439813.ece.
29. Adrian Levy and Catherine Scott-Clark. *Exile: The Flight of Osama Bin Laden*, Bloomsbury Publishing, 2018.
30. Biswajeet Banerjee. 'BJP's Poser to Congress and SP'. *The Times of India*, 3 February 2002, timesofindia.indiatimes.com/city/lucknow/BJPs-poser-to-Congress-and-SP/articleshow/732723049.cms
31. Subhash Mishra and Farzand Ahmed 'Prime Minister Atal Bihari Vajpayee's Remarks on a Temple in Ayodhya Rekindle an Old Issue'. *India Today*, 18 December 2000, www.indiatoday.in/magazine/nation/story/20001218-prime-minister-atal-bihari-

vajpayees-remarks-on-a-temple-in-ayodhya-rekindle-an-old-issue-778637-2000-12-18

32. 'POTA Bill Passed by Joint Session of Parliament'. Rediff.com, 26 March 2002, www.rediff.com/news/2002/mar/26poto7.htm

33. 'United Nations Security Council Resolution 1373 (2001): United Nations Security Council Counter-Terrorism Committee'. United Nations, 28 September 2001, www.un.org/sc/ctc/resources/databases/recommended-international-practices-codes-and-standards/united-nations-security-council-resolution-1373-2001/

34. Ananya Vajpeyi. 'The Bare Life of S.A.R. Geelani, Ph.D'. *Outlook*, 10 February 2005, www.outlookindia.com/website/story/the-bare-life-of-sar-geelani-phd/226458; N. Sathiya Moorthy. 'TN Police Arrests MDMK Leader Vaiko'. Rediff.com, 11 July 2002, www.rediff.com/news/2002/jul/11vaiko7.htm

35. 'Govt Is Firm on POTO, Says Advani'. *Times of India*, 23 March 2002, timesofindia.indiatimes.com/city/delhi/Govt-is-firm-on-Poto-says-Advani/articleshow/4693990.cms

36. Pallab Bhattacharya. 'Indian Govt Repeals "Controversial" Pota'. *Daily Star*, 12 August 2004, archive.thedailystar.net/2004/08/12/d40812130298.htm

37. A.K Verma. 'Political Prospects in UP Pointers from a Pre-Poll Survey'. *Economic & Political Weekly*, 6 February 2002, www.epw.in/journal/2002/06/commentary/political-prospects.html

38. Ibid.

39. Subhash Mishra and Ashok Malik. 'Uttar Pradesh Elections: A Game of Bluff between Rajnath Singh and Mulayam Singh Yadav'. *India Today*, 18 February 2002, www.indiatoday.in/magazine/cover-story/story/20020218-uttar-pradesh-elections-a-game-of-bluff-between-rajnath-singh-and-mulayam-singh-yadav-795904-2002-02-18

40. Vir Sanghvi. 'One-Way Ticket: My Take on the Godhra Tragedy When It Happened'. 2011, www.virsanghvi.com/Article-Details.aspx?key=611

41. Praveen Swami. 'Godhra Questions'. *Frontline*, 6 March 2002, frontline.thehindu.com/static/html/fl1906/19060120.htm

42. IANS. '2002 Gujarat Riots: SIT Report on Army Deployment Is "Blatant Lie", Says Retired Lt. General Zameer Uddin Shah'. *Free Press Journal*, 8 October 2018, www.freepressjournal.in/headlines/2002-gujarat-riots-sit-report-on-army-deployment-is-blatant-lie-says-retired-lt-general-zameer-uddin-shah/1371080

43. Ramakrishnan, Venkitesh. 'Convulsions in Uttar Pradesh'. *Frontline*, 28 April 2000, frontline.thehindu.com/static/html/fl1708/17080320.htm

Chapter 8: His Father's Son

1. 'The Saga of Ambedkar Memorial.' *Times of India*, 20 June 2002, timesofindia.indiatimes.com/city/lucknow/The-saga-of-Ambedkar-memorial/articleshow/13602492.cms?referral=PM.
2. Manuel Ciotti. 'Futurity in Words: Low-Caste Women Political Activists' Self-Representation and Post-Dalit Scenarios in North India'. *Contemporary South Asia*, 2010, www.tandfonline.com/doi/abs/10.1080/09584930903561622?journalCode=ccsa20
3. Vijay Singh. 'The Rediff Interview/Rajnath Singh'. Rediff.com, 25 October 2002, www.rediff.com/news/2002/oct/25inter.htm; Purnima Tripathi. 'Coalition Troubles'. *Frontline*, 14 March 2003, frontline.thehindu.com/static/html/fl2005/stories/20030314004204000.htm
4. Uday Mahurkar. 'Narendra Modi's Gaurav Yatra Acquires Sharper Political Edge as Gujarat Polls Draw Near'. *India Today*, 4 November 2002, www.indiatoday.in/magazine/states/story/20021104-narendra-modi-gaurav-yatra-acquires-sharper-political-edge-as-gujarat-polls-draw-near-794431-2002-11-04
5. Vijay Singh. 'The Rediff Interview/Rajnath Singh'. Rediff.com, 25 October 2002, www.rediff.com/news/2002/oct/25inter.htm
6. Ibid.
7. 'Rs 1,648.77 Cr. Aid for Drought-Hit States'. *The Hindu*, 24 March 2003, www.thehindu.com/2003/03/24/stories/2003032404961100.htm
8. Shankkar Aiyar and Amarnath K. Menon. 'Andhra Pradesh CM Chandrababu Naidu Squeezes National Resources for His State'. *India Today*, 27 May 2002, www.indiatoday.in/magazine/states/story/20020527-andhra-pradesh-cm-chandrababu-naidu-squeezes-national-resources-for-his-state-795179-2002-05-27
9. Sharad Joshi. 'The Tragi-Comedy in Agriculture'. *Hindu Business Line*, 16 May 2003, www.thehindubusinessline.com/2003/05/16/stories/2003051600010800.htm
10. 'No Bt Cotton, No GM Mustard: GEAC'. *Times of India*, 27 April 2003, timesofindia.indiatimes.com/india/No-Bt-cotton-no-GM-mustard-GEAC/articleshow/44701151.cms
11. Vimal Sumbly and Iqbal Singh. 'BJP Bid to Make Inroads into Rural Punjab'. *Tribune*, 28 September 2002, www.tribuneindia.com/2002/20020928/punjab1.htm
12. 'Separate Agriculture Lending Rate Mooted'. *The Hindu*, 8 July 2003, www.thehindu.com/2003/07/08/stories/2003070803061300.htm

13. 'System Soon to Ensure Ryots Get Soft Loans'. *The Hindu*, 28 July 2003, www.thehindu.com/2003/07/28/stories/2003072803641100.htm

14. 'Centre Is Anti-Farmer: Ajit Singh'. *Times of India*, 23 June 2003, timesofindia.indiatimes.com/city/hyderabad/Centre-is-anti-farmer-Ajit-Singh/articleshow/39573.cms

15. Charlotte Denny, et al. 'Blow to World Economy as Trade Talks Collapse'. *Guardian*, 15 September 2003, www.theguardian.com/world/2003/sep/15/business.politics

16. 'India Ups the Ante, Doha Failure Haunts Cancun'. Rediff.com, 10 September 2003, www.rediff.com/money/2003/sep/10wto.htm

17. 'Call Centre Scheme for Farmers on Anvil'. *Press Information Bureau of India*, 22 December 2003, pib.nic.in/newsite/printrelease.aspx?relid=438

18. Sharad Joshi. 'National Commission on Farmers, at Last'. *Hindu Business Line*, 3 March 2004, www.thehindubusinessline.com/2004/03/03/stories/2004030300160800.htm

19. 'National Federation of State Cooperative Banks Ltd. Memoranda Submitted'. National Federation of State Cooperative Banks Ltd., 16 January 2004, nafscob.org/org_struct/memo28.html

20. 'Ministry of Agriculture & Farmers Welfare'. *Press Information Bureau of India*, 7 February 2004, pib.nic.in/newsite/erelease.aspx?relid=991

21. Purnima Tripathi. 'The Battle Lines'. *Frontline*, 27 February 2004, frontline.thehindu.com/static/html/fl2104/stories/20040227007800400.htm

22. Swapan Dasgupta. 'BJP Chooses Path That Redefined Indian Politics but Becomes Victim of Its Own Novelty'. *India Today*, 15 April 2002, www.indiatoday.in/magazine/cover-story/story/20020415-bjp-chooses-path-that-redefined-indian-politics-but-becomes-victim-of-its-own-novelty-795510-2002-04-15

23. M.S. Swaminathan. 'National Policy for Farmers: Ten Years Later'. *Review of Agrarian Studies*, June 2016, ras.org.in/national_policy_for_farmers_ten_years_later

Chapter 9: The Party President Years

1. 'Swamy Digs out "Legal Bar" on Sonia Becoming PM'. Rediff.com, 3 May 2004, www.rediff.com/election/2004/may/03swamy.htm

2. Sonia Gandhi. 'The Inner Voice of Sonia'. *Outlook*, 18 May 2004, www.outlookindia.com/website/story/my-own-inner-voice/223952

3. A.P.J. Abdul Kalam. *Turning Points: A Journey Through Challenges*, HarperCollins *Publishers* India, 2012.
4. Hari Kumar. 'Sonia Gandhi's "Sacrifice"'. *New York Times*, 3 July 2012, india.blogs.nytimes.com/2012/07/03/sonia-gandhis-sacrifice/
5. K. Natwar-Singh. *One Life Is Not Enough: An Autobiography*, Rupa Publications India, 2014.
6. Vembu. 'Kalam Not Being Truthful on Sonia-as-PM Episode, Says Swamy'. *Firstpost*, 30 June 2012, www.firstpost.com/politics/kalam-not-being-truthful-on-sonia-as-pm-episode-says-swamy-362557.html
    'Why Dr Manmohan Singh and Not Sonia Gandhi Became the PM in 2004'. *Moneylife*, 4 May 2012, www.moneylife.in/article/why-dr-manmohan-singh-and-not-sonia-gandhi-became-the-pm-in-2004/25404.html
7. Sheela Bhatt and Onkar Singh. 'Advani Replaces Venkaiah Naidu as BJP Chief'. Rediff.com, 18 October 2004, www.rediff.com/election/2004/oct/18bjp1.htm
8. 'BJP Admits "India Shining" Error'. *BBC*, 28 May 2004, news.bbc.co.uk/2/hi/south_asia/3756387.stm
9. Amberish K. Diwanji. 'Vajpayee's Strategy, Advani's Tactics'. Rediff.com, 4 December 2003, www.rediff.com/election/2003/dec/04bjp1.htm
10. Neeraj Mishra. 'Chhattisgarh: Dilip Singh Judev Spycam Video Backfires on Congress'. *India Today*, 15 December 2003, www.indiatoday.in/magazine/cover-story/story/20031215-chhattisgarh-dilip-singh-judev-spycam-video-backfires-on-congress-791302-2003-12-15
11. 'Shibu Soren Sworn in as Jharkhand CM'. Rediff.com, 2 March 2005, in.rediff.com/election/2005/mar/02soren.htm
12. 'Munda Challenges Soren's Appointment in SC'. Rediff.com, 7 March 2005, in.rediff.com/election/2005/mar/07jhar.htm
13. Sheela Bhatt. 'Horse Trading: An Inside Look'. Rediff.com, 7 March 2005, www.rediff.com/election/2005/mar/07sheela.htm
14. Amberish K. Diwanji. 'How NDA Pulled Off Operation Decoy'. Rediff.com, 7 March 2005, www.rediff.com/election/2005/mar/03decoy.htm
15. J. Venkatesan. 'Supreme Court Orders Composite Floor Test in Jharkhand on Friday'. *The Hindu*, 10 March 2005, www.thehindu.com/2005/03/10/stories/2005031007940100.htm
16. Sanjay Kumar Jha. 'Jharkhand Political Drama Ends with Arjun Munda Winning Trust Vote'. *India Today*, 28 March 2005, www.indiatoday.in/magazine/states/story/20050328-jharkhand-political-drama-ends-with-arjun-munda-winning-trust-vote-788024-2005-03-28

17. 'CPI, CPI-M Leaders to Visit Pakistan'. *Dawn*, 19 November 2004, www.dawn.com/news/400231
18. Radhika Ramaseshan. 'Advani Salutes "Secular" Jinnah'. *Telegraph*, 4 June 2005, www.telegraphindia.com/india/advani-salutes-secular-jinnah/cid/873488
19. Aroon Purie and Prabhu Chawla. 'I Am Proud of My Hinduism, I Am Not against Muslims: LK Advani'. *India Today*, 16 January 2006, www.indiatoday.in/magazine/interview/story/20060116-i-am-proud-of-my-hinduism-i-am-not-against-muslims-lk-advani-786117-2006-01-16
20. Venkitesh Ramakrishnan. 'Advani Launches "Nyay Yatra at Varanasi'. *The Hindu*, 7 December 2005, www.thehindu.com/2005/12/07/stories/2005120709051200.htm
21. Mark Tully. 'Time to Settle Local Scores'. *Telegraph*, 25 April 2004, www.telegraphindia.com/india/time-to-settle-local-scores/cid/967115
22. Aman Sethi. 'Rule of the Outlaw'. *Frontline*, 17 December 2005, frontline. thehindu.com/static/html/fl2226/stories/20051230004301700.htm
23. Rajeev Dikshit and Pathikrit Chakraborty. 'Munna Bajrangi: Man Who Introduced Kalashnikov to UP Gang Wars'. *Times of India*, 10 July 2018, timesofindia.indiatimes.com/india/man-who-introduced-kalashnikov-to-up-gang-wars/articleshow/64925179.cms
24. Prabhu Razdan. 'Rajnath's Nyay Yatra Faces Uncertainty'. *Hindustan Times*, 22 January 2006, www.hindustantimes.com/india/rajnath-s-nyay-yatra-faces-uncertainty/story-KSc2u2JtW7r0vv0DnSn85N.html
25. Shekhar Iyer. 'Atal's Laxman Talk Leaves BJP Confused'. *Hindustan Times*, 31 December 2005, www.hindustantimes.com/india/atal-s-laxman-talk-leaves-bjp-confused/story-knK1fwmltWlp8y11pdxfTM.html
26. 'Mahajan Accepts Blame for BJP Debacle'. Rediff.com, 13 May 2004, www.rediff.com/election/2004/may/13pramod.htm
27. S. Prasannarajan and Priya Sahgal. 'Rajnath Singh Re-Elected BJP President, Aims to Restore Party's Glory'. *India Today*, 11 December 2006, www.indiatoday.in/magazine/nation/story/20061211-new-president-of-bjp-rajnath-singh-781811-2006-12-11
28. 'Aftermath: Lashkar-e-Qahab Owns up for Varanasi Blasts'. *Times of India*, 9 March 2006, timesofindia.indiatimes.com/india/Aftermath-Lashkar-e-Qahab-owns-up-for-Varanasi-blasts/articleshow/1444021.cms?referral=PM; 'Rajnath Kicks off Bharat Suraksha Yatra'. Rediff. com, 6 April 2006, www.rediff.com/news/2006/apr/06yatra4.htm
29. 'Indian Supreme Court Defends Assam Against "Bangladeshi Aggression"'. *WikiLeaks*, July 2005, wikileaks.org/plusd/cables/05NEWDELHI5913_a.html

30. 'BJP Cancels Bharat Suraksha Yatra'. *Daily News & Analysis*, 4 May 2006, www.dnaindia.com/india/report-bjp-cancels-bharat-suraksha-yatra-1027662
31. 'Pramod Mahajan Loses Battle for Life'. *The Hindu*, 4 May 2006, www.thehindu.com/todays-paper/pramod-mahajan-loses-battle-for-life/article3128386.ece
32. Priya Sahgal. 'Pramod Mahajan: Fastest Rising Leader of His Generation in BJP'. *India Today*, 8 May 2006, www.indiatoday.in/magazine/coverstory/story/20060508-pramod-mahajan-fastest-rising-leader-of-his-generation-in-bjp-785583-2006-05-08
33. S. Prasannarajan and Priya Sahgal. 'Rajnath Singh Re-Elected BJP President, Aims to Restore Party's Glory'. *India Today*, 11 December 2006, www.indiatoday.in/magazine/nation/story/20061211-new-president-of-bjp-rajnath-singh-781811-2006-12-11
34. Rajnath Singh. 'National Executive Presidential Address'. BJP National Convention, 23 December 2006, www.bjp.org/en/national-executive-2015/2006/?u=presidential-speech-by-sh-rajnath-singh-in-national-council-meeting-lucknow-uttar-pradesh-1
35. 'Muslims Must Have First Claim on Resources: PM'. *Times of India*, 9 December 2006, timesofindia.indiatimes.com/india/Muslims-must-have-first-claim-on-resources-PM/articleshow/754937.cms
36. Neeraj Mishra. 'Justice Sachar Presents Report on Status of Indian Muslims'. *India Today*, 4 December 2006, www.indiatoday.in/magazine/nation/story/20061204-justice-rajinder-sachar-present-the-committe-report-on-indian-muslims-2006-781990-2006-12-04
37. Somini Sengupta. 'Israelis Warned to Avoid Goa, a Longtime Favorite Tourist Destination for Young Travelers'. *New York Times*, 16 December 2006, www.nytimes.com/2006/12/16/world/middleeast/16goa.html
38. Syed Amin Jafri. 'Rajnath Extends Full Support for Telangana State'. Rediff.com, 18 March 2005, www.rediff.com/news/2006/mar/18rajnath.htm
39. Prabhu Chawla. 'BJP Leader Rajnath Singh Talks to Prabhu Chawla on Seedhi Baat'. *India Today*, 19 March 2007, www.indiatoday.in/magazine/seedhi-baat/story/20070319-rajnath-singh-in-an-exclusive-with-prabhu-chawla-for-india-today-748918-2007-03-19
40. Shankkar Aiyar and Puja Mehra. 'Price Rise Worries Trouble UPA Government'. *India Today*, 7 March 2007, www.indiatoday.in/magazine/cover-story/story/20070305-inflation-and-price-rise-the-prime-concern-of-common-man-government-need-to-tackle-748854-2007-03-05#

41. Prabhu Chawla. 'BJP Leader Rajnath Singh Talks to Prabhu Chawla on Seedhi Baat'. *India Today*, 19 March 2007, www.indiatoday. in/magazine/seedhi-baat/story/20070319-rajnath-singh-in-an-exclusive-with-prabhu-chawla-for-india-today-748918-2007-03-19

42. 'Committee Report on 33% Representation of Women in BJP at Organisational Level'. BJP National Convention, September 2007.

43. 'Women's Bill: What's the Fuss about?' Rediff.com, 24 August 2005, www.rediff.com/news/2005/aug/24spec2.htm

44. Shekhar Iyer. "Who Is BJP's PM-in-Waiting?" *Hindustan Times*, 8 September 2007, www.hindustantimes.com/india/who-is-bjp-s-pm-inwaiting/ story-Q1Y2v2PZwArslYxRj5pR7M.html

45. 'I'll Be Candidate for PM: Advani'. *iTimes of India*, 10 December 2006, timesofindia.indiatimes.com/india/Ill-be-candidate-for-PM-Advani/ articleshow/763314.cms

46. Priya Sahgal. 'Who Is the Leader?' *India Today*, 7 November 2007, www.indiatoday.in/magazine/nation/story/20070910-who-is-the-leader-733873-2007-09-07

47. 'VK Malhotra, Six Other BJP MPs Quit LS'. *Economic Times*, 17 December 2008, http://economictimes.indiatimes.com/news/ politics-and-nation/vk-malhotra-six-other-bjp-mps-quit-ls/ articleshow/3848805.cms?from=mdr

48. RSS' Stamp Finally Puts Rajnath under Advani's Thumb'. *Economic Times*, 5 January 2009, http://economictimes.indiatimes.com/news/ politics-and-nation/rss-stamp-finally-puts-rajnath-under-advanis-thumb/articleshow/3935641.cms?from=mdr

49. 'I Don't Expect Atal to Return Favour to Me: Advani'. *Daily News & Analysis*, 10 December 2006, www.dnaindia.com/india/report-i-don-t-expect-atal-to-return-favour-to-me-advani-1068589

50. Rajdeep Sardesai. 'We Did Not Feel That The Story Was Complete'. *Outlook*, Outlookindia.com, 29 July 2008, www.outlookindia.com/ website/story/we-did-not-feel-that-the-story-was-complete/238044

51. 'New Arrest in Indian "Cash for Votes" Scandal'. *BBC News*, 28 September 2011, www.bbc.com/news/world-south-asia-15086265

52. 'Political Bargaining Continues Prior to Key Vote in Parliament'. WikiLeaks, 17 July 2008, wikileaks.org/plusd/ cables/08NEWDELHI1972_a.html

53. 'BJP Makes a "Sankalp" in Bengaluru'. Rediff.com, 14 September 2008, specials.rediff.com/news/2008/sep/14sld1.htm

54. 'Now, Jaitley Endorses Modi as PM-in-Waiting after Advani'. NDTV. com, 25 April 2009, www.ndtv.com/india-news/now-jaitley-endorses-

modi-as-pm-in-waiting-after-advani-392755; Chowdhury, Neerja. 'Arun to Varun, BJP Image Takes a Beating'. *CurrentNews*, 23 May 2009, currentnews.in/arun-varun-bjp-image-takes-beating/

55. Aditi Phadnis. 'Mandal, Not Mandir'. *Business Standard*, 7 February 2009, www.business-standard.com/article/opinion/aditi-phadnis-mandal-not-mandir-109020700043_1.html

56. 'Treasury Targets Al Qaida and Lashkar-E Tayyiba Networks in Pakistan'. *U.S. Department of the Treasury*, 1 July 2009, http://www.treasury.gov/press-center/press-releases/Pages/tg192.aspx" www.treasury.gov/press-center/press-releases/Pages/tg192.aspx

57. Narayan Lakshman. 'U.S. Designates Terrorist Group Operating in India and Pakistan'. *The Hindu*, 7 August 2010, http://www.thehindu.com/news/international/U.S.-designates-terrorist-group-operating-in-India-and-Pakistan/article16123379.ece

58. B. Raman. 'Curiouser And Curiouser'. *Outlook*, 6 August 2010, http://www.outlookindia.com/website/story/curiouser-and-curiouser/266576

59. B. Raman. 'Why Politicizing the Malegaon Case Is Dangerous'. Rediff. com, 17 November 2011, http://www.rediff.com/news/slide-show/slide-show-1-why-politicising-the-malegaon-case-is-dangerous-raman/20111117

60. Bhavna Vij-Aurora. 'Hardselling Terror'. *India Today*, 20 November 2008, www.indiatoday.in/magazine/nation/story/20081201-hardselling-terror-738301-2008-11-20

61. Bharatiya Janata Party. 'BJP Manifesto: Lok Sabha Elections 2009'. 3 April 2009, www.bjp.org/en/documents/manifesto/manifesto-lok-sabha-election-2009

62. Lal Krishna Advani. '"एक कवि-हृदय राजनेता."' *Sahitya Amrita*, December 2018; Priya Sahgal. 'The Games Begin'. *India Today*, 15 October 2008, www.indiatoday.in/magazine/nation/story/20080929-the-games-begin-737634-2008-09-19

63. 'Varun Gandhi Arrested over Muslim Hate Speech'. *Reuters*, 29 March 2009, in.reuters.com/article/idINIndia-38758620090329

64. 'Congress Drops Jagdish Tytler, Sajjan Kumar'. *Economic Times*, 10 April 2009, economictimes.indiatimes.com/congress-drops-jagdish-tytler-sajjan-kumar/articleshow/4384398.cms

65. 'Manmohan Weakest PM Ever: Advani'. *India Today*, 24 March 2009, www.indiatoday.in/latest-headlines/story/manmohan-weakest-pm-ever-advani-42541-2009-03-24; M.D. Nalapat. 'Why the BJP Lost a Sure Election'. *The Jewish Institute for National Security of America*, 29 May 2009, www.jinsa.org/publications/research-articles/central-south-asia/why-bjp-lost-sure-election

66. M.D. Nalapat. 'Why the BJP Lost a Sure Election'. *The Jewish Institute for National Security of America*, 29 May 2009, www.jinsa.org/publications/research-articles/central-south-asia/why-bjp-lost-sure-election

67. Kenneth Bo Nielsen and Alf Gunvald Nilsen, editors. *Social Movements and the State in India Deepening Democracy?* Palgrave Macmillan, 2016.

68. 'Jaswant Questions BJP Leadership on Poll Loss'. News18, 11 June 2009, www.news18.com/news/politics/rebellion-in-bjp-jaswant-letter-318092.html

69. 'Strategy Mian'. *Outlook*, 22 September 2008.

70. 'Jaswant Questions BJP Leadership on Poll Loss'. News18, 11 June 2009, www.news18.com/news/politics/rebellion-in-bjp-jaswant-letter-318092.html

71. Arun Jaitley. 'Triumph of the Moderate'. *Indian Express*, 27 May 2009, archive.indianexpress.com/news/triumph-of-the-moderate/466421/0

72. 'Jinnah Was a Great Man: Jaswant Singh'. *Times of India*, 17 August 2009, timesofindia.indiatimes.com/india/Jinnah-was-a-great-man-Jaswant-Singh/articleshow/4900197.cms

73. Saba Naqvi. 'Advani Is Not Fit . . .To Serve The Interests Of The Country'. *Outlook*, 7 September 2009, www.outlookindia.com/magazine/story/advani-is-not-fitto-serve-the-interests-of-the-country/261553

74. Suman K. Jha. 'Shourie Dares: RSS Must Rebuild BJP, Chief Rajnath Is Alice in Blunderland: *Indian Express*'. *Indian Express*, 25 August 2009, archive.indianexpress.com/news/shourie-dares-rss-must-rebuild-bjp-chief-rajnath-is-alice-in-blunderland/506811/; 'Jaswant Blames Advani for Cash-for-Votes Scam'. News18, 28 August 2009, www.news18.com/news/politics/jaswant-blames-advani-for-cash-for-votes-scam-323614.html

75. Rajnath Singh. 'National Executive Presidential Address'. June 2009, www.bjp.org/en/national-executive-2015/2009/?u=presidential-speech-by-shri-rajnath-singh-at-the-national-executive-meeting-parliament-annexe-new-delhi-1

Chapter 10: Take It to the Voter

1. Aaron Smith. ' The Internet's Role in Campaign 2008'. *Pew Research Center: Internet, Science & Tech*, 15 April 2009, www.pewinternet.org/2009/04/15/the-internets-role-in-campaign-2008/

2. Arun Prabhudesai. 'Interesting Facebook India Statistics [Numbers, Growth, Brands]'. *Trak*, 30 October 2017, trak.in/tags/business/2011/06/24/facebook-india-statistics/

3. Nikhil Pahwa. 'Facebook Opens India Office; Users Mostly From Delhi & Mumbai'. *MediaNama*, 1 October 2010, www.medianama. com/2010/10/223-facebook-opens-india-office-users-mostly-from-delhi-mumbai/

4. T. Ramakrishnan. 'BJP's Focus Is on Development, Socio-Economic Reform, and Nationalism: Nitin Gadkari'. *The Hindu*, 12 April 2010, www.thehindu.com/opinion/op-ed/BJPs-focus-is-on-development-socio-economic-reform-and-nationalism-Nitin-Gadkari/ article16366188.ece

5. 'Deepening Economic Doubts in India'. *Pew Research Center's Global Attitudes Project*, 10 September 2012, www.pewglobal.org/2012/09/10/ deepening-economic-doubts-in-india/

6. Animesh Roul. 'After Pune, Details Emerge on the Karachi Project and Its Threat to India'. *CTC Sentinel*, April 2010, ctc.usma.edu/ after-pune-details-emerge-on-the-karachi-project-and-its-threat-to-india/

7. 'Somali Pirates Capture 120 Indian Sailors'. *Times of India*, 30 March. 2010, timesofindia.indiatimes.com/india/Somali-pirates-capture-120-Indian-sailors/articleshow/5741365.cms

8. 'BJP Slams Maya, Defends Maharaj on Stampede'. *Outlook*, 6 March 2010, www.outlookindia.com/newswire/story/bjp-slams-maya-defends-maharaj-on-stampede/675969

9. Reetika Khera. 'Wages of Delay'. *Frontline*, May 2010, frontline. thehindu.com/static/html/fl2710/stories/20100521271010500.htm

10. Himanshu, et al. 'NREGS in Rajasthan: Rationed Funds and Their Allocation across Villages'. *Economic and Political Weekly*, 5 February 2015, www.epw.in/journal/2015/6/special-articles/nregs-rajasthan.html

11. Piyush Srivastava. 'UP NREGA Scam Worth over Rs 10,000 Crore, Claims Sandeep Dixit'. *India Today*, 29 October 2011, www.indiatoday. in/india/north/story/nrega-scam-sandeep-dixit-144340-2011-10-29

12. '"Aadhaar", the Unique ID Project Goes Live!' *Gadget Now*, 29 September 2010, www.gadgetsnow.com/tech-news/Aadhaar-the-Unique-ID-project-goes-live/articleshow/6652043.cms

13. 'Cash Transfer of Subsidies in 51 Districts Begins on Jan 1'. *Tribune*, 25 November 2012, www.tribuneindia.com/2012/20121125/main1.htm

14. Promit Mukherjee. 'DBTL Helps Govt Save Rs 10,000 Crore as Illegal LPG Consumption Falls'. *Livemint*, 2 July 2015, www.livemint.com/ Industry/PGCreyRo9L9rCt3Vx3xyBO/DBTL-helps-govt-save-Rs10000-crore-as-illegal-LPG-consumpti.html; 'PM Narendra Modi Wants Integration of All Land Records with Aadhaar'. *Economic Times*, 24 March 2016, economictimes.indiatimes.com/news/economy/policy/

pm-narendra-modi-wants-integration-of-all-land-records-with-
aadhaar/articleshow/51535407.cms
15. *Press Trust of India.* 'Declare Pak A Rogue State, Rajnath Tells UN In
Hindi'. *India TV*, 7 October 2010, www.indiatvnews.com/news/india/
declare-pak-a-rogue-state-rajnath-tells-un-in-hindi-4968.html
16. 'PM Thanks Advani for BJP's Support on Nuclear Liability Bill'.
Times of India, 26 August 2010, timesofindia.indiatimes.com/india/
PM-thanks-Advani-for-BJPs-support-on-nuclear-liability-bill/
articleshow/6440143.cms
17. *Anna Hazare on Indefinite Fast over Stronger Lokpal Bill.* Web Archive,
5 April 2011, web.archive.org/web/20110410042738/http://www.
hindustantimes.com/Anna-Hazare-to-start-fast-unto-death-for-
strong-Lokpal-Bill/Article1-681415.aspx
18. 'Indian Activist Anna Hazare Begins Anti-Graft Fast'. *BBC News*,
5 April 2011, www.bbc.com/news/world-south-asia-12968151;
'Northeast Support to Hazare'. *Times of India*, 9 April 2011,
timesofindia.indiatimes.com/city/guwahati/Northeast-support-to-
Hazares/articleshow/7921183.cms?referral=PM
19. 'Government Issues Notification to Constitute a Joint Drafting
Committee to Prepare Draft Lok Pal Bill'. *Press Information Bureau of
India*, 9 April 2011, pib.nic.in/newsite/erelease.aspx?relid=71560
20. 'Midnight Police Swoop on Baba Ramdev Ends Protest'. *Times of
India*, 5 June 2011, timesofindia.indiatimes.com/india/Midnight-
police-swoop-on-Baba-Ramdev-ends-protest/articleshow/8730121.
cms
21. Bindu Shajan Perappadan. 'Rajbala, Seriously Injured in Ramlila
Crackdown, Dies'. *The Hindu*, 26 September 2011, www.thehindu.com/
news/cities/Delhi/rajbala-seriously-injured-in-ramlila-crackdown-
dies/article2486713.ece
22. 'Satyagraha at Rajghat: Shri Rajnath Singh'. *Bharatiya
Janata Party*, 6 June 2011, www.youtube.com/watch?time_
continue=377&v=eQzd6gkOZ2o
23. 'BJP Deputes Rajnath to Meet Farmers in Gurgaon over Land Row'.
Times of India, 5 August 2011, timesofindia.indiatimes.com/india/
BJP-deputes-Rajnath-to-meet-farmers-in-Gurgaon-over-land-row/
articleshow/9487301.cms
24. Sunit Dhawan. 'State Misusing Power to Loot Land: Rajnath'. *Tribune*,
6 August. 2011, www.tribuneindia.com/2011/20110806/haryana.
htm#1
25. Atiq Khan. 'BJP in Yatra Mode, Galaxy of Party Leaders to Descend
on U.P. This Week'. *The Hindu*, 9 October 2011, www.thehindu.com/

todays-paper/tp-national/bjp-in-yatra-mode-galaxy-of-party-leaders-to-descend-on-up-this-week/article2522676.ece
26. Piyush Srivastava. 'Uttar Pradesh Polls: Revolt in BJP over Promotion of Rajnath Singh's Son'. *India Today*, 23 January 2012, www.indiatoday.in/india/north/story/uttar-pradesh-revolt-bjp-promotion-rajnath-singh-pankaj-singh-90594-2012-01-23
27. Rajiv Srivastava. 'Denied Poll Ticket Thrice, Rajnath's Son Biding His Time'. *Times of India*, 28 August 2014, timesofindia.indiatimes.com/india/Denied-poll-ticket-thrice-Rajnaths-son-biding-his-time/articleshow/41031603.cms
28. Piyush Srivastava. 'Uttar Pradesh Polls: Revolt in BJP over Promotion of Rajnath Singh's Son'. *India Today*, 23 January 2012, www.indiatoday.in/india/north/story/uttar-pradesh-revolt-bjp-promotion-rajnath-singh-pankaj-singh-90594-2012-01-23
29. Shekhar Gupta, et al. 'The January Night Raisina Hill Was Spooked: Two Key Army Units Moved towards Delhi without Notifying Govt'. *Indian Express*, 4 April 2012, archive.indianexpress.com/news/the-january-night-raisina-hill-was-spooked-two-key-army-units-moved-towards-delhi-without-notifying-govt/932328/0
30. 'Command and Control'. *Courage and Conviction: An Autobiography*, by General V. K. Singh with Kunal Verma, Aleph Book, 2013, p. 751.
31. Mahapatra, Dhananjay. 'Gen. VK Singh Loses Battle for Age, Tries to Save Some Honour'. *Times of India*, 12 February 2012, timesofindia.indiatimes.com/india/Gen-VK-Singh-loses-battle-for-age-tries-to-save-some-honour/articleshow/11843085.cms
32. 'India Rejects Army Movement Sparked Coup Fears'. *BBC*, 4 April 2012, www.bbc.com/news/world-asia-india-17606834
33. Diana Owen. 'The New Media's Role in Politics'. *The Age of Perplexity: Rethinking the World We Knew*, Penguin Random House, 2017.
34. Amarnath Chattopadhyay. 'How BJP Rode On Social Media Towards A Sweeping Victory In 2014'. *Digital Vidya*, 16 July 2015, www.digitalvidya.com/blog/how-bjp-rode-on-social-media-towards-a-sweeping-victory-in-2014/
35. *Press Trust of India*. 'Birthday Bombshell: Advani Sets Tongues Wagging on PM Ambition'. *India Today*, 8 November 2012, www.indiatoday.in/india/story/advani-birthday-prime-minister-ambitions-120953-2012-11-08
36. Ramdutt Tripathi. "आडवाणी प्रधानमंत्री के लिए सबसे योग्य: उमा भारती." *BBC News*, 13 October 2011, www.bbc.com/hindi/india/2011/10/111013_up_bjp_yatra_adg
37. Minhaz Merchant. '2014: Winning India's 150 Million First-Time Voters'. *Economic Times*, 20 September 2013, economictimes.

indiatimes.com/blogs/headon/2014-winning-india-s-150-million-
first-time-voters/
38. Kiran Tare and Bhavna Vij-Aurora. 'Will BJP President Nitin Gadkari
    Get His Second Term in Office?' *India Today*, 5 November 2012,
    www.indiatoday.in/magazine/india/corruption-charges-against-nitin-
    gadkari/story/20121105-bjp-president-nitin-gadkari-second-term-in-
    office-is-unlikely-760348-1999-11-30
39. 'Nitin Gadkari's Corruption Charge Is BJP's Internal Matter, but RSS
    Tells Him to "Come Clean"'. *Indian Express*, 24 October 2012, archive.
    indianexpress.com/news/nitin-gadkaris-corruption-charge-is-bjp-s-
    internal-matter-but-rss-tells-him-to--come-clean-/1021466/
40. Ibid.
41. Bhavna Vij-Aurora. 'The Burden of Gadkari'. *India Today*, 25 January
    2013,   www.indiatoday.in/india/corruption-charges-against-nitin-
    gadkari/story/the-burden-of-gadkari-152504-2013-01-25
42. Ibid.

Chapter 11: Two in a Wave

1. B. Muralidhar Reddy. 'Rajnath Takes Charge of the '"Party of
   Differences"'. *Hindu*, 23 June 2013, www.thehindu.com/news/national/
   rajnath-takes-charge-of-the-party-of-differences/article4335476.ece
2. 'One Man, One Post: Jaitley Steps down as BJP Gen Secy'. *News18*,
   16 June 2009, www.news18.com/news/politics/jaitley-quits-jaitley-vo-
   nalin-kohli-chunk-318464.html
3. 'LK Advani Back in Prime Ministerial Race?' *Zee News*, 6 April 2013,
   zeenews.india.com/news/nation/lk-advani-back-in-prime-ministerial-
   race_840243.html
4. B.S. Yeddyurappa had been charged with corruption and left the party
   in 2011 to form his own party, the Karnataka Janata Paksha. However,
   in 2014, he merged his party with the BJP and was subsequently elected
   to the sixteenth Lok Sabha from the Shimoga constituency.
5. T.A. Johnson. 'The Charges against Yeddyurappa and His Defense'.
   Indian Express, 26 October 2016, indianexpress.com/article/opinion/
   web-edits/the-charges-against-former-karnataka-chief-minister-b-s-
   yeddyurappa-and-his-defense-3103674/
6. 'Sukhbir Badal Supports Modi as NDA's PM Candidate, Says Akalis
   with BJP in Its Decision'. *India Today*, 30 January 2013, www.
   indiatoday.in/india/north/story/sukhbir-badal-supports-narendra-
   modi-as-nda-pm-candidate-152871-2013-01-30
7. IANS. 'Shiv Sena to Support Modi or Any Other Candidate as BJP's
   PM Nominee'. *India Today*, 13 September 2013, www.indiatoday.in/

india/story/shiv-sena-to-support-modi-or-any-other-candidate-for-bjps-pm-nominee-210845-2013-09-13

8. 'Raj Thackeray Says He Will Support Narendra Modi for PM in 2014 Polls'. *India Today*, 26 March 2014, www.indiatoday.in/elections/highlights/story/will-support-narendra-modi-for-pm-says-mns-chief-raj-thackeray-184268-2014-03-09

9. 'Modi, Nitish Avoid Each Other as They Come Face-to-Face at CMs' Meet in Delhi'. *India Today*, 13 June 2013, www.indiatoday.in/india/north/story/nctc-meet-modi-nitish-avoid-each-other-165646-2013-06-05

10. Deepshikha Ghosh. 'Gujarat Court Accepts Clean Chit to Narendra Modi in 2002 Riots'. NDTV.com, 26 December 2013, www.ndtv.com/cheat-sheet/gujarat-court-accepts-clean-chit-to-narendra-modi-in-2002-riots-545759

11. Ibid.

12. Lakshmi Chaudhry. 'Nidhi Razdan vs Barry Gardiner: A Spectacle of Shamelessness'. *Firstpost*, 16 August 2013, www.firstpost.com/politics/nidhi-razdan-vs-barry-gardiner-a-spectacle-of-shamelessness-1038279.html

13. 'Advani Skips Goa Conclave; BJP Says "Wait till Tomorrow" for a "Major Announcement"'. *Hindustan Times*, 8 June 2013, www.hindustantimes.com/india/advani-skips-goa-conclave-bjp-says-wait-till-tomorrow-for-a-major-announcement/story-GCvBNIWJZx6bO5GnxtrZyH.html

14. 'NaMo Mantra to Dominate BJP's Meet in Goa but Consensus Eludes Party'. *India Today*, 7 June 2013, www.indiatoday.in/india/story/namo-mantra-to-dominate-bjps-meet-in-goa-consensus-eludes-party-165883-2013-06-07

15. Sahil Makkar, et al. 'Many Top BJP Leaders Call in Sick before Goa Conclave'. *Livemint*, 7 June 2013, www.livemint.com/Politics/DmZrJQLxnBkc8ijCP4A1EN/LK-Advani-to-skip-BJP-office-bearers-meeting-in-Goa.html

16. IANS. 'Goa Conclave Day 2: Narendra Modi Likely to Be Named BJP Election Chief Tomorrow'. *India Today*, 7 June 2013, www.indiatoday.in/india/north/story/goa-national-executive-meet-day-2-bjp-delays-decision-on-poll-campaign-committee-chief-166009-2013-06-07

17. Radhika Ramaseshan. 'Rajnath Grasps What Advani Would Not, More Mature in Fresh Innings'. *Telegraph*, 12 June 2013, www.telegraphindia.com/india/rajnath-grasps-what-advani-would-not-more-mature-in-fresh-innings/cid/288224

18. 'Narendra Modi Begins Month-Long Vivekanand Yuva Vikas Yatra'. *India Today*, 11 September 2012, www.indiatoday.in/india/west/

story/narendra-modi-begins-month-long-vivekanand-yuva-vikas-yatra-115742-2012-09-11

19. 'Modi's Gujarat Bags Tata's Nano'. *Business Standard*, 8 October 2008, www.business-standard.com/article/companies/modi-s-gujarat-bags-tata-s-nano-108100801044_1.html

20. 'JD (U) Ends 17-Year-Old Alliance with BJP, Quits NDA'. *Times of India*, 16 June 2013, timesofindia.indiatimes.com/india/JDU-ends-17-year-old-alliance-with-BJP-quits-NDA/articleshow/20616468.cms

21. 'Narendra Modi Anointed BJP PM Candidate, Advani Disappointed'. *Times of India*, 13 Sept. 2013, timesofindia.indiatimes.com/india/Narendra-Modi-anointed-BJP-PM-candidate-Advani-disappointed/articleshow/22554959.cms

22. 'How Modi Became BJP PM Candidate'. News18, 13 September 2013, www.news18.com/news/politics/advani-modi--638522.html

23. 'Election Results 2014: India Places Its Faith in Moditva'. *Times of India*, 17 May 2014, timesofindia.indiatimes.com/news/Election-results-2014-India-places-its-faith-in-Moditva/articleshow/35224486.cms

24. 'Rajnath Singh Surpasses Atal Bihari Vajpayee's Victory Margin in Lucknow'. *Daily News & Analysis*, 17 May 2014, www.dnaindia.com/india/report-rajnath-singh-surpasses-atal-bihari-vajpayee-s-victory-margin-in-lucknow-1989202

25. Dipanjan Roy Chaudhury. 'US Honours BJP Chief Rajnath Singh on Election Day in Lucknow'. *Economic Times*, 2 May 2014, m.economictimes.com/news/politics-and-nation/us-honours-bjp-chief-rajnath-singh-on-election-day-in-lucknow/amp_articleshow/34499613.cms#stickyBanner

Chapter 12: Set It Right

1. Praveen Swami. 'In a First, Modi Invites SAARC Leaders for His Swearing-In'. *The Hindu*, 21 May 2014, www.thehindu.com/news/national/in-a-first-modi-invites-saarc-leaders-for-his-swearingin/article6033710.ece

2. 'Karnataka No Longer Naxal Infested'. *Times of India*, 26 August 2010, articles.timesofindia.indiatimes.com/2010-08-26/hubli/28275788_1_police-station-naxal-activities-home-minister

3. Mahendra Kumar Singh. 'Development Plan for Naxal-Hit Districts Shows Good Response'. *Times of India*, 22 June 2011, timesofindia.indiatimes.com/india/Development-plan-for-Naxal-hit-districts-shows-good-response/articleshow/8958266.cms?referral=PM;

Maneesh Chhibber. 'Centre to Declare More Districts Naxal-Hit'. *Indian Express*, 5 July 2011, archive.indianexpress.com/news/centre-to-declare-more-districts-naxalhit/812671

4. Surabhi Malik. 'Sabyasachi Panda, Odisha's Most Wanted Naxal Leader, Arrested'. NDTV.com, 18 July 2014, www.ndtv.com/india-news/sabyasachi-panda-odishas-most-wanted-naxal-leader-arrested-590380

5. 'Rajnath to Undertake Aerial Survey of Flood-Hit Jammu and Kashmir Today'. *India Today*, 6 September 2014, www.indiatoday.in/india/story/floods-jammu-and-kashmir-rajnath-singh-aerial-survey-207465-2014-09-06

6. *Press Information Bureau of India*. 'Round-up of Rescue and Relief Operations in Flood-Hit J&K'. 12 September 2014, pib.nic.in/newsite/printrelease.aspx?relid=91945; *Press Information Bureau of India*. 'Union Government Provides Massive Relief in Flood Affected J&K'. 18 September 2014, pib.nic.in/newsite/printrelease.aspx?relid=109800

7. Toufiq Rashid. 'Flood Situation Grim in Kashmir, Army Cantonment Flooded'. *Hindustan Times*, 7 September 2014, web.archive.org/web/20140907103430/http://www.hindustantimes.com/india-news/-flood-situation-grim-in-kashmir-army-cantonment-flooded/article1-1261140.aspx

8. Nida Najar and Salman Masood. 'India and Pakistan Strain as Flooding Kills Hundreds'. *New York Times*, 8 September 2014, www.nytimes.com/2014/09/09/world/asia/hundreds-dead-in-flooding-in-india-and-pakistan.html

9. Aman Sharma. 'Home Minister Rajnath Singh Asks to Revamp CRPF to Fight Naxals'. *Economic Times*, 1 October 2014, economictimes.indiatimes.com/news/politics-and-nation/home-minister-rajnath-singh-asks-to-revamp-crpf-to-fight-naxals/articleshow/43967383.cms

10. Soudhriti Bhabani. '58 Terror Modules Operating from Illegal Madrasas in West Bengal, Reveals Probe'. *India Today*, 31 October 2014, www.indiatoday.in/india/east/story/west-bengal-madrasas-tterror-modules-burdwan-blast-bangladesh-nia-nsg-ib-225251-2014-10-31

11. Ibid.

12. Rupam Jain Nair. 'India Uncovers Suspected Plot to Assassinate Bangladeshi PM'. *Reuters*, 28 October 2014, in.reuters.com/article/india-bangladesh-plot-hasina/india-uncovers-suspected-plot-to-assassinate-bangladeshi-pm-security-officials-idINKBN0IH1HN20141028

13. 'NIA to Probe NDFB(S) Mass Killing in Assam: Rajnath Singh'. *Livemint*, 25 December 2014, www.livemint.com/Politics/JRz4YV6HAK5UCHnXigA3MM/Assam-attacks-Death-toll-rises-to-72-angry-Adivasis-retali.html

14. Pavan Dahat. '14 CRPF Men Die in Maoist Strike'. *The Hindu*, 1 December 2014, www.thehindu.com/news/national/13-crpf-men-killed-inmaoist-ambush-in-chhattisgarh/article6651913.ece; Fayaz Bukhari. 'Eleven Soldiers, Police Dead in Attack on Camp in Kashmir'. *Reuters*, 5 December 2014, in.reuters.com/article/india-kashmir-suicide-attack/eleven-soldiers-police-dead-in-attack-on-camp-in-kashmir-idINKCN0JJ0CK20141205?irpc=932

15. 'Officials: Boat Carrying Explosives Blows up off Indian Coast'. *Al Jazeera America*, 2 January 2015, america.aljazeera.com/articles/2015/1/2/india-pakistan-boat.html

16. Col (Retd) Anil Athale. 'The Boat Incident Could Have Led to Nuclear War'. Rediff.com, 7 January 2015, www.rediff.com/news/column/anil-a-athale-the-boat-incident-could-have-led-to-nuclear-war/20150107.htm

17. 'Pakistani Vessel Blow-up: DIG BK Loshali Dismissed by Indian Coast Guard'. *International Business Times*, India Edition, 14 December 2015, www.ibtimes.co.in/pakistani-vessel-blow-dig-bk-loshali-dismissed-by-indian-coast-guard-659452

18. Michael R. Gordon and Gardiner Harris. 'Kerry Lays Groundwork for Obama's Visit to India'. *New York Times*, 11 January 2015, www.nytimes.com/2015/01/12/world/asia/john-kerry-india-narendra-modi.html

19. '15 Things That India Achieved Due to Obama's Visit'. *Times of India*, 28 January 2015, timesofindia.indiatimes.com/india/15-things-that-India-achieved-due-to-Obamas-visit/articleshow/46037486.cms

20. 'Barack Obama, Narendra Modi Meet: 6 Key Takeaways from India Visit'. *Financial Express*, 27 January 2015, www.financialexpress.com/economy/narendra-modi-barack-obama-meet-key-takeaways-from-india-visit/35202/

21. Lisa Curtis. 'Takeaways from the Obama Visit'. *The Hindu*, 30 January 2015, www.thehindu.com/opinion/lead/takeaways-from-the-obama-visit/article6835420.ece

22. Kabir Taneja. 'Why Operation Rahat Is a Major Achievement For India'. HuffPost India, 8 April 2015, www.huffingtonpost.in/kabir-taneja/why-operation-rahat-is-a-_b_7023266.html?ec_carp=5339689712350719095

23. *Press Information Bureau of India*. Sushma Swaraj. 'Statement in Lok Sabha on "Recent Developments in the Republic of Yemen and Efforts Made for Safe Evacuation of Indian Nationals from There"'. 20 April 2015, pib.nic.in/newsite/PrintRelease.aspx?relid=118364

24. Ministry of External Affairs, Government of India. 'Press Release: Prime Minister's Telephonic Conversation with King Salman Bin Abdul Aziz Al Saud of Saudi Arabia'. 30 March 2015.

25. Pranav Kulkarni. 'Yemen: Naval Warship Sails into "Barrage of Bombs", Evacuates 349 Indians'. *Indian Express*, 1 April 2015, indianexpress. com/article/india/india-others/indian-navy-evacuates-nearly-348-indians-from-strife-torn-yemen/

26. *Press Information Bureau of India*. 'Rescue Operations by India'. 23 December 2015, pib.nic.in/newsite/printrelease.aspx?relid=133841

27. 'US among 26 Countries Asking India to Help Citizens Escape Yemen'. *Al Jazeera America*, 7 April 2015, america.aljazeera.com/ articles/2015/4/7/us-among-26-countries-asking-india-to-help-citizens-escape-yemen.html

28. Douglas Busvine and Katharine Houreld. 'India Ends Yemen Evacuation, Rescues People from 41 Countries'. Edited by Jeremy Laurence, *Reuters*, 10 April 2015, www.reuters.com/article/us-yemen-india-idUSKBN0N10Q320150410

29. Kanwal, Gurmeet. 'Operations Maitri and Rahat: How Indian Military Proved Efficiency in Disaster Response'. *DailyO*, 7 May 2015, www. dailyo.in/politics/operation-maitri-operation-rahat-nepal-earthquake-yemen-iaf-indian-navy-al-qaeda/story/1/3582.html

30. 'Astra Missile Launched Successfully'. *Indian Express*, 18 March 2015, indianexpress.com/article/india/india-others/astra-missile-launched-successfully/; Rajat Pandit. 'Govt Approves Construction of 7 Stealth Frigates, 6 Nuclear-Powered Submarines'. *Times of India*, 18 February 2015, timesofindia.indiatimes.com/india/Govt-approves-construction-of-7-stealth-frigates-6-nuclear-powered-submarines/articleshow/46281364.cms

31. Sanjeev Miglani. 'India Clears $8 Billion Warships Project to Counter Chinese Navy'. *Reuters*, 18 February 2015, in.reuters.com/article/india-defence-navy/india-clears-8-billion-warships-project-to-counter-chinese-navy-idINKBN0LM1A920150218

32. 'India Conducts Fourth Test Launch of Agni-V Missile'. *BBC News*, 26 December 2016, www.bbc.com/news/world-asia-india-38434944

33. 'Manifesto of the National Socialist Council of Nagaland'. *South Asian Terrorism Portal*, www.satp.org/satporgtp/countries/india/states/nagaland/documents/papers/manifesto_national_socialist_council_nagaland.htm

34. 'Myanmar Operation: 70 Commandos Finish Task in 40 Minutes'. *The Hindu*, 10 June 2015, www.thehindu.com/news/national/myanmar-operation-70-commandos-finish-task-in-40-minutes/article7302348.ece

35. Ibid.

36. Rishi Iyengar. 'Indian Army's Strikes in Burma Are a Message to Its Neighbors'. *Time*, 11 June 2015, time.com/3917362/india-burma-army-operation-militant-attack-pakistan-manipur/?%23

37. 'Is Myanmar Raid Indian Counter-Insurgency Shift?' *BBC News*, 10 June 2015, www.bbc.com/news/world-asia-india-33074776

38. 'Ex-Army Chief Dalbir Singh Praises PM Narendra Modi for Surgical Strikes in Pakistan, Myanmar'. *Economic Times*, 11 July 2018, economictimes.indiatimes.com/news/defence/ex-army-chief-dalbir-singh-praises-pm-narendra-modi-for-surgical-strikes-in-pakistan-myanmar/articleshow/60885703.cms

39. Reisang Vashum. 'Naga National Movement: A Historical Account (Since 1948)'. *Nagas' Rights to Self Determination: An Anthropological-Historical Perspective*, Mittal Publications, 2000, pp. 105–07.

40. 'PM Witnesses Signing of Historic Peace Accord between Govt of India and NSCN'. *Prime Minister's Office*, 3 August 2015, www.pmindia.gov.in/en/news_updates/pm-witnesses-the-signing-of-historic-peace-accord-between-government-of-india-and-nationalist-socialist-council-of-nagaland-nscn/

41. Samudra Gupta Kashyap. 'Towards the Govt-Naga Peace Accord: Everything You Need to Know'. *Indian Express*, 4 August 2015, indianexpress.com/article/explained/simply-put-towards-accord-step-by-step/

42. Narendra Modi. 'Today, We Mark Not Merely the End of a Problem but the Beginning of a New Future'. Twitter, 3 August 2015, twitter.com/narendramodi/status/628215598246309888

43. 'Rajnath to Discuss Security Cooperation in China'. *The Hindu*, 18 November 2015, www.thehindu.com/news/national/home-minister-rajnath-singh-sixday-visit-to-china/article7891234.ece

44. B.R. Deepak. *India and China: Foreign Policy Approaches and Responses*, Vij Books India Pvt. Ltd, 2016.

45. 'Joint Statement between the Ministry of Home Affairs and the Ministry of Public Security of the People's Republic of China'. *Press Information Bureau of India*, 21 November 2015, pib.nic.in/newsite/PrintRelease.aspx?relid=131765

46. Vikram Sood. 'Pathankot Attack: "Someone" Is Unhappy with Modi-Nawaz Talks'. Rediff.com, 3 January 2016, www.rediff.com/news/column/pathankot-attack-someone-is-unhappy-with-modi-nawaz-talks/20160103.htm

47. Rohan Dua. '+92 3000597212: Phone Number of Pathankot Attacker's "Ustaad" in Pakistan'. *Times of India*, 8 January 2016, timesofindia.

indiatimes.com/india/92-3000597212-Phone-number-of-Pathankot-attackers-ustaad-in-Pakistan/articleshow/50490489.cms

48. Bruce Riedel. 'The China-Pakistan Axis and Lashkar-e-Taiba'. The Brookings Institution, 28 July 2015, www.brookings.edu/opinions/the-china-pakistan-axis-and-lashkar-e-taiba/

49. Dexter Filkins. 'The Pakistani Dystopia'. New Yorker, 15 January 2016, www.newyorker.com/news/news-desk/the-pakistani-dystopia?intcid=mod-latest

50. 'JNU Event Had LeT Support: Rajnath'. Deccan Herald, 15 February 2016, www.deccanherald.com/national/jnu-event-had-let-support-rajnath-509558.html

51. 'JNU Row: Outsiders Raised Controversial Slogans, Says University Report'. India Today, 16 March 2016, www.indiatoday.in/india/story/jnu-row-outsiders-raised-controversial-slogans-says-university-report-313473-2016-03-16

52. Rituparna Chatterjee. '"They Were Not Carrying Arms, Just Ideas": Eyewitness Account of What Actually Happened At JNU'. HuffPost India, 15 February 2016, www.huffingtonpost.in/2016/02/15/jnu-arrest_n_9233910.html

53. John Wilson. 'ISI Fangs'. Pioneer, 30 June 1999.

54. Hein G. Kiessling. Faith, Unity, Discipline: The Inter-Service-Intelligence (ISI) of Pakistan. Hurst & Co. Ltd, 2016.

55. Bashaarat Masood. 'Guns 'n' Poses: The New Crop of Militants in Kashmir'. Indian Express, 26 July 2015, indianexpress.com/article/india/india-others/big-picture-guns-n-poses/

56. Ashiq Hussain. 'Last of Burhan Wani's Boys Killed, Marking End of the 11 Who Posed in Photo That Went Viral'. Hindustan Times, 6 May 2018, www.hindustantimes.com/india-news/last-of-burhan-s-boys-killed-marking-end-of-the-11-who-posed-in-viral-pic/story-Bn8f0IsDixrM4JvECFFhgN.html

57. Sandeep Unnithan. 'New Gun Mantra', India Today, 29 July 2016, www.indiatoday.in/magazine/the-big-story/story/20160808-overhaul-of-arms-rules-gun-licences-manufacturing-policy-829299-2016-07-27

58. 'Ministry of Home Affairs Relaxes Small Arms Manufacturing Rules to Boost Export, Employment Generation'. New Indian Express, 30 October 2017, www.newindianexpress.com/nation/2017/oct/30/ministry-of-home-affairs-relaxes-small-arms-manufacturing-rules-to-boost-export-employment-generati-1687319.html

59. Shaswati Das. 'Govt. Amends Arms Rules to Spur Make in India'. Livemint, 30 October 2017, www.livemint.com/Industry/

YlIC2Gmf90zjycWtsvN7LL/Govt-relaxes-Arms-Rules-to-boost-investment-in-manufacturing.html

60. 'Indian Army Set to Acquire Artillery Guns, Finally'. *India Strategic*, July 2016, www.indiastrategic.in/Indian_Army_Set_to_Acquire_Artillery_Guns_Finally.htm

61. Anna Ahronheim. 'India Clears Major Air Defense Deal with Israel Aerospace Industries'. *Jerusalem Post*, 24 February 2017, www.jpost.com/Israel-News/India-clears-major-air-defense-deal-with-Israel-Aerospace-Industries-482416

62. Ari Yashar. 'Israel and India at the Start of a New Era'. *Israel National News*, 6 November 2014, www.israelnationalnews.com/News/News.aspx/187153

63. 'India to Buy Armed Israeli Drones in $400M Deal'. *Times of Israel*, 11 September 2015, www.timesofisrael.com/india-to-buy-armed-israeli-drones-in-400m-deal/

64. 'India Chooses Israel for $525 Million Missile Deal'. *Israel National News*, 26 October 2014, www.israelnationalnews.com/News/News.aspx/186587

65. Zachary Keck. 'Israel Is On the Verge of Selling India 4,500 Spike Tank-Killer Missiles'. *National Interest*, 2 July 2018, nationalinterest.org/blog/buzz/israel-verge-selling-india-4500-spike-tank-killer-missiles-24807

66. 'Rajnath Singh to Visit Pakistan for SAARC Home Ministers Meet'. *News Minute*, 28 July 2016, www.thenewsminute.com/article/rajnath-singh-visit-pakistan-saarc-home-ministers-meet-47242

67. 'Home Minister Rajnath Singh Arrives in Pakistan for SAARC Meeting'. *Hindustan Times*, 3 August 2016, www.hindustantimes.com/india-news/home-minister-rajnath-singh-arrives-in-pakistan-for-saarc-meeting/story-L5kwbAJb6bA5vprAq1za0K.html

68. '"Undiplomatic" Treatment by Pakistan Made Rajnath Singh Leave Pakistan Earlier than Scheduled'. *Economic Times*, 6 August 2016, economictimes.indiatimes.com/news/politics-and-nation/undiplomatic-treatment-by-pakistan-made-rajnath-singh-leave-pakistan-earlier-than-scheduled/articleshow/53565061.cms

69. Narendra Modi. 'We Strongly Condemn the Cowardly Terror Attack in Uri. I Assure the Nation That Those behind This Despicable Attack Will Not Go Unpunished'. Twitter, 18 September 2016, twitter.com/narendramodi/status/777417302912430080

70. Shubhajit Roy and Yubaraj Ghimire. 'SAARC Summit to Be Called off as Dhaka, Kabul and Thimphu Too Slam Islamabad'. *Indian Express*, 29 September 2016, indianexpress.com/article/india/india-news-india/

dhaka-kabul-thimphu-too-blame-islamabad-saarc-summit-to-be-called-off-3054953/

71. Praveen Swami. 'In Posters Pasted on Gujranwala Streets, Lashkar Claims Responsibility of Uri Attack'. *Indian Express*, 26 Oct. 2016, indianexpress.com/article/india/india-news-india/exclusive-uri-attack-in-posters-pasted-on-gujaranwala-streets-lashkar-claims-responsibility-3101738/

72. Rishi Iyengar. 'Uri Attack: India, Pakistan's Kashmir Dispute Flares Again'. *Time*, 19 September 2016, time.com/4498891/kashmir-uri-attack-india-pakistan-military-conflict/

73. Hamzah Rifaat. 'Nawaz Sharif Takes on India, Kashmir at the United Nations'. *Diplomat*, 22 September 2016, thediplomat.com/2016/09/nawaz-sharif-takes-on-india-kashmir-at-the-united-nations/

74. Elizabeth Roche. 'Sushma Swaraj at UNGA: Terrorism Is Pakistan's Calling Card'. *Livemint*, 26 September 2016, www.livemint.com/Politics/YK1wU6Z24Ak9sWmamNZriK/Sushma-Swaraj-seeks-to-isolate-Pakistan-raises-Balochistan.html

75. Nitin A. Gokhale. *Securing India the Modi Way: Pathankot, Surgical Strikes and More*, Bloomsbury, 2017.

76. Saurav Bhanot. 'The Real Story of "Uri: The Surgical Strike" Movie: What Happened in the Uri Attack and How Did India Respond?' *GQ India*, 10 January 2019.

77. '4 Hours, Choppers and 38 Kills: How India Avenged the Uri Attack'. *Economic Times*, 29 September 2016, economictimes.indiatimes.com/news/defence/army-conducted-surgical-strikes-on-terror-launch-pads-on-loc-significant-casualties-caused-dgmo/articleshow/54579855.cms

78. Shiv Aroor and Rahul Singh. *India's Most Fearless: True Stories of Modern Military Heroes*, Penguin Random House), 2017.

79. 'Political Parties Hail Surgical Strikes across LoC, Mehbooba Strikes Note of Caution'. *Livemint*, 29 September 2016, www.livemint.com/

80. Ibid.
'Amid Protests, Kejriwal Defends Demand for Proof of Surgical Strikes'. *Hindustan Times*, 4 October 2016, www.hindustantimes.com/india-news/amid-protests-criticism-kejriwal-defends-demand-for-proof-of-surgical-strikes/story-LpFsrwCor8971mjt5A2cbM.html

81. '"Surgical Strikes": Journalists Flown to LoC to Debunk Indian Myth'. *Express Tribune*, 2 October 2016, tribune.com.pk/story/1192133/surgical-strikes-journalists-flown-loc-debunk-indian-myth/

82. 'Government Releases New Video of 2016 Surgical Strikes'. *Indian Express*, 28 September 2018, indianexpress.com/article/india/govt-releases-new-video-of-2016-surgical-strikes-5377317/

83. 'Pakistan's New Strategy: Exploit India's Fault Lines on Caste and
    Religion, Encourage Modi Baiters'. *India Today*, 18 October 2016,
    www.indiatoday.in/india/story/nawaz-sharif-pakistan-senate-
    strategy-uri-attack-surgical-strikes-india-muslims-dalits-narendra-
    modi-347035-2016-10-17
84. Muhammad Saleh Zaafir and Mumtaz Alvi. 'Parliament Should
    Monitor National Security, Foreign Policy'. *News International*, 8
    October 2016, www.thenews.com.pk/print/155822-Parliament-
    should-monitor-national-security-foreign-policy
85. Smita Sinha. 'One Year of Note Ban: The Ultra-Secret Move That No
    One Came to Know for Several Months'. *Economic Times*, 7 November
    2017, economictimes.indiatimes.com/news/politics-and-nation/one-
    year-of-note-ban-the-ultra-secret-move-that-no-one-came-to-know-
    for-several-months/articleshow/61528334.cms
86. Romita Datta. 'Mamata Banerjee to Rally against Demonetisation in
    Kolkata on November 28'. *India Today*, 25 November 2016, www.
    indiatoday.in/india/story/mamata-banerjee-demonetisation-kolkata-
    pm-modi-trinamool-congress-354027-2016-11-25; 'Demonetization
    Is Nothing but a Big BJP Scam: Kejriwal'. *Business Standard*, 12 November
    2016, www.business-standard.com/article/news-ani/demonetization-
    is-nothing-but-a-big-bjp-scam-kejriwal-116111200849_1.html;
    'Kerala CM Pinarayi Vijayan, Ministers Stage Dharna Outside RBI
    Office'. *Daily News & Analysis*, 18 November 2016, www.dnaindia.
    com/india/report-kerala-cm-pinarayi-vijayan-ministers-on-dharna-
    say-demonetisation-destroying-cooperative-sector-2274629; 'Bihar
    CM Nitish Kumar Supports Decision to Withdraw Rs 1000, Rs
    500 Notes'. *Indian Express*, 9 November 2016, indianexpress.com/
    article/india/india-news-india/bihar-cm-nitish-supports-decision-to-
    withdraw-demonetisation-currency-rs-1000-rs-500-notes-4366034/;
    'Chandrababu Naidu Welcomes Demonetization Move'. *New Indian
    Express*, 8 November 2016, www.newindianexpress.com/states/andhra-
    pradesh/2016/nov/08/chandrababu-naidu-welcomes-demonetisation-
    move-1536401.html
87. Neeraj Chauhan. 'Demonetization Leads to Highest Ever Surrender
    of Maoists in a Month'. *Times of India*, 29 November 2016,
    timesofindia.indiatimes.com/india/Demonetisation-leads-to-largest-
    Maoist-surrenders/articleshow/55675983.cms; Mausami Singh.
    'Demonetization Cuts Terror Attacks by 60 per Cent in Kashmir,
    Hawala Business by 50 per Cent'. *India Today*, 7 January 2017, www.
    indiatoday.in/india/story/demonetisation-cuts-terror-attacks-hawala-
    business-fake-currency-953685-2017-01-07

88. 'GDP Grows at 5-Quarter High of 7.2% in Oct-Dec'. *Times of India*, 1 March 2018, timesofindia.indiatimes.com/business/india-business/gdp-grows-at-5-quarter-high-of-7-2-in-oct-dec/articleshow/63118408.cms

Chapter 13: The Sky As a Shelter

1. '45% Fall in Infiltration after Surgical Strikes: Rajnath Singh'. *Times of India*, 3 June 2017, timesofindia.indiatimes.com/india/45-fall-in-infiltration-after-surgical-strikes-rajnath-singh/articleshow/58973164.cms
2. 'Sukma Attack Cold-Blooded, Govt Will Review Naxal Policy: Rajnath Singh'. News18, 25 April 2017, www.news18.com/news/india/rajnath-singh-pays-homage-to-25-crpf-men-killed-in-naxal-ambush-in-sukma-1383001.html
3. Rituparna Chatterjee. 'How 300 Maoist Guerrillas, Including Women Wielding AK-47s, Ambushed A CRPF Team In Sukma'. HuffPost India, 25 April 2017, www.huffingtonpost.in/2017/04/24/how-300-maoist-guerrillas-including-women-wielding-ak-47s-ambu_a_22054104/
4. 'After Sukma Attack, CRPF Set to Overhaul Anti-Naxal Operations in Bastar'. *Economic Times*, April 2017, economictimes.indiatimes.com/news/defence/after-sukma-attack-crpf-set-to-overhaul-anti-naxal-operations-in-bastar/articleshow/58401240.cms
5. Press Trust of India. 'UAV Base Shifted to Maoist-Controlled Bastar'. *The Hindu*, 8 October 2017, www.thehindu.com/news/national/uav-base-shifted-to-maoist-controlled-bastar/article19824298.ece
6. 'Year End Review 2017: Ministry of Home Affairs'. *Press Information Bureau of India*, 28 December 2017, www.pib.gov.in/PressReleseDetail.aspx?PRID=1514455
7. *Press Information Bureau of India*. 'Development Schemes in the Naxal Affected Districts'. 4 March 2015, pib.nic.in/newsite/PrintRelease.aspx?relid=116427
8. Dipankar Ghose. 'Echo from the Hills of Chhattisgarh: "We Are the First Bastariya Battalion"'. *Indian Express*, 22 May 2018, indianexpress.com/article/india/echo-from-the-hills-of-chhattisgarh-we-are-the-first-bastariya-battalion-5185799/
9. Jugal R. Purohit and Ashok Upadhyay. 'Tackling the Maoists: Why 2018 May Be a Deciding Year'. *DailyO*, 2 January 2018, www.dailyo.in/politics/maoists-left-wing-extremists-india-naxal-surrender-tribals/story/1/21498.html

10. Yunus Y. Lasania. 'Central Committee Member of Banned Maoist Outfit Surrenders with Wife in Telangana'. *Livemint*, 25 December 2017, www.livemint.com/Politics/VNcLhJWjoi6P9PL06LxhfL/Central-committee-member-of-banned-Maoist-outfit-surrenders.html

11. 'Left Wing Extremism Shrinks: Centre Redraws Red Corridor, Removes 44 Districts from List of Naxal-Hit'. *Financial Express*, 16 April 2018, www.financialexpress.com/india-news/left-wing-extremism-shrinks-centre-redraws-red-corridor-removes-44-districts-from-list-of-naxal-hit/1134508/

12. 'Internal Security Improved Vastly in Last Four Years: Rajnath Singh'. *Indian Express*, 16 December 2018, indianexpress.com/article/india/internal-security-improved-vastly-in-last-four-years-rajnath-singh-5496159/

13. Ganesh Kanate and Vijay Singh. '56 NGOs Raising Funds, Cadres for Naxals in State'. *Daily News & Analysis*, 17 March 2008, www.dnaindia.com/mumbai/report-56-ngos-raising-funds-cadres-for-naxals-in-state-1156453

14. Aman Malik. 'Government Identifies 128 Front Organizations for Naxals'. *Livemint*, Livemint, 7 October 2013, www.livemint.com/Politics/B9Pmu3NurDrcRdD9ttb6JP/Government-identifies-128-front-organizations-for-Naxals.html

15. Vicky Nanjappa. 'Kashmir: Relief of Rs 600 Cr Used to Finance Terror, Says NIA'. Rediff.com, 7 August 2013, www.rediff.com/news/report/trust-raised-rs-600-cr-in-kashmir-to-finance-terror-nia/20130807.htm

16. Vijaita Singh. 'Greenpeace India's Registration Cancelled'. *The Hindu*, 4 September 2015, www.thehindu.com/news/national/greenpeace-indias-registration-cancelled/article7613184.ece.

17. *Press Information Bureau of India.* 'Year-end Review 2017: Ministry of Home Affairs'. 28 December 2017, www.pib.gov.in/PressReleseDetail.aspx?PRID=1514455

18. Neeraj Chauhan. '3,292 NGOs Have 15 Days to Comply with FCRA Rules or Have Their Licences Cancelled'. *Times of India*, 28 April 2018, timesofindia.indiatimes.com/india/3292-ngos-have-15-days-to-comply-with-fcra-rules-or-have-their-licences-cancelled/articleshow/63956761.cms

19. Stewart Bell and Sean Craig. 'Government Revokes Group's Charity Status, Audit Cites Possible Funding of Pakistani Militants'. *Global News*, 19 July 2017, globalnews.ca/news/3606224/government-revokes-groups-charity-status-audit-cites-pakistani-militants/

20. Dalip Singh. 'Rajnath Singh Launches Online Tool to Monitor Foreign-Funded NGOs'. *Economic Times*, 2 June 2018, economictimes. indiatimes.com/news/politics-and-nation/rajnath-singh-launches-online-tool-to-monitor-foreign-funded-ngos/articleshow/64423819. cms

21. 'Rajnath Singh Leads All-Party Delegation to Kashmir'. HuffPost India, 4 September 2016, www.huffingtonpost.in/2016/09/04/rajnath-singh-leads-all-party-delegation-to-kashmir_a_21465128/

22. 'Rajnath Clears Use of Chilli-Filled PAVA Shells as Alternative to Pellet Guns'. *The Hindu*, 18 October 2016, www.thehindu.com/news/national/Rajnath-clears-use-of-chilli-filled-PAVA-shells-as-alternative-to-pellet-guns/article14621892.ece

23. Malini Parthasarathy. 'Understanding Kashmir's Stone Pelters'. *The Hindu*, 4 November 2016, www.thehindu.com/opinion/lead/Understanding-Kashmirs-stone-pelters/article16120870.ece

24. Jamshed Adil Khan and Sushant Pathak. 'Stone Pelters on Hire in Kashmir: *India Today* Nails Valley's Insidious Villains'. *India Today*, 30 March 2017, www.indiatoday.in/india/story/jammu-and-kashmir-stone-pelters-hizbul-mujahideen-burhan-wani-968402-2017-03-29

25. Animesh Roul. 'Indian Investigations Reveal Funding System for Promoting Jihad in Kashmir'. *Jamestown Foundation*, 4 April 2014, jamestown.org/program/indian-investigations-reveal-funding-system-for-promoting-jihad-in-kashmir/

26. Rajesh Ahuja. 'Terror Funding Case: Kashmiri Separatist Leaders Mentioned in NIA Charge Sheet but No Formal Charges'. *Hindustan Times*, 3 February 2018, www.hindustantimes.com/india-news/nia-charge-in-terror-funding-case-mentions-top-kashmiri-separatists-but-has-no-formal-charges/story-zMKGbj3FdEucZ1fEuFJapM.html

27. 'Pakistan's ISI Paid Kashmiri Separatists Rs 800 Crore to Fuel Unrest in Kashmir, Says Intelligence Bureau Report'. *India Today*, 4 April 2017, www.indiatoday.in/india/story/jammu-and-kashmir-india-inter-services-intelligence-pakistan-isi-separatists-kashmir-unrest-969395-2017-04-04; Pamela Constable, 'Pakistan's Kashmir Solidarity Day Co-Opted by Supporters of Detained Muslim Cleric'. *Washington Post*, 6 February 2017, www.washingtonpost.com/world/in-pakistan-kashmir-solidarityday-is-tinged-with-a-more-ambivalent-message/2017/02/06/c9d19b42-ea22-11e6-903d-9b11ed7d8d2a_story.html?utm_term=.e51e446aab1f

28. Fareed Rahman. 'India PM Narendra Modi Begins Historic Visit to UAE'. *Gulf News*, 16 August 2015, gulfnews.com/uae/government/india-pm-narendra-modi-begins-historic-visit-to-uae-1.1567527;

K.P.M. Basheer, 'UAE's $75-Billion Investment Offer Could Be the Largest for India so Far'. *Hindu Business Line*, 18 August 2015, www.thehindubusinessline.com/economy/uaes-75billion-investment-offer-could-be-the-largest-for-india-so-far/article7554390.ece

29. Arunabh Saikia. 'Rajnath Singh Flies to Bahrain in Attempt to Sway OIC Sentiment against Pakistan'. *Livemint*, 23 October 2016, www.livemint.com/Politics/cutes3W1uCiV0sq3r7xVFI/Rajnath-Singh-flies-to-Bahrain-in-attempt-to-sway-OIC-sentim.html

30. Ministry of External Affairs, Government of India. 'India–Saudi Arabia Joint Statement during the Visit of Prime Minister to Saudi Arabia'. 3 April 2016

31. Tokyo Foundation. 'Embracing Diversity: Asian Experts Offer Insights into Region's Shared Values and Democracy'. 14 March 2016, www.tokyofoundation.org/en/articles/2016/embracing-diversity

32. Steven Lee Myers, et al. 'How India and China Have Come to the Brink Over a Remote Mountain Pass'. *New York Times*, 26 July 2017, www.nytimes.com/2017/07/26/world/asia/dolam-plateau-china-india-bhutan.html

33. Bhairavi Singh and Nidhi Razdan. 'After Meeting China Ambassador, Rahul Gandhi Says "My Job To Be Informed".' NDTV.com, 10 July 2017, www.ndtv.com/india-news/chinese-embassy-claims-then-deletes-that-rahul-gandhi-met-ambassador-1722875

34. Simon Denyer and Annie Gowen. 'India, China Agree to Pull Back Troops to Resolve Tense Border Dispute'. *Washington Post*, 28 August 2017, www.washingtonpost.com/world/india-withdraws-troops-from-disputed-himalayan-region-defusing-tension-with-china/2017/08/28/b92fddb6-8bc7-11e7-a2b0-e68cbf0b1f19_story.html?utm_term=.ca6193330408

35. Dipanjan Roy Chaudhury. 'India's Geopolitical Status Goes up after Doklam Standoff Ends'. *Economic Times*, 13 July 2018, economictimes.indiatimes.com/news/defence/indias-geopolitical-status-goes-up-after-doklam-standoff-ends/articleshow/60282585.cms

36. 'Rajnath Singh to Lead Indian Delegation at Shanghai Cooperation Organisation Meet in August'. *Daily News & Analysis*, 17 August 2017, www.dnaindia.com/india/report-rajnath-to-lead-indian-delegation-participating-in-sco-member-states-meeting-in-aug-2533033

37. Dipanjan Roy Chaudhury. 'Home Minister Rajnath Singh May Attend Bilateral Meet at SCO Summit on Disaster'. *Economic Times*, 24 August 2017, economictimes.indiatimes.com/news/politics-and-nation/home-minister-rajnath-singh-may-attend-bilateral-meet-at-sco-summit-on-disaster/articleshow/60199104.cms

38. Saurav Jha. 'The India-Russia-US Energy Triangle'. *Diplomat*, 12 July 2018, thediplomat.com/2018/07/the-india-russia-us-energy-triangle/
39. Irina Slav. 'The New Oil Cartel Threatening OPEC'. *Oil Price*, 3 July 2018, oilprice.com/Energy/Crude-Oil/The-New-Oil-Cartel-Threatening-OPEC.html
40. Cyril Widdershoven. 'The Overlooked Factor That Could Derail the OPEC Deal'. *Oil Price*, 17 April 2018, oilprice.com/Energy/Crude-Oil/The-Overlooked-Factor-That-Could-Derail-The-OPEC-Deal.html
    'Venezuela Willing to Accept Oil Payments in Rupees: Envoy'. *Economic Times*, 22 May 2018, economictimes.indiatimes.com/industry/energy/oil-gas/venezuela-willing-to-accept-oil-payments-in-rupees-envoy/articleshow/64277053.cms
41. https://globalriskinsights.com/2018/06/china-india-oil-buyers-club-opec/
42. '"OPEC to Consider Views of PM Modi, Other World Leaders before Cutting Oil Production," says Saudi Minister.' *Business Today*, 7 December 2018, www.businesstoday.in/latest/opec-to-consider-views-of-pm-modi-other-world-leaders-before-cutting-oil-production-says-saudi-minister/story/298226.html
43. Munkhchimeg Davaasharav and Henning Gloystein. 'Mongolia Launches Construction of First Oil Refinery with Indian Aid'. *Reuters*, 22 June 2018, www.reuters.com/article/mongolia-refinery/mongolia-launches-construction-of-first-oil-refinery-with-indian-aid-idUSL4N1TO1TO
44. G. Parthasarathy. 'Energy Diplomacy to Power South Asia'. *Pioneer*, 15 August 2014, www.dailypioneer.com/2014/columnists/energy-diplomacy-to-power-south-asia.html; Indrani Bagchi. 'Away from OBOR, India Pushing for "Energy Diplomacy" in Neighbourhood'. *Economic Times*, 15 May 2017, economictimes.indiatimes.com/industry/energy/away-from-obor-india-pushing-for-energy-diplomacy-in-neighbourhood/articleshow/58678035.cms
45. Yogesh Joshi. 'Bhima–Koregaon Violence: Police Arrest 5 with Alleged Maoist Links for Inciting Riots'. *Hindustan Times*, 6 June 2018, www.hindustantimes.com/india-news/bhima-koregaon-violece-lawyer-3-others-with-alleged-maoist-links-arrested-professor-s-house-searched/story-yfDDMI6zOdESFRsQtRP0IM.html
46. T.N. Raghunatha. 'Maoists Plotted to Kill Modi in Rajiv Style'. *Pioneer*, 9 June 2018, www.dailypioneer.com/2018/page1/maoists-plotted-to-kill-modi-in-rajiv-style.html
47. Yatish Yadav. 'Bhima–Koregaon Raids: MHA Puts "Urban Naxalism" under Scanner, Flags Spread of Maoist Agenda from Jungles to Cities'.

Firstpost, 29 August 2018, www.firstpost.com/india/bhima-koregaon-raids-mha-puts-urban-naxalism-under-scanner-flags-spread-of-maoist-agenda-from-jungles-to-cities-5066601.html

48. Aneesha Mathur. 'Bhima–Koregaon Case: SC Says "Dissent Is the Safety Valve of Democracy", Puts All 5 Accused under House Arrest'. *Times Now*, 29 August 2018, www.timesnownews.com/india/article/bhima-koregaon-violence-maoists-supreme-court-urban-naxals-maharashtra-pune-police-gautam-navlakha-sudha-bharadwaj-varavara-rao-vernon-gonsalves-arun/277011

49. Samanwaya Rautray. 'Bhima-Koregaon Case: Supreme Court Refuses to Interfere with Arrests of Five Activists'. *Economic Times*, 28 September 2018, economictimes.indiatimes.com/news/politics-and-nation/koregaon-bhima-case-sc-refuses-to-interfere-with-arrests-of-five-activists/articleshow/65990909.cms

50. 'Repeated Same Order Existing since 2009: Jaitley on MHA Surveillance Order'. *Asian News International*, 21 December 2018, www.aninews.in/news/national/general-news/repeated-same-order-existing-since-2009-jaitley-on-mha-surveillance-order201812211707270001/

51. 'NIA Busts ISIS-Inspired Module, Arrests 10 People from UP and Delhi.' *Economic Times*, 27 December 2018, economictimes.indiatimes.com/news/defence/nia-searches-16-places-in-delhi-up-over-new-is-module/articleshow/67252785.cms

52. 'In a First, CRPF Deploys Women Commandos for Anti-Naxal Ops'. *Economic Times*, 13 July 2018, economictimes.indiatimes.com/news/defence/in-a-first-crpf-deploys-women-commandos-for-anti-naxal-ops/articleshow/55438106.cms

53. 'Rajnath Singh Launches App for Paramilitary Forces to Air Grievances'. *Indian Express*, 11 May 2017, indianexpress.com/article/india/rajnath-singh-launches-app-for-paramilitary-forces-to-air-grievances-4651547/

54. 'Govt to Ensure Minimum Rs 1 Crore Compensation to CAPFs Martyrs: Rajnath Singh'. *Economic Times*, 11 July 2018, economictimes.indiatimes.com/news/defence/govt-to-ensure-minimum-rs-1-crore-compensation-to-capfs-martyrs-rajnath-singh/articleshow/58097663.cms; Film actor Akshay Kumar donated Rs 9 lakh each to the families of the twelve CRPF personnel who lost their lives in the Sukma ambush.

55. Ajit Kumar Dubey. 'India Prepares Israeli SPYDER Air Defence Missile System for Pakistan Border'. *India Today*, 28 February 2017, www.indiatoday.in/mail-today/story/india-pakistan-border-iaf-spyder-israel-air-defence-missile-system-963021-2017-02-28

56. *Press Information Bureau of India*. 'Year End Review 2018–Ministry of Home Affairs'. 14 December 2018, pib.nic.in/PressReleseDetail. aspx?PRID=1555980

57. Surender Sharma. 'Pathankot Terror Attack: HC Raps MHA over Inaction on BSF Report'. *Hindustan Times*, 13 January 2016, www. hindustantimes.com/punjab/pathankot-terror-attack-hc-raps-mha-over-inaction-on-bsf-report/story-LppUJK1EHTTpUjckvoAS7J.html

58. 'Entire Effort of MHA Seems to Be to Destroy National Register of Citizens, Says Supreme Court'. *Business Standard*, 5 February 2019, www.business-standard.com/article/news-ani/entire-effort-of-mha-seems-to-be-to-destroy-national-register-of-citizens-says-supreme-court-119020500966_1.html

59. 'Lok Sabha Passes Citizenship Bill amid Protests, Seeks to Give Citizenship to Non-Muslims from 3 Countries'. *India Today*, 9 January 2019, www.indiatoday.in/india/story/citizenship-amendment-bill-passed-lok-sabha-assam-protests-1426345-2019-01-08

60. Pallab Bhattacharya. 'A Visit beyond Usual Trappings'. *Daily Star*, 19 July 2018, www.thedailystar.net/opinion/perspective/visit-beyond-usual-trappings-1607392

Acknowledgments

As always, the list of people to whom I owe my heartfelt gratitude for their help with writing this book is incomplete. In the course of writing for years, I have accumulated a lot of debt that can never be repaid, let alone adequately acknowledged. I owe my first debt of thanks to Shri Rajnath Singh for letting me enter a space very few have been previously allowed. This book would not have been possible had Rajnathji not shared the story of his life and career. The conversations with Rajnathji have been enriching and, through the course of my writing, he rarely ceased from being open and insightful but most importantly, made no demands and imposed no restrictions. I remain grateful for his benevolence and patience that contributed immensely to this book.

I'm grateful to many friends and family who have endured my conversations, read and commented on this work, either in part or in some cases on the entire manuscript. Special thanks to Shri Hardeep Singh Puri, Shri Swapan Dasgupta and Gaurav Goel, BJYM, Chandigarh for their help and guidance.

The warmth and love of the whole team at Penguin Random House made writing this book an enjoyable experience. Thank you, Milee Ashwarya, my publisher, for making me feel at home and the invaluable insight you brought to the manuscript. A special shout out to Saksham Garg and Neeraj Nath for the brilliant cover. I remain thankful to Bidisha Srivastava for her work on the manuscript. This is my fourth book with my editor and friend Shantanu Ray Chaudhuri, who remains an unwavering advocate of my work. I can never thank him enough for bringing a 'fog-dispelling human sense' to my writing.

As always I remain indebted to my parents Kavita and Ashok Chintamani and my parents-in-law Kawal and Ajit Bhinder for all their support. In the end, I would like to thank my wife and partner-in-crime, Amrita, without whom nothing is ever possible. Last but not the least, thank you, Buddy, our six-year-old Labrador, who continues to cuddle up at my feet while I write and unfailingly forces me to write a few more words before I break his sleep.

Index